T0301251

Industrial Relations in Emerging Economies

Industrial Relations in Emerging Economies

The Quest for Inclusive Development

Edited by

Susan Hayter

International Labour Office, Switzerland

Chang-Hee Lee

ILO Country Office for Viet Nam

Cheltenham, UK • Northampton, MA, USA

International Labour Office

Geneva, Switzerland

Published by
Edward Elgar Publishing Limited
The Lypiatts
15 Lansdown Road
Cheltenham
Glos GL50 2JA
UK

Edward Elgar Publishing, Inc.
William Pratt House
9 Dewey Court
Northampton
Massachusetts 01060
USA

In association with
International Labour Office
4 route des Morillons
CH-1211 Geneva 22
Switzerland
ISBN 978-92-2-130383-1 (paperback)

A catalogue record for this book
is available from the British Library

Library of Congress Control Number: 2017953271

This book is available electronically in the **Elgar**online
Economics subject collection
DOI 10.4337/9781788114387

ISBN 978 1 78811 437 0 (cased)
ISBN 978 1 78811 438 7 (eBook)

Typeset by Servis Filmsetting Ltd, Stockport, Cheshire
Printed and bound in Great Britain by TJ International Ltd, Padstow

Contents

Contributors

Janine Berg is a Senior Economist at the International Labour Office, Switzerland. She received her PhD in Economics from the New School for Social Research, USA.

Aziz Çelik is a full-time Professor and Head of the Industrial Relations Division in the Department of Labour Economics and Industrial Relations at the Kocaeli University, Turkey. He holds a PhD from Marmara University, Turkey.

Susan Hayter is a Senior Specialist on Industrial Relations at the International Labour Office, Switzerland. She received an MSc in Industrial Relations from the London School of Economics in the United Kingdom.

Chang-Hee Lee is the Director of the ILO Country Office for Viet Nam and a former industrial relations specialist at the ILO. He holds a PhD in Sociology from the Seoul National University, Republic of Korea.

Nicolas Pons-Vignon is a Senior Researcher in the School of Economics and Business Sciences at the University of the Witwatersrand, South Africa. He received his PhD from the École des hautes études en sciences sociales (EHESS), Paris, France and the University of the Witwatersrand, South Africa.

Uma Rani is a Senior Development Economist at the International Labour Office, Switzerland. She holds a PhD in Development Economics from the University of Hyderabad, India.

Eduardo Schneider is a Technical Officer with DIEESE, the Inter-Union Department of Socioeconomic Statistics and Studies, Brazil. He completed his PhD in Economic Studies at the Universidade Federal do Rio Grande do Sul, Brazil.

Ratna Sen, PhD, is a retired Professor of Human Resource Management and Industrial Relations at the Indian Institute of Social Welfare and Business Management, University of Calcutta, India.

1. Industrial relations in emerging economies*

Susan Hayter

1.1 INTRODUCTION

Industrial relations is as relevant in emerging economies as it is in developed economies. The five emerging economies that are the subject of this volume – Brazil, China, India, South Africa and Turkey – together comprise 41 per cent of the world's population and 42 per cent of the world's labour force. Three of these countries – Brazil, China and India – are also among the world's largest economies. Each country liberalized its product markets in the hope of accelerating the country's growth and development. In some, this was accompanied by democratic transition, with organized labour playing a key role in the process of political change. High degrees of informality and late or limited industrial development produced patterns of industrial relations that differ from those in advanced economies.

These developments raise important questions about the institutionalization of industrial relations in emerging economies and its contribution to development. Is it meaningful to talk of an 'industrial relations system' in emerging economies? Can we trace the institutional trajectory of industrial relations over the course of a country's industrial development, and do the studies in this volume suggest that these trajectories converge? What about outcomes? Does the institutionalization of industrial relations in emerging economies contribute to inclusive development? This volume aims to shed light on these questions by examining industrial relations across very diverse national systems.

We have chosen to call this volume *Industrial Relations in Emerging Economies* because it focuses on the institutionalization of employment relations. This volume provides information about the institutions that are the traditional subject of industrial relations: trade unions, employers' organizations and collective bargaining. It also reveals the paucity of a traditional industrial relations perspective in a developing-country context where work in the informal economy is as significant, if not more significant in terms of the numbers of workers, than formal employment. In fact, as we show, the evolution of these institutions is closely intertwined with 'labour relations' involving all who work, including those in low-quality employment and own account workers in the informal economy.

This chapter begins with a brief overview of the theoretical perspectives that inform the study of industrial relations (section 1.2). It then examines empirical literature on industrial relations in developing economies (section 1.3). Section 1.4 considers the insights that emerge from the comparative analysis of the country studies in this volume. Comparative analysis of the very different institutional settings of the countries examined in this volume, provides important insights about the similar external factors shaping national industrial relations systems and, perhaps more importantly, the internal factors that constrain the contribution of these institutions to inclusive development. Industrial relations has always had an interdisciplinary orientation, employing methods of economics, sociology, political science and law; so too do the contributors to this volume. The chapter concludes that in examining industrial relations in emerging economies, it is necessary to expand the analysis and focus on the broader concept of labour relations.

1.2 THEORETICAL PERSPECTIVES ON THE INSTITUTIONALIZATION OF INDUSTRIAL RELATIONS

Theoretical perspectives of industrial relations have their origins in the response to the 'labour problem' that emerged in industrializing countries in the late nineteenth and early twentieth centuries. Faced with child labour, low wages, long working hours and hazardous working conditions, early trade unions used the 'method' of collective bargaining to improve working conditions (Webb and Webb, 1897). The gradual and incremental structuring of production relations through processes such as collective bargaining was seen as a means of 're-balancing the institutions of capitalism in order to bring about more stability, efficiency, justice and human values to the employment relationship' (Kaufman, 2010, p. 76).

Industrial relations developed as a study of this structuring of production relations and institutionalization of employment relations. For Dunlop (1958 [1993]), as he explains in his influential book *Industrial Relations Systems*, this includes the 'actors', 'contexts' and 'web of rules' created to govern work. Flanders (1965) understood industrial relations as the 'analysis of job regulation' and the ways in which the relations between employers and employees were managed within the substantive rules of industrial relations. Industrial relations is thus concerned with both job regulation and with the broader context in which the employment relationship is determined. For Flanders, the development of an industrial relations system was not systematic but emerged in a piecemeal and haphazard manner.

Fox (1974) identified three 'frames of reference' in industrial relations that held very different assumptions about the nature of work, employment relations and conflict, resulting in different theoretical and explanatory approaches: unitarism, pluralism and Marxism (also known as the radical approach). The unitarist perspective assumes that there is no difference in interests between an employer and employee. All actors and organizations share the same goals. Industrial relations is thus characterized by the ordering of common interests, the outcome of which is harmonious employment relations. This view is typical of human resource management according to which it is possible for employment policies and practices to align the interests of employees and employers (Lewin, 2001).

A pluralistic approach accepts conflict as an innate characteristic of employment relations and seeks pragmatic means to contain it (see, e.g., Fox, 1966; Clegg, 1979). According to this perspective, workers and employers with different interests require processes that help identify both common ground and potential trade-offs. Collective bargaining is seen as a principal means for keeping conflict within tolerable bounds. The incremental structuring of employment relations occurs as the result of an ongoing compromise between employers and employees, and their representative organizations. Employment relations is embedded in a stable system within which the interests of employers and workers can be reconciled. This institutionalization of employment relations also constitutes part of the broader corporatist social contract and is seen as the 'ideal' form for managing industrial conflict in the course of a country's economic development. From this perspective, a rise in unofficial 'wildcat' strike action or social disorder is simply an indicator of an institutional lag.

A radical perspective of industrial relations sees conflict as an inherent characteristic of employment relations, and inevitable given the nature of capitalist development. The focus is on the nature of the capitalist society and the fundamental division between capital and labour. Employment relations under capitalism involves the control and deployment of labour in order to generate profit so that firms can continue to accumulate capital. The field of industrial relations is concerned with the 'study of the process of control over work relations' (Hyman, 1975, p. 12). Trade unions balance the inherent imbalance of power in the workplace, and provide a form of opposition against capitalist production processes (Hyman, 2001). Rather than focusing on the processes that reconcile different interests, employment relations should be understood as a process of 'structured antagonism' between capital and labour (Edwards, 1986).

From this perspective, industrial relations may result in stability and the containment of conflict, but its value is also to be found in the processes of contestation, resistance and instability that the institutionalization of employment relations inevitably produces. This reveals fundamental contradictions, such as rising inequality, that in turn threaten the long-run viability of capitalist development. As a critique of the pluralist tradition, the radical perspective also points to a fundamental paradox which renders the institutionalization of employment relations inherently unstable and incomplete: the role of trade unions as actors on the one hand, and as architects of the industrial relations system on the other. By participating in the institutionalization of employment relations, unions are incorporated into the system, dependent on its formal procedures and integrated into structures of managerial control (Hyman, 1989). The institutional security they derive from the system may displace the need to continuously organize – and represent – the shop floor (Purcell, 1993). Growing dissatisfaction at the workplace and a lacuna in formal institutions for representation and collective action may result in the emergence of other forms of collective representation, the search for new sources of power and ongoing contestation in work relations (Hyman, 2015).

Considerable attention has been given to patterns of institutional development in the comparative industrial relations literature. Early theories of convergence argued that as countries move through distinct stages of development, a 'logic of industrialization' prevailed, production relations were structured along similar lines and employment relations started to resemble a common model ('pluralistic industrialism') (Kerr et al., 1964). Crouch's (1993 [2003]) seminal account of the historic development of European industrial relations institutions shows that after industrialization, the pattern tends to be one of institutional continuity within countries, and diversity across countries. He uses a common theoretical framework to explain these divergent yet nationally distinct patterns. Recent comparative studies of developed economies also find evidence of divergence in national patterns of employment relations (e.g., Katz and Darbishire, 2000; Bamber et al., 2010).

There has been some theorizing about continuity and discontinuity in the development of industrial relations institutions. Erickson and Kuruvilla (1998) in their evolutionary description of change in industrial relations, make a distinction between discontinuous change, and more incremental and adaptive change. Much of the literature emphasizes the role that economic restructuring plays in fundamentally transforming industrial relations. Since industrial relations institutions are socially constructed, they reflect the balance of class power at the time of their construction. There can be long periods of continuity as long as the economic interests of workers and employers are balanced which in turn rests on stable patterns of economic growth. When that economic pattern changes, interests and power resources change and industrial relations systems experience some instability until a new compromise is reached.[1] Howell (2005) argues that insufficient attention has been given in pluralist accounts of industrial relations to the role of the state in institutionalizing industrial relations. Broad shifts in the patterns of economic growth may trigger reforms to industrial relations systems:

> State actors play a central role in the construction of industrial relations institutions by virtue of a set of unique public capacities, of which I emphasize the following: enforcing and systematizing institutional change; narrating an authoritative interpretation of industrial relations crisis; solving the collective action problems of employers and unions; and anticipating and crafting alliances among private industrial actors, though it is important not to forget the state's overt coercive power. (p. 37)

The field of comparative political economy, particularly the institutionalist analysis within it that focuses on state traditions, has been very influential. Hall and Soskice's (2001) variety of capitalisms framework addresses the relationship between different institutions (including industrial relations institutions) in advanced capitalist economies and distinguishes between two types: a coordinated market economy (CME) and a liberal market economy (LME). Complementary institutions develop in different sub-spheres of the political economy at the national level (for example, financial systems and industrial relations systems). These undergird the strategic choices made by economic actors. Interactions between this set of institutions reinforce a certain path-dependence. This analytical framework is used to explain why globalization had different effects on industrial relations systems. For example, trade unions were weakened by business initiatives and labour market deregulation in LMEs, but remained strong in CMEs where different coalitions ensured their survival and their continued role in wage coordination. Other scholars in this tradition have emphasized 'critical junctures' in the development of (industrial relations) institutions, during which new configurations can emerge between different institutions, which in turn forges a new institutional trajectory (Thelen, 2009).

For the purposes of this volume, it is also interesting to consider the perspective of development economists. Freeman (2009), in considering the effects of labour market institutions (including unions and collective bargaining) on efficiency and equity, argues that where the share of formal sector employment is small, then these institutions will only affect aggregate outcomes if they have very large effects on the formal economy, there are sizeable spillovers to the informal economy, or they are located in sectors that are particularly important for economic development (for example, traded goods).

Literature on the role of the development state in economic transformation in Asia highlights the role that governments play in promoting cooperative labour–management relations, in addition to building economic infrastructure through education, training and research, and creating comparative advantage (Öniş, 1991). The importance of participatory institutions and cooperative employment relations in transforming work relations and processes was also emphasized by Stiglitz (2000) in his keynote address to the Industrial Relations Research Association (Boston, January 2000). In his view, development strategies needed to pay greater attention to the role of organized labour in the transformation of industrial relations, including through the creation of high-trust and high-involvement systems at the workplace.

1.3   THE INSTITUTIONALIZATION OF INDUSTRIAL RELATIONS AND DEVELOPMENT

What insights can we draw from the empirical literature on industrial relations in emerging economies?[2] Unlike the rich comparative literature that exists on developed economies, the study of the institutionalization of industrial relations in emerging economies is a less-developed subject of enquiry. Comparative studies on the role of trade unions in development from the 1950s and 1960s focused on the question of whether the growth of independent trade unions and collective bargaining contributed to, or impaired, development.[3]

One view held that effective unions would secure a wage that was higher than the marginal product of labour and thus divert the scarce resources available for investment into consumption (Mehta, 1957). Moreover, the labour-intensive production on which these economies relied to generate economic growth would be frustrated if hours of work were too short and wages above internationally competitive levels. Unions would also make it difficult to fire unproductive workers. According to this view, collective bargaining was only appropriate after a sufficient level of industrialization had been achieved.

Galenson (1959, 1962), in comparative studies on the role of labour in developing countries, came to a very different view. Independent trade unions did not impair the investment function, instead they played an important role in securing a committed workforce (through improvements in working conditions and job security). The positive engagement of workers in production and change would offset any consumptionist pressure:

> Independent trade unionism and satisfactory economic development are by no means antithetical. On the contrary, we believe that independent unions can make a major contribution to development by giving the individual worker a sense of personal dignity and a means of redressing his grievances. It is quite understandable for government leaders who are concentrating on the achievement of economic goals in the face of what must sometimes appear to be impossible odds to be impatient with intractable, 'irresponsible' representatives of workers. There is an ever-present temptation to silence them and to substitute paternalism for bargaining and conflict. But the price may be very high indeed: the loss to the nation of the creative energies of free men who feel themselves masters of their own fates rather than cogs in a vast, impersonal machine. (Galenson, 1962, p. 10)

Despite such views, concerns over the effects of unions on wages and labour costs continued to inform development strategies and structure the relationship between the state and organized labour. State actors tended to prioritize economic policies over labour policies and restrict the growth of independent unions. The interests of labour were viewed as subordinate to the interests of the state (Galenson, 1992).

A number of comparative studies in Asia, including on China and India, focused on the impact of a country's industrialization strategy, and of global economic integration, on national systems of industrial relations in the 1980s and 1990s. For example, Kuruvilla (1996) shows that policies of import substitution relied heavily on the maintenance of peace and stability by the state. A low-cost, export-oriented strategy tended to be associated with cost containment and union suppression. As countries shifted to higher value-added exports, their policy orientation toward labour changed and greater emphasis was placed on skills development and achieving flexibility. This was often accompanied by an increase in foreign direct investment and the growing importance of multinational enterprises (as new actors in industrial relations). Other studies in the region also highlighted the manner in which states intervened in industrial relations as they navigated the path of industrialization. They emphasize the role of external constraints in the transformation of national systems of industrial relations (see, e.g., Kuruvilla and Erickson, 1997, 2002; Frenkel and Harrod, 1995). Bhattacherjee (2001), in examining the evolution of industrial relations in India, considered it necessary for comparative studies to extend analysis beyond the effects of development strategies and international economic integration, to examine a broader range of socio-economic and cultural factors, as well as patterns of historical development.

Indeed, while it is important to understand the external factors that shape industrial relations, it is equally important to examine the historic process by which industrial relations have been institutionalized and the manner in which these shape future institutional trajectories. The experience of colonialism and the struggle for independence has had a profound influence on the manner in which industrial relations systems evolved in affected countries (Kuruvilla and Mundell, 1999; Koçer and Hayter, 2011). For example, in South Africa the newly independent state reproduced the system of control and exclusion that had developed under the colonial powers. The industrialization strategy in the twentieth century was closely related to the system of racial repression that ensured the availability of a cheap and disciplined labour force (Webster, 1978; Hayter and Pons-Vignon, Chapter 3 in this volume).[4] Even where workers were guaranteed certain rights and protections by post-colonial states, the majority of workers tended to be unemployed or to work in the informal economy and thus excluded from these protections (Webster and Bhowmik, 2014).

In Latin America, where organized labour had been a part of the struggle for independence, it was integrated into the post-colonial state in a form of state corporatism. When protests over conditions of work challenged the stability of these post-colonial political regimes, governments sought to extend labour rights and institutionalize labour conflict. Where these labour reforms coincided with the transition from an autocratic to a democratic state – such was the case in Brazil and Argentina – this led to the strengthening of collective rights (Cook, 1998). Organized labour enjoyed a generally favourable political context. The different strategies that were used by states to incorporate labour led to very different trajectories of political change and produced distinct constitutional legacies (Collier and Collier, 1991).

With economic restructuring in the 1980s and 1990s, the system of state corporatism came under increased pressure. The liberalization of markets posed new demands for labour market flexibility, which in turn eroded employment security at the core (of labour markets). The economic reforms generated higher levels of unemployment and inequality and the context for organized labour became increasingly unfavourable. Unions were often portrayed as 'privileged special-interest groups' and 'market-distorting institutions' that pushed up wages at the cost of all those excluded from the labour market and surviving at the periphery. This legitimized policies to remove and reduce union power (rather than expand labour protection to those excluded). In countries such as Chile and Peru, where unions were already weak, labour market reforms gave significant power to employers over individual workers and unions. In Brazil and Argentina, where labour was stronger, labour reforms affected individual employment relations but not collective industrial relations. Moreover, the recognition by the governments of Brazil and Argentina of the legitimacy of labour's collective interests led to the design of labour laws and policies that addressed labour market issues in a more integrated manner. In countries such as Chile, flexibility-driven reforms led to changes that were piecemeal and met with resistance from unions. They also exacerbated inequality (Cook, 2007).

Three factors determined the capacity of collective industrial relations institutions to withstand future attempts to weaken the power of labour: the initial incorporation of labour in the society; the position of labour during dictatorships and the subsequent transition to democracy; and the nature of reforms to labour legislation. Institutional legacies determined the capacity to respond to the effects of economic liberalization on the labour market. Cook (2007) has argued that of these institutions, a legacy of state corporatism and the protection of collective rights provided organized labour with the best institutional setting for its survival:

> Brazil and Argentina demonstrate the importance of strong unions in defending collective rights and protections. But more important, perhaps these cases suggest that the organizational resources and collective rights established in national labour law can provide a beachhead from which labour unions could weather political and economic storms. (Cook, 2007, p. 104)

Studies from the 2000s of industrial relations in emerging economies also point to the effect of the democratic incorporation of organized business and labour interests on the coherence between economic and social policies. Tripartite social dialogue between the state, peak employers' organizations and trade unions proved instrumental in some countries in focusing attention on the social costs of market-oriented reforms and resulted in measures to mitigate these. These included: agreement to moderate the pace of liberalization; packages to facilitate adjustment through training and support to industries; and reinforcement of social protection (Fraile, 2010). There are concerns that in some instances, the political inclusion of organized labour in policy-making was premised on co-option rather than concertation, and closed a channel for dissent. In these cases it served the interests of labour leaders, some of who subsequently moved into government and failed to address the interests of the broader working class (Alémán, 2010).

One of the issues that is not sufficiently addressed in the literature on industrial relations in emerging economies is the effect of internal constraints – including prevailing labour market conditions – on the direction of institutional change. Labour markets in these countries continue to be characterized by high levels of unemployment, underemployment and informal employment. The lack of broader social transformation, together with job and income insecurity, function as primary constraints on the institutionalization of work and employment relations, and the subsequent contribution of these institutions to development (for the example of the Philippines, see Erickson et al., 2003 and Hutchinson, 2016). These conditions lead to a questioning of the role that industrial relations plays in development. The narrative is often one in which privileged 'insiders' enjoy rights and protections at the expense of 'outsiders'. This argument is then used to justify reforms that deregulate protections for collective industrial relations, rather than to support the development of more inclusive labour relations institutions.

Another issue that deserves more attention is the fact that contestation over the 'labour problem' is not necessarily institutionalized. For example, a number of significant strikes and protests by unions have occurred outside of the formal industrial relations system. These include strikes in the construction industry in Brazil between 2011 and 2013; the strikes in the automobile sector in India in 2011 and 2012; the strikes of farmworkers in South Africa in 2012 and 2013, and mineworkers in 2014; the strikes of autoworkers in Turkey in 2015; and in China, starting with the 19-day strike at Honda and subsequently in other factories in Guangdong (Chan and Hui, 2012; Nowark, 2015; Campos and Dobrusin, 2016; and relevant chapters in this volume). Demands are similar: a better quality of life and fairer distribution of income. Many were sparked by the increase in insecurity that workers experience as a result of a rise in the use of contract labour.

Similarly, while there are notable accounts of unions organizing informal workers (for example, see Agarwala, 2013 for India) and lobbying for the extension of labour protection (for example, in Brazil, to domestic workers), we have also seen the emergence of new actors. Some authors consider this to be the result of the growing inadequacies of traditional industrial relations institutions to address the interests of the working class in these countries (Cook, 2011; Cook and Wood, 2011; Ness, 2016). Examples include self-employed workers organizing and engaging in solidarity-based collective action to improve the conditions in which they work (Routh, 2016; Webster and Bhowmik, 2014).

1.4   INDUSTRIAL RELATIONS IN EMERGING ECONOMIES

Despite their significance in the global economy, there are few studies of industrial relations in emerging economies (Barry and Wilkinson, 2011). This volume contributes to that literature and examines the evolution of industrial relations in these countries, the degree to which institutional trajectories have been shaped by economic and political transition, and the role these industrial relations institutions play in forging patterns of inclusive development. For the purposes of this volume we consider inclusive development to mean patterns of economic growth that contribute to reductions in working poverty and inequality.

This volume includes country chapters from very different regions: Southern Asia (India), East Asia (China), Africa (South Africa), Latin America (Brazil) and Europe/Western Asia (Turkey). Manufacturing output has been steadily increasing and, until recently, many of these countries were experiencing moderate to rapid economic growth. Yet the extent to which this resulted in structural transformation and sustainable reductions of poverty remains an open question. As the figures in Table 1.1 show, the proportion of those in informal employment remains significant in many of these countries. Income inequality is high, and there has been a rise in insecure forms of employment, whether 'labour brokering' in South Africa, 'dispatched labour' in China or 'outsourced' labour in Brazil.

Each of these countries experienced significant economic restructuring in the 1980s and 1990s as they integrated into the global economy. In some, the liberalization of the economy was accompanied by political transition (a return to democracy in Brazil, 1985; democratic transition in

Table 1.1   Population, income, growth and labour markets, 2016 or latest

Country	Population (000)	GDP (PPP) per capita – constant 2011 $	Inequality (Gini)	GDP growth (%)	Trade (% GDP)	Labour force participation (rate)	Informal employment (% of total)
Brazil	207 653	14 023	51.48	−3.6	24.6	62.0	43.0
China	1 378 665	14 339	42.16	6.7	37.1	70.9	51.9
India	1 324 171	6092	35.15	7.1	39.8	53.9	90.6
South Africa	55 908	12 260	63.40	0.3	60.4	54.7	34.0
Turkey	79 512	23 756	40.04	3.2	46.8	52.0	31.7

Source: World Bank (WDI), UNDP (HDI) and ILO (informal employment).

South Africa, 1994); in others, political change was more modest (India, Turkey). With the exception of China, all are now political democracies. All these countries are fairly integrated into the global economy (see Table 1.1).

What is perhaps notable for the purposes of this volume, are the differences in industrial relations systems and the relationship of the state to organized business and labour interests (see Table 1.2). Not all countries have ratified the ILO Freedom of Association and Protection of the Right to Organise Convention, 1948 (No. 87) and the Right to Organise and Collective Bargaining Convention, 1949 (No. 98). Corporatism is a mechanism used by governments to integrate the associations and organizations of different interest groups, such as trade unions and employers' organizations (Schmitter, 1974). South Africa can be described as corporatist, in the government's use of national institutional processes to integrate employers' and workers' collective interests into policy-making, particularly in respect of labour market policy. Brazil is described as state corporatist, given the central role the state has played in the regulation of the affairs of both unions and employers' organizations and the integration of their interests. China can be described as a model of state corporatist unitarism, in that the state maintains indirect control over the official trade union, business associations and employers' organizations, aligning their interests in order to ensure harmonious industrial relations (Unger and Chan, 2015).

These corporatist models can be counterpoised with pluralist ones involving a multiplicity of interest groups, free market competition and conflict. In Turkey, the collective rights of workers and collective disputes are constrained by the state, subordinate to economic policies, and can thus be described as a form of state pluralism. In India, industrial relations evolved from a post-independence system of state pluralism, where the interests and rights of workers were constrained by state-led industrialization, to a system of industrial pluralism, where these interests are now constrained by the exercise of managerial power at the workplace, as well as conditions in the large unorganized informal economy (Bhattacherjee, 2001).

These differences raise important questions. Are there common patterns and experiences of the institutionalization of industrial relations across these countries? Can we trace the institutional trajectory of industrial relations over the course of a country's industrial development, and do the countries examined in this volume suggest that these trajectories converge?

Table 1.2 Industrial relations indicators, 2015/16

Country	Industrial relations	Tripartite social dialogue	Trade union density (%)	Trade union structure	Collective bargaining coverage (%)	Structure of collective bargaining
Brazil	State corporatist	Council for Economic and Social Development (CDES) National Labour Forum (FNT)	17.7	Single union (*unicidade syndical*) craft unionism	65.7	Territorial by occupation
China	State corporatist unitarism	National Tripartite Consultatve Committee (NTCC)	42.6	State-sponsored monopoly union	40.6*	Enterprise level and some by sector or territory
India	Industrial pluralism	Indian Labour Conference (ILC) Standing Labour Committee (SLC) Industrial committees	12.8	Multiple union structures (craft, industry, general etc.)	6.0	Enterprise level (private sector), centralized (public sector)
South Africa	Corporatism	National Economic Development and Labour Council (NEDLAC)	28.2	Largely industrial unionism	30.0	Sectoral bargaining councils, multi-employer bargaining and enterprise level
Turkey	State pluralism	Economic and Social Council (ESC)	8.2	Industrial unionism	5.9	Enterprise level

Note: * For China this is an indicator of coverage of 'collective negotiation agreements' and not CBAs.

Source: Author and ILOSTAT.

1.4.1   Institutional Continuity and Discontinuity

Each of the authors in this volume place the existing industrial relations institutions in historic context. They examine the different process
by which employment relations became institutionalized. They provide
evidence of periods of institutional restructuring, followed by periods
of institutional stability: of continuity and discontinuity. Discontinuity
is often explained by periods of political or economic transition. To use
the analogy developed by Erickson and Kuruvilla (1998), the transition
to a democratic regime was often associated with discontinuous change.
Economic transition and integration into the global economy tended
to result in incremental change and the adaption of industrial relations
institutions rather than their dramatic transformation.

Comparative analysis shows that rather than economic liberalisation
being an exogenous factor – driving systemic change through increases
in foreign direct investment (FDI), a rise in manufacturing exports and
the intensification of competition – it amplified certain endogenous
forces. Growing economic insecurity and inequality within the labour
market places as much pressure on institutionalized industrial relations
(from the periphery, so to speak) as the functional requirements (for
example, flexibility, competitive labour costs) of a particular development strategy.

Berg and Schneider (Chapter 4 in this volume) show that there has been
little change in the main features of Brazil's industrial relations system
since these were first instituted in the 1930s during the Vargas era. The
government of the time, which adopted an ambitious industrialization
agenda supported by a state corporatist system of industrial relations,
relied heavily on the legislative branch to regulate labour markets and
labour disputes to ensure labour peace. The structure in which a single
union represents union members of a given occupational category and
territory (*unicidade syndical*), supported by a union tax that finances
unions, remained stable for decades. A transition to democratic rule in
1946 and the passage of a new Constitution enhanced labour rights but
retained the state corporatist system and union structure. After a period of
military dictatorship and state intervention in union activities, the return
to democracy and adoption of a new Constitution in 1988 left these pillars
of the industrial relations system intact.

In South Africa, the transition to democratic rule in 1994 marked a shift
from a form of state pluralism premised on exclusion, to a corporatist
system premised on inclusion. Nevertheless, it retained the institutional
features of collective bargaining at the industry level first established in
law in 1924 (Hayter and Pons-Vignon, Chapter 3 in this volume). Rani

and Sen (Chapter 2 in this volume) also show significant continuity in legal and institutional frameworks from the British colonial system in India. Economic shocks in the 1980s and the different union strategies (some of which were politically affiliated, others independent) resulted in the emergence of a variety of industrial relations systems at the state level.

Lee (Chapter 5 in this volume) provides a brief description of the fundamental transition in China from a centrally planned to a market economy, and from an agricultural to increasingly industrial society. This was also marked by discontinuous change in institutions of employment relations, from lifelong employment in state-owned enterprises to an individual contract system. There has been remarkable continuity in two institutions. First, China's adoption of economic reforms from the early 1980s saw the revival of the workers' congress system first instituted in the 1920s (Hong, 1984). Second, the All China Federation of Trade Unions (ACFTU) maintains its monopoly representation, despite the transition to a socialist market economy. Since the 2000s, Lee identifies a process of top-down 'cloning' of labour market institutions on the one hand, yet divergent patterns of industrial relations across different regions on the other.

1.4.2 Political Transition

In some of the countries studied, the transition to democratic rule provided unions with a new source of institutional power. In Brazil and South Africa, the political inclusion and incorporation of organized labour gave unions a degree of political influence and was accompanied by the strengthening of labour rights. There were also significant attempts by the state to foster tripartite policy dialogue (in South Africa after 1994, and in Brazil after 2002) in order to respond to labour market challenges and possible reforms.

Organized labour in Brazil played an important role in protests calling for an end to the dictatorship. When democratic rule was re-established in 1985, it was followed by the enactment of a new Constitution (1988) that ended interference by the state in the associational governance of unions and recognized the right to strike. At the same time, it maintained the structure of union organization and union finance (with some modifications). This provided labour with important organization resources. The new government in 2002, headed by a former trade unionist, Luiz Inácio 'Lula' da Silva, sought to reach consensus on changes to collective labour law. The emphasis on tripartism and policy concertation marked a departure in practice from previous governments. Among the most important were the Councils for Economic and Social

Development (CDES), a multipartite structure for discussions on labour social security and tax reforms, and the National Labour Forum (FNT) on labour law reform. Considerable time was spent on potential labour law reforms. Debates on a bill proved difficult; organized employer interests blocked proposals to regulate subcontracting and reduce working hours. Nevertheless a law was finally adopted in 2008 that recognized the role of central unions in tripartite dialogue and provided modalities for their financing through the union tax. The Lula Government also advanced social policy in a number of other areas, including increases in the minimum wage and the expansion of social protection. More recently, there has been a reversal in government support and proposals to reform the core pillars of the labour code (the CLT) (Berg and Schneider, Chapter 4 in this volume).

In South Africa, the independent unions had been key actors in the fight for democracy. A 'tripartite alliance' was established between the largest union confederation, COSATU; the ruling party, the African National Congress (ANC); and the South African Communist Party. When the new democratically elected ANC government came into power in 1994, it had already been engaging union confederations and organized business in designing a new corporatist system of industrial relations. This led to the establishment of the National Economic and Development, Labour and Social Council (NEDLAC). The mid- to late 1990s saw significant changes to labour market policies and regulations that extended both individual and collective workers' rights to all workers. New bargaining institutions were established in the public sector. In 2013, there was tripartite dialogue in NEDLAC on labour law amendments to ensure the protection of workers working for 'labour brokers'. In 2016, tripartite social dialogue over low wages, wage inequality and violent and protracted labour disputes led to an agreement in February 2017 to a new national minimum wage, a Code of Good Practice on Collective Bargaining, Industrial Action and Picketing, and amendments to be introduced to the Labour Relations Act. Nevertheless, as Hayter and Pons-Vignon (Chapter 3 in this volume) point out, significant tensions within the labour movement over the terms of the 'tripartite alliance' with the ruling political party have undermined the unity of organized labour. Employers' organizations are also challenged by the diversity of enterprises and difficulty articulating common interests.

In India, the transition to democracy took place with independence in 1947. Rani and Sen (Chapter 2 in this volume) provide an account of a government that intended to pave the way for a 'labour-inclusive development state'. Given the state's reliance on domestic capital, it tended to support the interests of employers and intervened in industrial relations in order to maintain industrial peace.

Turkey's transition to multi-party democracy was interrupted by military *coups d'état* in 1960, 1971 and 1980. Nevertheless, the adoption of a new Constitution in 1961, after the 1960 *coup d'état*, expanded workers' rights and ushered in organizational and collective bargaining rights. Industrial relations became increasingly institutionalized and income inequality declined in the two decades that followed. However, the 1980 *coup d'etat* and suspension of the Constitution dealt a severe blow to the nascent industrial relations system. Under the new Constitution enacted in 1982, union freedoms and collective rights were restricted. This legislation remained in force for almost 30 years without any major changes, until the 2010 amendments to the Constitution. In 2012, new labour laws made it easier to establish unions and be recognized for collective bargaining, but also easier for the government to curb industrial action. While the government established a tripartite Economic and Social Council (ESC) in 1995 after discussions regarding potential accession to the European Union, this has not played a key role in shaping labour policy and a number of strikes have been banned by the government on the grounds that they were prejudicial to national security (Çelik, Chapter 6 in this volume).[5]

1.4.3 Economic Liberalization and Industrial Relations Institutions

The liberalization of the economy had a significant impact on industrial relations institutions in all countries studied. There was increased pressure for flexibility at the workplace (numerical, functional and wage flexibility). Whereas political change had a transformative effect on industrial relations systems (perhaps with the exception of Brazil), the change arising from the integration into global markets can be described as incremental. The direction of that change depended to some degree on the organizational strength and power resources available to organized labour. Close alliances with the government provided an important source of institutional power. In some instances, such as South Africa and Brazil, organized labour was able to influence the direction of change and industrial relations institutions played a role in 'regulating flexibility'. In India and Turkey, organized labour was not able to draw on organizational strength or institutional power. The result was the further weakening of labour as market pressures undermined bargaining power.

In Brazil, liberalization during the 1990s led to a significant decline in employment in sectors that were traditionally highly unionized, including manufacturing and banking. Unions shifted their focus from wage increases to job security. The increasing trend toward outsourcing and subcontracting weakened the bargaining power of labour. Labour reforms introduced in the 1990s focused on achieving greater flexibility in employment (for example, easing hiring of temporary workers) and working conditions (for example, banked hours and other flexible working time schemes). However, efforts to change the corporatist system of industrial relations, and to remove the union tax and *unicidade*, were unsuccessful and unions retained their core organizational resources. The government also introduced an Executive Order in 2004 concerning Profits and Results (PLR) that provided an incentive to increase productivity in the form of a collectively negotiated bi-annual non-taxable bonus payment to workers. The adoption of banked hours was also subject to collective negotiations. This enhanced the role of bipartite negotiations in a traditionally corporatist system, but did little to change its basic tenets. As Berg and Schneider (Chapter 4 in this volume) show, it opened a space for unions to enter into dialogue on technology, qualifications and other topics, thus expanding the scope of the bargaining agenda. The measure became an important feature of industrial relations in Brazil. Unions were able to represent labour interests in the face of demands for the intensification of work and increases in productivity. It is still too early to tell what the outcomes of the proposed reforms to the labour code will be. At the time of writing, unions are in defensive mode and fighting to hold on to the gains of the earlier period, as well as to maintain their institutional space in labour relations (Berg and Schneider, Chapter 4 in this volume).

In South Africa, the post-apartheid vision for labour market policy was one of balancing economic and social policies through policy concertation in NEDLAC and achieving 'regulated flexibility' in labour markets through 'voice'. The agenda for labour law reform sought to reinforce the role of industry-level bargaining councils and introduce statutory workplace forums to encourage workplace cooperation and 'world-class manufacturing'. As Hayter and Pons-Vignon (Chapter 3 in this volume) show, unions have played a key role in stemming the rise in insecure forms of employment ('labour broking') both through tripartite social dialogue on labour law reforms on temporary employment, and through collective agreements that regulate non-standard forms of employment in different ways. However, while collective bargaining plays an important role in balancing flexibility and insecurity in some industries and enterprises, this is limited in the face of high structural unemployment and labour market insecurity. As is discussed below, this is placing considerable pressure on institutionalized industrial relations, despite the relative strength of organized labour. At a policy level, there has been considerable tripartite dialogue on labour market policy, including the new Labour Relations Act of 1995 (and subsequent amendments), the signing of a number of social pacts (for example, on skills and youth employment), and most recently on the introduction of a national minimum wage. By contrast, there has been a dearth of concertation over macroeconomic policy.

In India, shortly after coming to power in 1984, the government of Rajiv Gandhi began to liberalize the economy. These initial steps were intensified under the International Monetary Fund (IMF) Stabilization and Structural Adjustment Programme in 1991. Restructuring in the private sector led to an increase in managerial demands for functional flexibility and a shift to productivity-linked bargaining. As a result, the industrial relations system has been progressively decentralized to the enterprise level. There has been a change in the union structure marked by the proliferation of enterprise unions (due in part to the opposition of party-affiliated unions to decentralization) and a decline in the bargaining power of unions. This is accompanied by an increase in inter-state and inter-city variations in industrial relations (Rani and Sen, Chapter 2 in this volume).

The liberalization of Turkey's economy from 1980s onwards, and large-scale privatization, coincided with the military coup, limiting of labour rights and weakening of industrial relations institutions. Organized labour has not been able to achieve a balance in the face of powerful business interests (Çelik, Chapter 6 in this volume).

China underwent the most dramatic economic transition in the 1980s, from a centrally planned to a market economy. Lee (Chapter 5 in this volume) argues that the formal industrial relations institutions were not prepared to address the challenges of new market-based employment relations. During the 1990s there were almost no enterprise unions in most enterprises in the burgeoning non-state sector. Those that did exist tended to be management appointees. A bifurcation occurred between 'institutions' and 'voice', and workplace relations were increasingly characterized by flexibility and insecurity. Rising protests led to attempts to stabilize and build 'harmonious labour relations'. Concerted efforts were made to expand coverage by collective contracts. While the author identifies both hybrid forms of representation and 'institutional thickening' that have improved the working conditions and terms of employment for those covered, the overall picture remains one of a bifurcated system.

1.4.4   Industrial Relations and Inclusive Development

The question that remains is the degree to which industrial relations institutions contributed to inclusive development. One important issue that emerges from this comparative study, with important implications for inclusive growth and development, is the complementarity between labour market institutions and policies in the country. In Brazil and China, this complementarity contributed to the formalization of employment and a reversal of income inequality in the 2000s.

Brazil included organized labour and business in discussions on reforms to the labour code as well as increases in the national minimum wage, thus reinforcing complementarities between labour market institutions. As Berg and Schneider (Chapter 4 in this volume) show, the reinvigoration of the minimum wage policy and the PLR had a favourable influence on collective bargaining, which in turn delivered real wage increases and compressed the wage distribution. The state corporatist system allowed for a high degree of coordination. A union campaign that led to an increase in the minimum wage, and the extension of workers' rights to domestic workers, also played an important role in reducing income inequality. Unions and their collective action did not act as a brake on development. On the contrary, labour market developments were characterized by a growth in formal employment, a decline in unemployment, a decrease in the numbers of informal workers and a reduction in poverty in the 2000s. With the transition to a new government and worsening economic context, the pendulum has once again swung in the other direction, shrinking labour's space in national debates and weakening their position at the bargaining table.

In South Africa, complementarities between particular industrial relations institutions (NEDLAC and bargaining councils) appear to be addressing rising insecurity in the employment relationship. Collective bargaining is compressing wage structures and reducing wage inequality among those covered. However high unemployment and rising inequality has limited the potential contribution of these institutions to inclusive development. Nevertheless, organized labour, organized employers and the state continue to play a key role in shaping labour market policies, including the regulation of temporary employment and approval by Cabinet of a National Minimum Wage Bill in November 2017, aimed at addressing poverty and inequality.

In Turkey, industrial relations institutions deliver gains for the workers covered, but make little contribution to a more inclusive development path. In India, the role of industrial relations institutions is marginal, in part due to the limited organizational resources of unions and their capacity to represent the unorganized sector or informal economy. As Rani and Sen (Chapter 2 in this volume) show, other measures such as the Mahatma Gandhi National Rural Employment Guarantee Act (MGNREGA), which provides 100 days of employment per year to those willing to work, have raised the incomes of households in rural areas. New workers' organizations are also being formed in the informal economy.

A paradox that emerges is that while organized labour gained institutional and organizational power in Brazil and South Africa, and was able to influence broader economic and social policies, this has not necessarily been accompanied by institutional deepening in respect of employment relations at the workplace. The continued bifurcation in China between 'institutions' and 'voice', and absence (India and Turkey) or hollowing out (South Africa) of collective representation at the workplace has resulted in an observable increase in spontaneous non-procedural protests, disputes and work stoppages. In China, Lee (Chapter 5 in this volume) points to the widely reported Honda strike in 2010 and the spate of wildcat strikes since. In India, women workers from garment factories in Bengaluru in 2016, protesting over changes to provident funds, were not members of a trade union. Hayter and Pons-Vignon (Chapter 3 in this volume) show similar examples of strikes that took place in mining and agriculture in South Africa. Despite the institutionalization of industrial relations and highly regarded dispute resolution processes and institutions, in 2016, 59 per cent of strikes were unprotected. The authors argue that the lack of broader economic and social transformation and high dependency ratios weigh heavily on the bargaining agenda and are placing pressure on the industrial relations system.

As Figure 1.1 shows, industrial relations institutions covering those in formal 'employment relations', and those in non-standard forms of

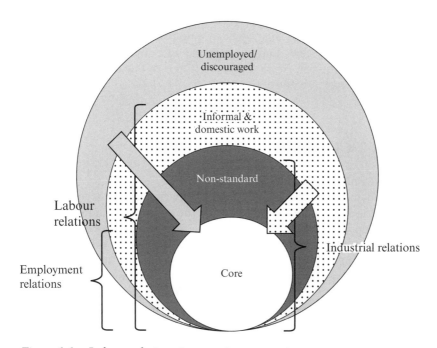

Figure 1.1   Labour relations in emerging economies

employment do not exist in an enclave. Pressure from the surrounding 'labour relations' context can lead to discontinuous change. Rather than 'insiders' at the core protecting their members against 'outsiders', these 'insiders', where they have the organizational resources to do so, do act in solidarity to improve the conditions of the so-called 'outsiders'. In Brazil and South Africa, unions have engaged in solidarity action, lobbying for changes in social policy to improve the lives of workers on the periphery. At the same time, conditions in the wider labour market place pressure on formal processes of collective bargaining and ultimately erode the institutionalization of industrial relations at the core. Those covered by formal industrial relations institutions and processes continually face the prospect that the labour protections they enjoy will be deregulated.

In India and Turkey, the organizational resources of unions are very limited. As Rani and Sen (Chapter 2 in this volume) show, not only have unions in India been turning their attention to organizing the informal economy and forging coalitions with other actors, but new workers' organizations have emerged representing home-based workers, street vendors, *beedi* workers, waste-pickers and construction workers. These representational gaps and organizational challenges limit the contribution of industrial relations institutions to stability and inclusive development. In order to understand the contribution of the organized interests of workers and employers to development, it is thus necessary to broaden our concepts and analysis and to examine 'labour relations' involving all those who work, including those in low-quality jobs in the informal economy, own-account workers and those engaging in unpaid family work.

1.5   CONCLUSION

The contributions to this collection show patterns of continuity and change in industrial relations. Despite significant changes in policies, many features of industrial relations in the countries examined tend to be path-dependent: their development determined by the original legal framework and institutions. Democratic transition was often accompanied by the inclusion of labour in the polity. In some countries, processes of inclusion and incorporation enhanced the influence of organized labour in economic and social policy with favourable outcomes. In others, this was either confined to a very narrow agenda or remained inconsequential. The liberalization of economies put industrial relations systems under significant pressure. The degree to which they have been able to contribute to inclusive development depended on their capacity to influence labour and social policy (for example, the minimum wage) as well as on the complementarity between labour market institutions and policies. It also depended on the capacity to enhance the quality of employment relations at the workplace, a process which has been far more limited in the countries studied.

As the various chapters in this volume show, unemployment, informal employment and income insecurity pose internal constraints on the capacity of industrial relations institutions to balance the interests of capital and labour. This has important implications for efforts to forge an inclusive development path. One is that conflict may not be institutionalized, and thus while delivering short-run 'wins', does not deliver sustainable improvements in the conditions of labour or harness the commitment of the labour force. Another is a deepening representational gap. This is characterized on the one hand by resource-constrained unions that do not have the capacity to organize or represent those in the informal economy or the growing numbers of insecure contract workers; and on the other hand, the emergence of new actors. Without a concerted effort to expand labour protection through institutions of *labour relations* that can cover all who work, industrial relations at the core will continue to be eroded, constraining in its ability to contribute to inclusive development.

This reveals the paucity of a traditional industrial relations perspective in a developing-country context where work in low-quality jobs in the informal economy is as, if not more, significant than work in formal employment. As the contributions to this volume show, the evolution of industrial relations institutions is closely intertwined with that of *labour relations* involving all those who work. It is thus necessary to expand our analysis and focus on the broader concept of *labour relations* and the actors, processes and alliances that address the 'labour problem', balance work relations and improve the conditions of all who work.

NOTES

* The author thanks Janine Berg and Uma Rani for their comments, contributions and suggestions and those of the two anonymous reviewers.
1. These power resources may be associational (for example, membership), structural (for example, having organized sectors important for the economy) or institutional (for example, alliances with and political resources derived from the state).
2. The term 'emerging economies' is used rather than 'emerging markets'. These countries are categorized by intermediate levels of income and experienced significant economic transformation as they integrated into the global economy. See Vercueil (2012).
3. For a review of the debates on 'labour freedom versus growth' literature of the 1950s and 60s, see Levin (1964).

4. South Africa gained partial independence when the Union of South Africa was formed on 31 May 1910, and the Republic of South Africa was declared on 31 May 1961 under minority rule during apartheid.
5. The European Parliament voted to suspend accession negotiations with Turkey in November 2016.

REFERENCES

Alemán, J. 2010. *Labour Relations in New Democracies*. Basingtoke, UK and New York: Palgrave Macmillan.

Bamber, G.J., Lansbury, R.D. and Wailes, N. 2010. *International and Comparative Employment Relations: Globalisation and Change*. London: SAGE.

Barry, M. and Wilkinson, A. (eds). 2011. *Research Handbook of Comparative Employment Relations*. Cheltenham, UK and Northampton, MA, USA: Edward Elgar Publishing.

Bhattacherjee, D. 2001. 'The evolution of Indian industrial relations: A comparative perspective', *Industrial Relations Journal*, **32**(3), pp. 244–63.

Campos, L. and Dobrusin, B. 2016. 'Labour conflict in Argentina and Brazil: Challenging an alliance?', *Workers of the World: International Journal on Strikes and Social Conflicts*, **1**(8), pp. 99–121.

Chan, C.K.C. and Hui, E.S.I. 2012. 'The dynamics and dilemma of workplace trade union reform in China: The case of the Honda workers' strike', *Journal of Industrial Relations*, **54**(5), pp. 653–68.

Clegg, H.A. 1979. *The Changing System of Industrial Relations in Great Britain: A Completely Rewritten Version of the System of Industrial Relations in Great Britain*. Oxford: Blackwell.

Collier, R.B. and Collier, D. 1991. *Shaping the Political Arena: Critical Junctures, the Labour Movement and Regime Dynamics in Latin America*. Princeton, NJ: Princeton University Press.

Cook, F.L. and Wood, G. 2011. 'Symposium on employment relations and new actors in emerging economies', *Relations Industrielles*, **66**(1), pp. 3–6.

Cook, M.L. 1998. 'Toward flexible industrial relations? Neo-liberalism, democracy, and labor reform in Latin America', *Industrial Relations: A Journal of Economy and Society*, **37**(3), 311–36.

Cook, M.L. 2007. *The Politics of Labour Reform in Latin America: Between Flexibility and Rights*. University Park, PA: Penn State University Press.

Cook, M.L. 2011. 'Unions and labor policy under left governments in Latin America', *Revista Trabajo*, **5**(7), pp. 55–73.

Crouch, C. 1993 (reprint 2003). *Industrial Relations and European State Traditions*. Oxford: Clarendon Press.

Dunlop, J.T. 1958 [1993]. *Industrial Relations Systems* (revised edn 1993). Boston, MA: Harvard Business School Press.

Edwards, P.K. 1986. *Conflict at Work: A Materialist Analysis of Workplace Relations*. Oxford: Blackwell.

Erickson, C.L. and Kuruvilla, S. 1998. 'Industrial relations system transformation', *Industrial and Labour Relations Review*, **52**(1), pp. 3–21.

Erickson, C.L., Kuruvilla, S., Ofreneo, R.E. and Ortiz, M.A. 2003. 'From core to periphery? Recent developments in employment relations in the

Philippines', *Industrial Relations: A Journal of Economy and Society*, **42**(3), pp. 368–95.

Flanders, A. 1965. *Industrial Relations: What is Wrong with the System? An Essay on Its Theory and Future*. London: Faber & Faber.

Fox, A. 1966. 'Industrial sociology and industrial relations', Royal Commission on Trade Unions and Employer Association Research Paper 3. London: Her Majesty's Stationary Office.

Fox, A. 1974. *Beyond Contract: Work, Power and Trust Relationships*. London: Faber & Faber.

Fraile, L. (ed.). 2010. *Blunting Neoliberalism: Tripartism and Economic Reforms in the Developing World*. Basingstoke, UK and Geneva: Palgrave Macmillan and ILO.

Freeman, R. 2009. 'Labor regulations, unions, and social protection in developing countries: Market distortions or efficient institutions?', National Bureau of Economic Research (No. 14789).

Frenkel, S. and Harrod, J. (eds). 1995. *Industrialization and Labor Relations: Contemporary Research in Seven Countries*. Ithaca, NY: Cornell University Press.

Galenson, W. (ed). 1959. *Labour and Economic Development*. New York: John Wiley & Sons.

Galenson, W. (ed). 1962. *Labour in Developing Economies*. Berkeley and Los Angeles: University of California Press.

Galenson, W. (ed). 1992. *Labour and Economic Growth in Five Asian Countries: South Korea, Malaysia, Taiwan, Thailand and the Philippines*. New York: Greenwood Publishing Group.

Hall, P. and Soskice, D. 2001. *Varieties of Capitalism: The Institutional Foundations of Comparative Advantage*. Oxford and New York: Oxford University Press.

Hong, N.S. 1984. 'One brand of workplace democracy: The workers' congress in the Chinese enterprise', *Journal of Industrial Relations*, **26**(1), pp. 56–75.

Howell, C. 2005. *Trade Unions and the State: The Construction of Industrial Relations Institutions in Britain, 1890–2000*. Princeton, NJ and Oxford: Princeton University Press.

Hutchinson, J. 2016. 'The state and employment relations in the Philippines', *Journal of Industrial Relations*, **58**(2), pp. 183–98.

Hyman, R. 1975. *Industrial Relations: A Marxist Introduction*. London: Macmillan.

Hyman, R. 1989. *Strikes*. London: Palgrave Macmillan.

Hyman, R. 2001. *Understanding European Trade Unionism: Between Market, Class and Society*. London: SAGE.

Hyman, R. 2015. 'Three scenarios for industrial relations in Europe', *International Labour Review*, **154**(1), pp. 5–14.

Katz, H.C. and Darbishire, O.R. 2000. *Converging Divergences: Worldwide Changes in Employment Systems* (Vol. 32). Ithaca, NY, USA and London: Cornell University Press.

Kaufman, B. 2010. 'The theoretical foundation of industrial relations and its implications for labour economics and human resource management', *Industrial and Labour Relations Review*, **64**(1), pp. 74–108.

Kerr, C., Harbison, F., Dunlop, J.T. and Myers, C.A. 1964. *Industrialism and Industrial Man*. New York: Oxford University Press.

Koçer, R.G. and Hayter, S. 2011. 'Comparative study of labour relations in African countries', Amsterdam Institute for Advanced Labor Studies Working Paper, 116.

Kuruvilla, S. 1996. 'Linkages between industrialization strategies and industrial relations/human resource policies: Singapore, Malaysia, the Philippines, and India', *Industrial and Labor Relations Review*, **49**(4), pp. 635–57.

Kuruvilla, S. and C.L. Erickson. 1997. 'Industrial relations system transformation', *ILR Review*, **52**(1), pp. 3–21.

Kuruvilla, S. and C.L. Erickson. 2002. 'Change and transformation in Asian industrial relations', *Industrial Relations*, **41**, pp. 171–227.

Kuruvilla, S. and Mundell, B. (eds). 1999. *Colonialism, Nationalism, and the Institutionalization of Industrial Relations in the Third World*. Stamford, CT: Jai Press.

Levin, S. 1964. 'Conceptions of trade unionism in economic and political development', *Economic Development and Cultural Change*, **12**(2), pp. 215–19.

Lewin, D. 2001. 'IR and HR perspectives on workplace conflict: What can each learn from the other?', *Human Resource Management Review*, **11**(4), pp. 453–85.

Mehta, A. 1957. 'The mediating role of the trade union in underdeveloped countries', *Economic Development and Cultural change*, **6**(1), pp. 16–23.

Ness, I. 2016. *Southern Insurgency*. London: Pluto Press.

Nowark. J. 2015. 'Mass strikes in Brazil, South Africa and India after 2008', in Bieler, A., Roland Erne, R., Golden, D., Helle, I., Kjeldstadli, K., Matos, T. and Stan, S. (eds), *Labour and Transnational Action in Times of Crisis*. London and New York: Rowman & Littlefield.

Öniş, Z. 1991. 'The logic of the developmental state', *Comparative Politics*, **24**(1), pp. 109–26.

Purcell, J. 1993. 'The end of institutional industrial relations', *Political Quarterly*, **64**, pp. 6–23.

Routh, S. 2016. 'Informal workers' aggregation and law', *Theoretical Inquiries in Law*, **17**, pp. 283–320.

Schmitter, P.C. 1974. 'Still the century of corporatism?', *Review of Politics*, **36**(1), pp. 85–131.

Stiglitz, J. 2000. 'Democratic development as the fruits of labour', keynote address at the Industrial Relations Research Association, Boston, January. Reproduced in *Perspectives on Work*, **4**(1), pp. 31–8.

Supriya, R. 2016. 'Informal workers' aggregation and law', *Theoretical Inquiries in Law*, **17**(1), pp. 283–320.

Thelen, K. 2009. 'Institutional change in advanced political economies', *British Journal of Industrial Relations*, **47**(3), pp. 471–98.

Unger, J. and Chan, A. 2015. 'State corporatism and business associations in China: A comparison with earlier emerging economies of East Asia', *International Journal of Emerging Markets*, **10**(2), pp. 178–93.

Vercueil, J., 2012. 'Les Pays Émergents: Brésil, Russie, Inde, Chine', *Mutations Économiques Et Nouveaus Défis* (3rd edn, 17 July). Paris: Bréal.

Webb, S. and Webb, B. 1897. *Industrial Democracy* (1st edn). London, New York and Bombay: Longmans, Green & Co.

Webster, E. (ed.) 1978. *Essays in Southern African Labour History* (Vol. 1). Johannesburg: Ravan Press.

Webster, E. and Bhowmik, S. 2014. 'Work, livelihoods and insecurity in the South', in Fakier, K. and Ehmke, E. (eds), *Socio-Economic Insecurity in Emerging Economies: Building New Spaces*. London: Routledge.

2. Labour relations and inclusive growth in India: New forms of voice

Uma Rani and Ratna Sen

2.1 INTRODUCTION

India has experienced high growth rates since the mid-1990s: gross domestic product (GDP) grew on average by nearly 7 per cent a year, and there have been periods when the annual growth rate reached almost 10 per cent. As a result of this growth, poverty has been somewhat reduced in certain regions; however, over the past decade to 2012 consumption expenditure inequality has increased, and income inequality is quite high when compared to other emerging economies and is second-highest after South Africa (Rani and Furrer, 2016). The quality of employment seems not to have improved, with the proportion of low-paid workers increasing (Rani and Belser, 2012a). There has also been an increase in casualization of labour, with greater use of subcontracting arrangements, fixed-term contracts and casual work (Srivastava, 2016).

Real wages have been growing for both salaried (formal) and casual (informal) workers in rural and urban areas, though there are wide variations in its growth across the different segments of the labour market. The role of industrial relations (IR) institutions – chiefly collective bargaining and minimum wages – has also been transformed since the mid-1990s, despite their very limited scope and coverage of workers mainly in the organized (formal) sector. Yet questions remain about the role of these institutions in securing labour market outcomes. To what extent are wage gains attributable to the prevailing economic environment rather than the effectiveness of the IR system? How instrumental were unions in influencing government policies and in ensuring more inclusive growth? This chapter analyses the IR system in India and evaluates the contribution of trade unions and collective bargaining to labour market outcomes.

The following section briefly describes the origins and evolution of the IR system in India, and its development after independence from state-controlled political bargaining to decentralized enterprise bargaining. It also highlights the key changes in economic and labour market policies over the past two decades to 2012, some of which led to changes in the IR system. Section 2.3 assesses the contribution of IR to the creation of a fairer labour market in terms of more equal income distribution and better job quality, and considers how far the benefits of growth have percolated through to a larger proportion of the workforce, including those in the informal economy. Section 2.4 assesses the role of labour institutions in influencing government policies for inclusive development. Section 2.5 offers some concluding reflections.

2.2 THE INDUSTRIAL RELATIONS SYSTEM IN INDIA

The development of India's industrial relations system shows a transition from centralized bargaining during the first three decades of planned industrialization to decentralized bargaining when the economy was partially liberalized in the mid-1980s, opening it up to greater domestic and international competition. The continued liberalization process after 1991 put further pressure on the union–management bargaining relationship.

2.2.1 The Evolution of Industrial Relations in India, 1947–90[1]

Soon after independence the Indian Government adopted a development strategy aimed at achieving an egalitarian society through economic growth, with self-reliance, social justice and alleviation of poverty as the main objectives. The focus was on rapid state-led industrialization of heavy industry, and an economic strategy of import substitution. The state was directed to frame legislation or economic plans to achieve this objective (Punekar, 1966). The legal and institutional frameworks of industrial relations and collective bargaining inherited from the British colonial administration, which aimed primarily at dispute resolution, were largely retained. Some of the legislation was adopted unchanged,[2] other measures were consolidated into the Industrial Disputes Act (IDA) of 1947[3] and some of the labour laws regulating pay were adopted.[4]

In order to achieve economic growth, maintaining 'industrial peace' became a priority. The Industrial Truce Conference, 1947, placed greater emphasis on the prevention and settlement of industrial disputes and paved the way for a 'labour-inclusive development state'; but its resolution was repudiated by the capitalist class.[5] As the state was reliant on domestic capital to achieve its goal of rapid industrialization, it had to protect the interests of the employers (who wanted labour discipline) rather than those of labour, despite sympathy with the latter (Chibber, 2005). The state frequently intervened in industrial disputes, relying largely on a system of compulsory conciliation and adjudication rather than mediation and arbitration. The intrusion of the state in industrial relations was also due to the 'weakness of the trade union movement[6] and its growth along political lines' (Punekar, 1966, p. 29) and the need to fulfil social and economic objectives. The close proximity of the labour movement to the political alliance also led to a shift in the agenda of the 'rights of labour' from '*class compromise* in which labour would promise industrial peace in exchange for some concessions from employers on the shop floor and distributive issues' to '*class accommodation* . . . which ensures that labour's interests were merely accommodated' (Chibber, 2005, p. 54).

The state intervention through adjudication also had an impact on wage determination, which was 'influenced by administrative and legislative factors' (Jackson, 1972, p. 184),[7] and the levels of wages, allowances and bonuses were set by industrial courts, thus distorting the patterns and levels of wages in industry (Punekar, 1966). Subsequently, tripartite wage boards were constituted to cover an entire industry or a specific region. In order to pursue the social objective, there were 'political commitments to raising wages', and 'emphasis was placed on improving the position of the lower-paid worker' (Jackson, 1972, p. 185). The most significant measure in the field of wages was the enactment of the Minimum Wages Act 1948 to improve the conditions of workers in certain industries and agriculture, and it empowered the states to fix minimum wages. However, the 'interval between setting any particular minimum wage and its revision was quite long', nine years on average, and given the difficulties of implementation and its confinement to certain industries and regions, the effect was very limited (Jackson, 1972, p. 190).

These provisions were supplemented by the extension of social security provisions including sickness, maternity, employment injury and old age,[8] which is an important landmark in the evolution of state policy in the field of labour (Punekar, 1966). During this period three kinds of agreements could be observed in industrial relations: '*ad hoc* agreements on disputed issues, often at the stage of compulsory conciliation or during proceedings before the tribunals; agreements between an employers' association and the union . . . and finally collective agreements at the firm or plant level' (Kannappan, 1966, p. 50). As agreements based on adjudication were most prevalent, the nature of industrial relations transcended from 'free collective bargaining to the pace of legal sophistry' (Punekar, 1966, p. 29). However, there were a number of attempts at amending labour legislation in such a way as to promote genuine collective bargaining,[9] but none was enacted (Bhattacherjee, 2001).

The period 1966–79 was one of turbulence for India, reflected in industrial relations. Industrial stagnation between 1965 and 1975, high inflation, widespread shortages of essential goods leading to food riots in many states, industrial unrest and the oil shock in 1973 slowed down the economy and unemployment soared. These pressures culminated in a massive railway strike called by railway department employees in May 1974, which destabilized the economy (Nayar, 2006; Bhattacherjee, 2001). In response, the Government implemented a deflationary policy package in 1974, switching the course of economic policy from the pursuit of social justice to economic orthodoxy (Nayar, 2006).

Structural changes in the economy in this period had a marked impact on industrial relations. Disillusionment with the Indian National Trade Union Congress (INTUC) in representing the union voice at enterprise level led to a proliferation of new unions related to a variety of radical political organizations based on religion, caste and language (Oommen, 2009; Hill, 2009; Bhattacherjee, 2001). Several states, including Maharashtra, Gujarat, Rajasthan and Madhya Pradesh, passed their own laws on union recognition in the early 1970s (Mathur, 1992).[10] This pluralism led to 'fractionalization within the organized labour movement', even within its left-wing component (Bhattacherjee, 2000, p. 3760). The Emergency that was declared in 1975 had serious implications for industrial relations, as the 'right to strike was suspended, wage increases were frozen, minimum annual bonus was reduced, and increments in the cost of living allowance were transferred to a compulsory savings scheme' (Hill, 2009, p. 398). There were two direct interventions in the industrial relations system: first, a National Apex Body and state-level bodies were formed to conduct bipartite consultations between unions and employers to resolve disputes; second, the IDA of 1947 was amended in 1976, requiring state permission for lay-offs in firms employing 300 or more workers (Bhattacherjee, 2001).

The nationalization of 14 major private banks and the insurance sector in 1969 led to the proliferation of unions in the public sector units (PSUs). Bargaining in industries with capacity to pay moved towards decentralization from industry to enterprise level, resulting in a shift of focus in certain segments of the union movement from 'rights' (centralized lobbying) to 'interest' (decentralized collective bargaining) (Bhattacherjee, 2001, p. 252). With enterprise- and plant-level bargaining in private sector organizations growing during this period and no uniform collective bargaining procedure, differences in wage levels emerged between public and private and traditional and modern industries (Dayal, 1980). Comprehensive reviews of industrial relations were carried out by the central Government in 1967–69 and 1978–79, aiming 'to minimise inter-union rivalry, make collective bargaining more viable and reduce government interference in industrial relations' (Sheth, 1993, p. 233). Their recommendations were then formulated into a bill; however, the scope and content of the bill proved controversial each time it was introduced in the Parliament, and eventually the Government put it on hold (Rao, 1980; Sheth, 1993).

The economic shocks continued after 1980. In 1979 the country experienced a severe drought, which resulted in inflation, followed by recession in 1980–81; and higher oil imports led to deterioration in the balance of payments. The Government negotiated a US$5 billion loan from the International Monetary Fund (IMF), lifted licensing restrictions on several industries, 'increased the ceiling of investment for big business houses, relaxed the regulations on technology imports, replaced quantitative trade restrictions with tariffs, simplified tax rules, and reduced marginal tax rates on personal and corporate income and announced that public sector reform was necessary' (Varshney, 2001, p. 241).

The early 1980s saw industrial unrest in response to the reforms related to new technologies. For example, major PSUs in Bangalore went on strike for 77 days during 1980–81, and there were nationwide strikes contesting computerization and labour rationalization in nationalized banks. The Government responded with the Essential Services Maintenance Ordinance of 1981 (later converted into an Act), which put severe restrictions on strikes; it also attempted to use this ordinance to regain some control over the IR system by unilaterally streamlining the wage structure of Life Insurance Corporation employees. In 1982–83 the textile industry in Mumbai (formerly Bombay) saw the longest strike in Indian labour history. The main demand of the striking workers (led by the independent union) was that the Rashtriya Mill Mazdoor Sangh (RMMS, National Mill Workers' Union), which was affiliated to INTUC and seen as an instrument of management, no longer be recognized as the sole bargaining agent for all textile workers; instead, they wanted decentralized wage bargaining at the mill level (Hill, 2009; Debroy and Kaushik, 2005; Bhattacherjee, 2001; Candland, 1996). The strike was defeated; the closure of many textile mills followed, with huge job losses, and thereafter in the more profitable mills negotiations were carried out through decentralized bargaining arrangements (Bhattacherjee, 2001, p. 254).

Another significant change of the 1980s was the 1982 amendment of the IDA 1947, which disallowed forced confinement of managerial personnel and unfair labour practices (that is, refusal of the employer to bargain collectively with recognized trade unions), and made government permission mandatory for lay-offs in firms employing 100 or more workers. These new legal restrictions prompted companies to reduce standard employment in a number of new ways, including subcontracting and outsourcing, as well as by natural attrition and redeployment. This trend was especially strong in the electrical, consumer non-durables and pharmaceutical industries in western India, where companies such as Pfizer, Cadbury, Hindustan Lever (Soaps and Detergents), Rallifan, Murphy and Bush subcontracted out their production. As a result, the proportion of production subcontracted out in these industries rose from under 15 per cent in 1980 to between 15 and 100 per cent in 1993 (Shrouti and Nandkumar, 1994, p. 11).

The amendment led to huge loss of labour and there was a ban on recruitment in many private sector industries in several states during the 1980s (Prasad, 1994, p. 17). In West Bengal, many jobs were lost in traditional industries such as jute, cotton and engineering; under pressure, the unions 'agreed to the terms of settlements in the 1980s that were unthinkable earlier', where it was accepting job losses and retaining higher levels of wages for those who kept their jobs despite lower levels of productivity compared to other industrially developed states (Chakravarty, 2010, p. 47). This type of concession bargaining became quite prevalent in certain sectors and industries in some of the regions.

The 1980s saw the emergence of different industrial relations systems at the state level:

> Politically affiliated left unions dominated in West Bengal; more enterprise level non-affiliated, independent unions in Maharashtra; union-free enterprises in the new, non-traditional, high-tech industries in Bangalore; unions affiliated to regional political parties in Tamil Nadu and Andhra Pradesh; 'footpath unionism' where lawyers organized seven disgruntled employees and went for 'contingent litigation' appeared in Gujarat; radical social movements using militant means undermined mainstream unions in the backward districts of Andhra Pradesh and Bihar; and small and medium enterprise unions in Orissa. (Venkata Ratnam, 2006, p. 277)

There were also variations in industrial relations between the cities, with independent non-affiliated unions and management bargaining bilaterally in Mumbai, company-based unions and bargaining in Bangalore, and political industry-wide unions in Kolkata (formerly Calcutta) (Ramaswamy, 1988).

2.2.2 The Industrial Relations System in India since 1991

In 1991, a crisis in the balance of payments led to another large IMF loan with conditions and a substantial devaluation of the rupee. The old structure of licences, controls and regulations was dismantled and a number of industry and trade policy reforms were introduced (Ghosh, 2008; Chandrasekhar and Ghosh, 2002). The private sector entered industries previously reserved for the public sector; import quotas were reduced and tariff barriers were lowered (Das, 2003: Nouroz, 2001). Foreign direct investment (FDI) was allowed up to 51 per cent of equity in 34 priority industries, subject to certain guidelines. The number of products that were reserved for production in small-scale industries were reduced and the ceiling on investment was raised five-fold, allowing small-scale and micro industries to expand. Other fiscal measures included easier credit policies and reduced taxation with the aim of promoting economic growth (Unni and Rani, 2008).

The labour market reforms of this period included disinvestment in public sector enterprises (PSEs), privatization of public sector industries and restructuring or closure of unviable units; the introduction of programmes for redeployment, retraining and appropriate compensation of laid-off workers, for which a National Renewal Fund was created, and voluntary retirement schemes (VRS); and there was a halt on recruitment at lower levels in the public sector (Ghosh, 2008; Bhattacherjee, 2001; Mathur, 1993). The state government's policies to attract capital by establishing Special Economic Zones and relaxing labour law implementation, and the emergence of informal workers in the formal sector, contributed to a climate that is still not favourable to the collective bargaining process for securing fair wages and working conditions in an otherwise growing economy (Reddy, 2016).

These reforms brought about a change in the IR system. Roychowdhury (2003a), analysing three PSEs in Bangalore, showed that there was a shift in IR practice from 'management versus worker' to a more 'participatory and consensus-oriented management–worker relationship' as enterprises tried to rationalize labour. The companies set up joint committees, with representatives from both the management and the unions, 'to enact, coordinate and implement critical restructuring decisions' (p. 38). If the unions opposed a decision, a solution was arrived at through a collaborative problem-solving approach; in other words, concession bargaining. It was further pointed out that although unions were critical of the VRS as it displaced workers, they accepted it on the pragmatic ground that the alternative was often closure or privatization, both of which were potentially more threatening than labour reduction (Roychowdhury, 2003a).

In PSEs, the centralized wage bargaining process was frozen for a couple of years after the reforms (Roychowdhury, 2003a; Bhattacherjee, 2001) and wage bargaining took place at enterprise level, as the central Government was not willing to take on the burden of additional wage increases (Bhattacherjee, 2001). At the company level, when the new rounds of negotiations began, 'the unions were told that they must suggest ways and means of funding any pay hike in the new settlement' (Roychowdhury, 2003a, p.41). The Fifth Central Pay Commission (1997), which reviewed civil service pay in the mid-1990s, recommended that the civil service personnel be reduced by 30 per cent (Venkata Ratnam, 2001).

In the private sector, the reforms led to restructuring through mergers and acquisitions, subcontracting and outsourcing, technological modernization, more use of casual and contract workers and the reduction of permanent employment through voluntary and compulsory retirement (Sundar, 2008; Ghosh, 2008; Deshpande et al., 2004). Venkata Ratnam (2003), in his analysis of 215 collective agreements in both private and public sectors in the 1990s, noted increased decentralization of bargaining, with a shift towards productivity-linked cooperative bargaining and long-term agreements extending for up to ten years. In Andhra Pradesh, in private enterprises, it was found that wages of the permanent employees were fixed through collective bargaining, and for the 'contract' workers there was no recognition of unions and the wages were linked to statutory minimum wages fixed by the state (Reddy, 2016). In Maharashtra,[11] the small and medium enterprises generally avoided collective bargaining by paying differentiated wages on the basis of actual work effort or productivity or on the basis of their skills, experience and qualifications. The payment of higher wages to skilled and experienced workers was also used as a strategy to avoid collective bargaining and to weaken the solidarity among the workers (Jagannathan, 2015). Roychowdhury (2003a) argues that 'the new IR structures which seek to create space for worker participation are a product of management's strategic thinking and initiatives', and while they seemed to incorporate workers in the decision-making process, actually the 'participatory practices … produced by these structures are largely controlled, that is, defined by management's broad interests' (p. 44).

Technological advances along with productivity bargaining also led to the introduction of new human resource management (HRM) and quality control practices such as total quality management (Krishnan, 2010), which entered India through the Japanese joint ventures in the automobile industry and spread across a number of other sectors, as well as small and medium-sized enterprises. Das (2010) observed that in enterprises of all sizes in both traditional (unionized) manufacturing and (non-unionized) information technology there was a shift from tripartite agreements to HRM or 'joint team based' patterns of employer–employee relations. He argued that the shift in IR strategy, including the Japanese-style HRM practices that were widely prevalent in these companies, could be due to competitive pressures forcing employers and workers to cooperate.

The industrial relations system in India today represents a mix of different bargaining levels and a variety of union structures (Bhattacherjee, 2001). Most of the enterprise-based, industry-wide unions are organized into confederations at the state or national level, and are affiliated to political parties. These include the following: Bhartiya Mazdoor Sangh (BMS); the Indian National Trade Union Congress (INTUC); the All India Trade Union

Table 2.1   Trade union density in India, 1993/94–2011/12 (%)

	1993/94	2004/05	2009/10	2011/12
All workers	10.0	10.5	10.9	10.7
Non-agricultural workers	16.0	20.9	18.7	17.7
Wage workers (casual and salaried)	16.2	14.1	13.4	13.4
Salaried workers	46.5	35.4	31.1	28.8
Self-employed workers	4.7	7.7	8.2	8.0

Source: Authors' estimates, based on raw data from National Sample Survey Organisation (NSSO) Employment–Unemployment Survey, respective years.

Congress[12] (AITUC); Hind Mazdoor Sabha (HMS) and the Centre of Indian Trade Unions (CITU). There are also enterprise-based unions (these are mostly politically affiliated) in the formal sector, such as the All India United Trade Union Centre,[13] the Trade Union Co-ordination Centre (TUCC), the All India Central Council of Trade Unions (AICCTU), the Labour Progressive Federation (LPF), the United Trade Union Congress (UTUC), the National Front of Indian Trade Unions – Dhanbad (NFITU-DHN) and the National Front of Indian Trade Unions – Kolkata (NFITU-KOL). In the informal sector, there are independent unions that represent certain categories of workers, such as the Self Employed Women's Association[14] (SEWA) (Datt, 2008). In all, there are 13 unions or federations that have the status of central trade union organizations (CTUOs).[15] In 2001, an amendment was made to the Trade Union Act 1926, requiring 10 per cent of workers or 100 workers (whichever is the smaller) in an establishment as the minimum membership for registering a union, to stop the proliferation of unions.

Union density, which covers members of both trade unions and other associations, depends upon what is taken as the denominator. Union density across the total workforce stood at 10.7 per cent in 2011/12, increasing marginally compared to the 1993/94 level (Table 2.1). Union density among female workers was half of that of male workers. Among non-agricultural workers, union density was 17.7 per cent in 2011/12, increasing marginally compared to 1993/94. Among wage workers (casual and salaried), union density fell since 1993/94, by three percentage points to 13.4 per cent. Union density among salaried workers fell precipitously since 1993/94, by 17.7 percentage points to 28.8 per cent, while among the self-employed workers it increased to around 8 per cent (approximately 14.7 million). Overall, trade union density in India is relatively low compared to other emerging economies such as Brazil and South Africa, which indicates the limited scope unions have to bargain for improvements in working conditions. However, although the trade union density in absolute numbers is quite high, the tendency to act is quite low due to close political affiliation. While a greater proportion of salaried workers are represented by unions than any other category, the salaried workers comprised only 17.8 per cent of the workforce in 2011/12. It is difficult to gauge the extent of collective bargaining coverage in India, as no reliable estimates are available; nevertheless, it would be fair to assume that it is lower than trade union density rates and concentrated in large enterprises.

The lead employers' organization is the Council of Indian Employers (CIE), which ensures cooperation and coordination between the All India Organization of Employers (AIOE), the Employers' Federation of India (EFI) and the Standing Conference on Public Enterprises (SCOPE). The objective of AIOE is to educate employers in the best IR practices; SCOPE represents public sector enterprises at central and state level; and the EFI protects, promotes and champions the interests of employers, mainly in the areas of human resources, industrial relations, and labour problems. The CIE also represents Indian employers at the International Labour Conference and in other international forums.

Patterns of bargaining vary according to sector and industry. In the private sector, enterprise-level bargaining takes place with enterprise-based unions, which may be either affiliated to political parties or independent. Within an enterprise there may be separate unions for shop-floor workers, support staff (attendants, drivers, clerks, and so on) and supervisory staff. If there are several unions in an enterprise, they are proportionally represented on the 'bargaining council or negotiating committee', so that the management does not have 'to negotiate individually with each registered union' (Ahn, 2010, p. 64). In the private sector, such as in cotton, jute and textile industries, tea plantations, ports and docks, bargaining takes place at industry and/or regional level; while for public sector enterprises such as banks, coal, steel, ports and docks, and oil, where the central Government is the major employer, sector-based collective bargaining is conducted at national level through a coordination committee with representatives of the Government and trade unions. Even within the public sector there exist multiple unions, and having four to five unions is quite common. For central and state Government employees in the service sector (transportation, postal services, insurance, and so on), wages and working conditions are determined through pay commissions; these workers belong to unions that are affiliated to political parties which lobby with the pay commissions at national level (Ahn, 2010).

The wages of casual and unskilled workers are regulated by the Minimum Wages Act 1948, which clearly specifies that workers in sectors not covered by collective bargaining are covered by schedules of employment under the Act. However, the criterion for inclusion in the list of scheduled employments is that there should be at least 1000 workers engaged in that activity in that state (Belser and Rani, 2010). The minimum wage rates for each scheduled type of employment are fixed by the appropriate government in its jurisdiction at intervals not exceeding five years. Two methods are used: the committee method and the notification method. In the former, the appropriate government sets up committees and subcommittees to hold inquiries and make recommendations with regard to the level and revision of minimum wages; in the latter, the government proposals are published in the official gazette. After considering the advice of the committees and sub-committees, or all the submissions by representatives of people affected, the appropriate government publishes the new or revised minimum wage levels in its official gazette. There is no uniformity in the wage structure across states or scheduled employments. Some pay consolidated wages, including basic pay and 'dearness allowance' (DA); others report DA as a separate component (GOI, 2015). There also exist advisory boards at both the central and state level, with the Central Advisory Board coordinating the work of the State Advisory Board. However, the minimum wage revisions and adjustments have not been in accordance with the law, and the revisions are done every five years, taking inflation into consideration. Deshpande et al. (2004), in their survey of 1300 manufacturing firms across nine industry groups, find that in most firms, statutory minimum wages prevail by and large as basic wages, as collective bargaining plays an insignificant role in determining basic wages. This was also found in the case of the cotton textile industry, which is among the most unionized industry.

At present, the central Government sets 45 minimum wage rates for different job categories, including work in agriculture, mining, oil extraction and any corporation under its ownership; while various state governments determine minimum wage rates for 1709 job categories across the sectors scheduled in the Act. Hence, there currently exist in India a total of 1754 different minimum wage rates, covering around two-thirds of all wage earners (Rani et al., 2013). Multiple minimum wage rates increase administrative complexity, and can make it difficult for workers and employers to determine the rate applicable to them. In Andhra Pradesh, there are about 20 to 40 categories for each scheduled employment, which would demand considerable time and effort in revision and implementation. Further, workers also often feel discriminated against when they do not see much difference in the work performed in certain operations differentiated by minimum wages (Reddy, 2016).

There has been a lot of debate since the late 1970s about simplifying and extending the minimum wage to all workers, and finally in 1991 the National Commission on Rural Labour (NCRL) recommended the concept of national floor level (NFL) wages to replace this multiplicity of minimum wages with a uniform wage structure, and in 1991 a NFL minimum wage was introduced. It is statutory and universal but not binding (Belser and Rani, 2010), and is revised at intervals no longer than two years, taking inflation rates into account. The national trade unions have launched a campaign for a statutory national minimum wage floor at a higher threshold than the currently non-statutory national minimum wage. And, more recently, the Government of India approved a new wage code bill, which consolidates four Acts,[16] which also makes a recommendation for a binding national minimum wage, which will ensure a minimum wage across all sectors. The extent to which it will gain political support and is implemented remains to be seen. Beyond these legislative steps, there is a range of challenges to implementing an effective wage policy, including some level of consensus on the need to ensure broader coverage of minimum wages, setting the level of the minimum wage, simplification of the minimum wage structure and measures to improve implementation.

For instance, there is no proper enforcement mechanism for minimum wages, as the task falls to the inspection staff who are already entrusted with monitoring implementation of other labour legislation (GOI, 2015). Furthermore, the inspection policy has changed since 2014, with inspections only carried out in the event of a complaint, as was observed in Karnataka. Even in domains where inspection is a legitimate activity, lack of infrastructure constitutes a serious impediment to the effective implementation of laws (Roychowdhury, 2016). In 2009/10, only about 62.7 per cent of the workers covered by the minimum wage legislation received the prescribed levels of pay. The level of compliance is quite high in other emerging countries such as Brazil (80 per cent), where the simplicity of minimum wages (national), along with investments in enforcement machinery, has ensured better compliance (Rani et al., 2013).

2.3   ECONOMIC GROWTH, INCLUSIVENESS AND LABOUR OUTCOMES

One of the main objectives of the economic reforms of the 1990s was to achieve high rates of economic growth that would create more employment and wealth that would eventually trickle down to the poor. While implementing the reforms, the Government also tried to maintain anti-poverty measures, and there has been some increase in social sector spending irrespective of the political party in power. The logic behind this strategy of piecemeal welfare provision was to ensure social peace and stability to enable wide-ranging neoliberal economic reforms to be implemented (Roychowdhury, 2003b, p.5278). Thus the state has been able to sustain economic growth at quite high levels, averaging 5.8 per cent in the 1990s,

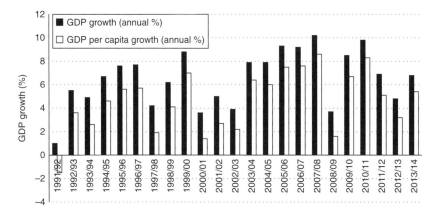

Source: Government of India, *Economic Survey, 2014–15* (2015).

Figure 2.1   GDP and per capita GDP growth in India, 1991/92–2013/14

although per capita income grew more slowly, averaging only 3.7 per cent over the same decade (Figure 2.1).

After 2000, while continuing the reform process, the Government came under pressure from coalition partners, which included left-wing parties, to pursue inclusive growth and reduce poverty. As a result, some rights-based developmental initiatives were implemented as part of the minimum needs programme, such as the National Rural Employment Guarantee Act (NREGA; later renamed after Mahatma Gandhi as the MGNREGA) in 2005, the Unorganised Sector Social Security Act 2008, the National Food Security Act 2013, and the Aadhar card 2013, which provides minimum health insurance cover.

High growth rates in the late 1990s and 2000s were accompanied by a decline in poverty rates in both rural and urban areas (Table 2.2).[17] However, income inequality, in respect of which India sits between the more equal East Asia and the highly unequal Latin America, rose, especially in urban areas.

2.3.1   Labour Outcomes: Employment

High economic growth in India was not translated into more quality employment between 1993/94 and 2004/05. Such job growth as did occur was largely in informal employment; indeed, between 1999/2000 and 2004/05 formal jobs, which are regular, protected and well paid, actually fell by 1.8 per cent. This decline reflected the contraction of public sector employment in the wake of liberalization, which led to the downsizing of government agencies

Table 2.2   Poverty and inequality in India, 1993/94–2011/12

	Poverty (Headcount ratio)		Inequality (Gini)	
	Rural	Urban	Rural	Urban
1993/94	50.1	31.8	28.6	34.4
2004/05	41.8	25.7	29.7	37.3
2009/10	33.8	20.9	27.0	38.1
2011/12	25.7	13.7	30.8	37.2

Sources: Figures for poverty based on Government of India Planning Commission estimates; figures for inequality computed from raw NSSO data, various years.

Table 2.3   Growth of employment in formal and informal sectors, all sectors and manufacturing sector

	Formal	Informal	Total	Average annual GDP growth (%)
	Total employment growth (%)			
1993/94–1999/2000	0.5	1.8	1.6	5.6
1999/2000–2004/05	–1.8	1.4	0.9	6.2
2004/05–2009/10	–4.3	–0.4	–0.9	6.9
	Manufacturing sector employment growth (%)			
1993/94–1999/2000	0.4	1.0	1.0	
1999/2000–2004/05	–0.2	0.0	0.2	
2004/05–2009/10	1.2	–0.2	–0.2	

Source: Authors' estimates, based on raw data from NSSO Employment–Unemployment Survey, respective years.

through voluntary retirement schemes, closure of poorly performing units and withdrawal from commercial activities (ILER, 2014; Ghosh, 2008). While economic growth accelerated during the latter half of the 2000s to 6.9 per cent, employment declined by 0.9 per cent (Table 2.3). There has also been a huge decline in the female labour force participation rate, from 42.7 per cent (1993/94) to 31.2 per cent (2011/12); a number of reasons have been advanced for this, including household income effect,[18] increased enrolment in higher education, and methodological issues (Dasgupta and Verick, 2016; Kapsos et al., 2014; Dasgupta and Goldar, 2005) and the figures are still under scrutiny and require further research.

The structure of employment has changed little over the two decades to 2012 (Table 2.4). A large proportion of the labour force continued to work

Table 2.4   Structure of employment in India, 1993/94–2011/12 (%)

	1993/94	1999/2000	2004/05	2009/10	2011/12
Employer	1.9	1.1	1.3	1.2	1.4
Self-employed					
Own account workers	29.6	30.3	31.3	31.3	32.8
Unpaid/contributing family helpers	23.2	21.5	24.3	18.5	17.9
Wage workers					
Casual workers	32.0	33.1	28.9	33.4	30.1
Salaried workers:					
Regular formal workers[1]	13.2	5.2	7.9	9.1	9.9
Regular informal workers[1]		8.7	6.3	6.5	7.9

Note: 1. 'Regular formal workers' denotes those workers who are classified as 'salaried' in the survey and have either a 'contract or paid leave or social security benefit' for the years 2004/05, 2009/10 and 2011/12. For 1999–2000, apart from the worker being classified as 'salaried', we take into consideration whether they have a 'provident fund' or not. Workers who do not have any of these provisions are classified as 'regular informal workers'. For 1993/94, there is no variable in the survey that helps us to distinguish between formal and informal status.

Source: Authors' estimates, based on raw data from NSSO Employment–Unemployment Survey, respective years.

in the informal sector, either in self-employment (32.8 per cent) or as casual labour (30.1 per cent), and these proportions remained stable. Unpaid or contributing family helpers declined from 23.2 per cent of the workforce in 1993/94 to 17.9 per cent in 2011/12, but still accounted for a substantial part of the workforce. The proportion of salaried formal workers rose from 5.2 per cent in 1999/2000 to 9.9 per cent in 2011/12, representing a modest improvement in the quality of employment (Table 2.4).

According to the latest data available, in 2011/12, the labour force in India comprises 429 million people: 420 million employed and 9 million unemployed. As in many developing countries, unemployment is quite low, as lack of unemployment insurance forces workers to resort to whatever paid employment may be available to sustain their livelihoods. Self-employment constitutes about 52 per cent of all employment (219.5 million workers), with a substantial proportion working as unpaid family helpers; and 30 per cent (125.8 million) are casually employed, which makes them part of the informal workforce. The 75 million salaried workers comprise 17.8 per cent of the workforce; 41.6 million of them (9.9 per cent of the total workforce) have some form of protection (contracts, social security and/or paid leave), while the remaining 33.4 million do not have any protection.[19]

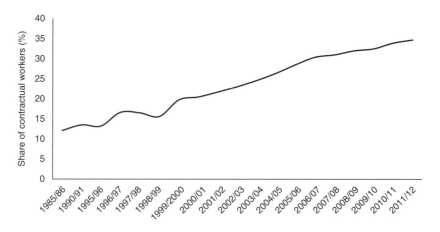

Source: Authors' estimates based on Annual Survey of Industries (ASI) data, respective years.

Figure 2.2   Share of contractual workers in the organized manufacturing sector, 1985/86–2011/12

Much of the increase that has taken place in salaried formal employment involves work arrangements of a contractual nature, that is, short-term or fixed-term contracts. Figure 2.2 shows the sharp and sustained rise in the share of contractual workers in the organized manufacturing sector from 14 per cent in 1990/91 to 34.7 per cent in 2011/12. A number of states amended the Contract Labour Act 1970 to facilitate this trend in the interests of the 'market-friendly' business economy (Roychowdhury, 2003b). Andhra Pradesh, for example, did so in 2003, allowing the employment of contract labour in certain 'non-core' and 'core' activities depending upon the situation (Sundar, 2011); other states opened the way to contract labour by redefining certain 'core' activities as 'non-core' activities. Many states also set out to attract foreign capital and sustain growth by relaxing their labour laws, as well as providing tax holidays and other incentives (see Box 2.1), further encouraging the use of flexible labour.

2.3.2   Labour Outcomes: Wages and Incomes

The empirical evidence on the growth of wages since the 1990s is quite mixed, as there was a wide variation in the growth of real wages across the different segments of the labour market (Sarkar and Mehta, 2010; Sundaram and Tendulkar, 2006; Himanshu, 2005). At the overall economy-wide level, average real wages in both rural and urban areas rose,

BOX 2.1　INDUSTRIAL RELATIONS IN THE AUTOMOBILE
　　　　　INDUSTRY

The automobile industry in India is one of the fastest-growing industries, contributing 7 per cent to gross domestic product (GDP) and employing 19 million people
directly and indirectly, according to Society of Indian Automobile Manufacturers
(SIAM). The first multinational corporation (MNC) entry was in the early 1980s,
through a joint venture between Suzuki Motors of Japan and Maruti Udyog, an
enterprise of the Government of India. The implementation of the Phased
Manufacturing Programme (PMP) by the Government enabled the auto component
industry to introduce new technologies, which facilitated them to develop and create
highly capable, competent and quality-conscious components and allowed them to
effectively localize the component base (Bhasker, 2013). Since the mid-1980s a
number of policy measures were introduced: 'broad branding', which permitted
manufacturers to produce different kinds of vehicles instead of one kind; delicens-
ing of the auto ancillary industry allowing capacity expansion; and importing capital
equipment for replacement. The economic reforms in 1991 and the 2002
Automobile Policy gave a further boost to this industry as it removed restrictions on
FDI, stipulations on requirements of local content (major attraction to invest), export
obligation, and foreign exchange neutralization (Unni and Rani, 2008).

　　As a result a number of MNCs (Hyundai, Honda, General Motors, Ford,
Mitsubishi, Toyota, and so on) entered the market and the inflow of foreign direct
investment doubled between 2007/08 and 2011/12 to US$1200 million. Production
increased from INR196 billion in 2001/02 to 530 billion in 2011/12 and exports
increased almost ten times in the decade to 2011/12 (from INR216 billion in
2001/02 to 2063 billion in 2011/12) (Bhasker, 2013).

　　To attract FDI in the automobile sector, both central and state governments
amended some provisions of labour law pertaining to industrial disputes, retrenchment, and migrant and contract labour, so as to facilitate outsourcing activities. For
example, Karnataka amended Schedule I of the IDA 1947 in 2001 to include
automobiles and components in the list of public utility services, thereby requiring
14 days' notice for strike. Even the Contract Labour Act was relaxed so as to
facilitate outsourcing and employment of contract workers without any restrictions
(Das and George, 2006). There has been intense competition among states to
attract investment, which was recently observed in the case of the Nano car project
in 2008 when it withdrew from West Bengal after protests by farmers. A number of
states – Karnataka, Andhra Pradesh, Maharashtra and Gujarat – offered them
packages (free land, infrastructure, employee training programmes, tax and other
fiscal incentives) to set up their plants, and after reviewing the different proposals
the project was based in Gujarat.

　　To enhance competitiveness, the Automotive Mission Plan 2006–16 also made
recommendations towards reforming labour laws. This included granting exemptions to all export-oriented units (EOUs) and special economic zones (SEZs) in
Sections 51, 54 and 56 of the Factories Act 1948 and to increase working hours from
48 to 60 per week (Section 51), from 9 to 11 per day (Section 54), and spread over
from 10.5 to 13.0 hours per day (Section 56) (p. 43). The policy also recommended
to allow contract labour and fixed-term employment contracts in core activities, and
to introduce flexibility to recruit workforces to meet the market demand.

In general, enterprise-based unions are quite common in this sector. However, enterprises such as Escorts and Toyota Kirloskar in Bangalore have unions which are politically affiliated, while Hero Puch has an independent union. Maruti Employees Suzuki Union was an independent union, which was de-recognized after the labour unrest in 2011 and replaced by the management-friendly Maruti Udyog Kamgar Union (Bose and Pratap, 2012). Although some of these unions are successful in negotiating increased wages and benefits, two issues that elude them are: revoking of suspension of workers, and removal of contract labour systems on the main production line.

This sector has observed a lot of industrial unrest or strife, and wildcat strikes since 2005. If one were to understand the reasons for such unrest, in many cases, 'there is no demand for even a wage rise; just to form a union or to be able to gain the right to organize' (Das, 2011). Almost every strike at the numerous factories in the Gurgaon–Manesar region since 2005 had started with companies refusing to recognize the demand of workers to form an independent union: Maruti in 2000, Honda Motorcycles and Scooters India (HMSI) in 2005, and Rico Auto in 2009. This continuing trend would undoubtedly lead to higher productivity and profits for MNCs, but at a huge cost to labour rights and welfare of the workers. The case of the automobile sector shows that although there are regulations and formal institutions, the lack of enforcement or modification of regulations, which is quite widespread in this sector and elsewhere, also shape industrial relations (Ford and Gillan, 2016).

but with varying benefit to salaried (formal) and casual (informal) workers, respectively. The greatest gains accrued to salaried workers in urban areas, whose wages increased faster than those of their rural counterparts and of casual labourers (Figure 2.3). Casual workers earned just above one-third of the wages of regular salaried workers in urban areas in 2011–12, while in rural areas they earned almost half of the regular salaried workers. The rural wages have improved since 2004/05, partly as a result of agricultural growth along with periodic revision of support prices, and partly as a result of the implementation of the Mahatma Gandhi National Rural Employment Guarantee Act (MGNREGA), which stipulated minimum wages as part of social spending (Jose, 2016).

The widening wage differentials were reflected in increasing wage inequality between 1993/94 and 2004/05 (Table 2.5). The small reversal of this trend in 2011/12 could be due to the increase in wages of casual workers, partly as a result of the implementation of the MGNREGA, which stipulated minimum wages (see section 2.4.3 below). Wage inequality is higher among salaried workers than among casual workers, indicating greater variations in skills, education and the nature of work (ILER, 2014; Mazumdar and Sarkar, 2008; Banerjee, 2005). The sharp rise in the Gini coefficient of wage inequality among salaried workers from 0.41 in 1993/94 to 0.49 in 2011/12 is attributable to changes in government

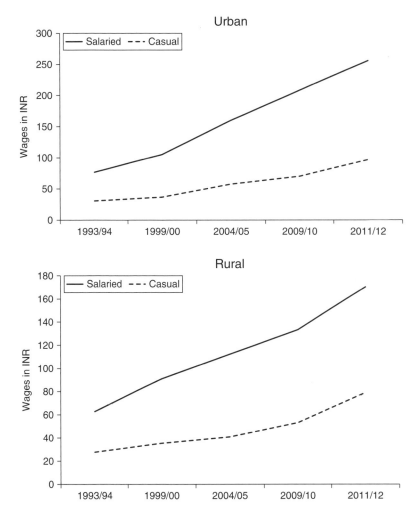

Source: Authors' estimates based on raw data from Employment–Unemployment Surveys, various dates.

Figure 2.3   *Divergence of real wages, salaried and casual workers, urban and rural areas, 1993/94–2011/12*

policy, including the dismantling of trade protection, the de-reservation of products, and the differences in the wages between skilled and unskilled workers (Unni and Rani, 2008).

Within the formal manufacturing sector, the proportion of gross value added paid out in wages and salaries fell from 32 per cent in 1991/92 to 25 per

Table 2.5   Wage inequality in India, 1993/94–2011/12 (Gini)

	Salaried	Casual	Total
1993/94	0.41	0.30	0.46
1999/2000	0.45	0.29	0.49
2004/05	0.49	0.28	0.50
2009/10	0.49	0.26	0.49
2011/12	0.49	0.26	0.47

Source: Authors' estimates based on raw data from NSSO Employment–Unemployment Survey, respective years.

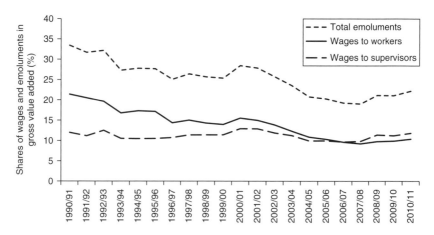

Source: Authors' calculations from ASI, various years.

Figure 2.4   Share of total emoluments, wage of workers and wages of supervisors in gross value added, manufacturing sector, 1990/91–2010/11

cent in 2004/05. The share of workers' wages declined much faster than that of supervisors' pay: the former was almost halved from 23 per cent in 1991/92 to 12 per cent in 2004/05, the latter virtually unchanged at around 12 per cent (Figure 2.4), while their respective numerical proportions remained almost constant. The decline in the share of wages paid to workers could be due in part to falling employment as a result of technological changes, but also due to the increased flexibility in the labour market with a rising proportion of contract workers (Banerjee, 2005); some have argued that the decline in the share of wages has been felt most acutely by low-paid blue-collar workers (Kannan and Raveendran, 2009). The rise in total emoluments after 2006 has

Table 2.6   *Factor incomes in the organized (formal) manufacturing sector (%)*

Period	Total emoluments	Rent payments	Interest payments	Profits	Net value added
1990/91 to 1994/95	43.4	2.0	29.2	25.3	100
1995/96 to 1999/2000	36.3	2.7	26.8	30.8	100
2000/01 to 2004/05	38.5	2.3	22.0	37.2	100
2005/06 to 2010/11	28.3	1.8	11.6	58.3	100

Source: Computed from Annual Survey of Industries (ASI), various years.

been driven largely by the increases in wages to supervisors, whose share of the total has exceeded that of wages to workers since 2007 (Figure 2.4).

The analysis of factor incomes shows that the share of wages in net value added in the organized manufacturing sector declined quite sharply from 43.4 per cent in 1994/95 to 28.3 per cent in 2010/11 (Table 2.6). The wage share declined in the 1990s despite the increase in employment (Table 2.3), and then declined again in the 2000s when employment fell. Meanwhile, the share of profits has increased steeply, almost doubling from 25.3 per cent in 1994/95 to 58.3 per cent in 2010/11. The proportion of rents remained almost unchanged, while interest payments declined by almost two-thirds.

The picture in the unorganized (informal) sector is somewhat different. Across all sectors, the share of wages to workers has actually increased by 5 percentage points over the decade to 2009/10 (Table 2.7); however, the highest gains were in high-skilled services (7 percentage points) and transport (5 percentage points). This is consistent with what happened in the overall economy, where wages of casual workers increased in both rural and urban areas (Figure 2.3). While overall the share of profits fell by 1.3 percentage points, it increased in the high-skilled services sector alone.

As for the self-employed, who comprised almost 50 per cent of the workforce in 2009/10, their incomes overall have grown, most strongly in transport, storage and communications, and in low-skilled services (Table 2.8); although self-employed workers in high-skilled services have seen their incomes fall. The increase in incomes for the self-employed in the manufacturing sector is largely due to outsourcing and subcontracting arrangements with the formal sector, which also gave a boost to the transport, storage and communications sector. The increase in incomes among the salaried and managerial class led to increased demand for personal services, which are low-skilled in nature, thus leading to a rise in the incomes of those providing them. Some of the improvement is also

*Table 2.7   Factor incomes in the unorganized (informal) sector,
1999/2000, 2009/10*

	Total emoluments	Rent paid	Interest paid	Profits	Net value added
1999/2000					
All sectors	*32.6*	*59.0*	*4.3*	*4.1*	*100*
Manufacturing	42.1	51.5	3.4	3.0	100
Transport, storage and communications	31.9	58.1	3.8	6.2	100
Wholesale and retail trade, repair services	22.8	66.9	4.8	5.6	100
Low-skilled services	38.9	53.5	5.7	1.9	100
High-skilled services	36.7	56.0	5.4	1.9	100
2009/10					
All sectors	*37.6*	*55.0*	*4.7*	*2.8*	*100*
Manufacturing	45.5	48.1	3.9	2.5	100
Transport, storage and communications	37.4	54.4	2.1	6.1	100
Wholesale and retail trade, repair services	24.8	66.6	5.6	3.0	100
Low-skilled services	39.8	51.7	6.9	1.6	100
High-skilled services	44.1	49.2	4.1	2.6	100

Source: Authors' estimates, based on raw data from NSSO Employment–Unemployment Survey, respective years.

*Table 2.8   Incomes of self-employed in the overall economy, in real terms
(annual)*

	1999/2000 (INR)	2009/10 (INR)	Growth (%)
All industries	24035	27424	1.3
Manufacturing	16700	18804	1.2
Transport, storage and communications	24584	31044	2.3
Wholesale and retail trade, repair	29929	34185	1.3
Low-skilled services	19689	24919	2.4
High-skilled services	30303	29050	−0.4

Source: Authors' estimates, based on raw data from NSSO Employment–Unemployment Survey, respective years.

the result of initiatives by self-employed unions such as SEWA, and new forms of organizations that have tried to ensure income security for these workers, which are discussed in the next section.

2.4 LABOUR RELATIONS AND INCLUSIVE DEVELOPMENT: THE ROLE OF LABOUR INSTITUTIONS

Given the transformation of labour relations in India over recent decades, outlined above, what has been the role of labour institutions in influencing government policies with a view to ensuring more inclusive development? This section looks at the role of traditional unions in ensuring workers' rights since the onset of the economic reforms of the 1990s, given that a significant proportion of workers are engaged in the informal economy, with 'informal (uncodified) institutions, such as unwritten norms, conventions or codes of behaviour' (Witt and Redding, 2013; Harriss-White, 2010), and these institutions can simply supersede the formal institutions in protecting the workers. This section examines the role of the new workers' organizations and other initiatives that have been taken to address the welfare and rights of workers in the informal sector. It also examines how state action and social policies interact with formal and informal industrial relations. The new forms of organization that have arisen to address the issues of workers in the informal sector are not just specific to India but can be observed in other countries too (see Webster et al., 2016 for a detailed account).

2.4.1 Traditional Unions

The trade union movement in the 1990s was able to mount resistance to major reforms, especially privatization, and in collaboration with consumer and environmental organizations (Uba, 2008) its efforts substantially slowed down the process. Despite differences in approach which made consensus-building difficult, several sectoral alliances, including the Road Transport Workers Federation, the Joint Action Council of Textile Trade Unions and the Railways Anti-Privatization Campaign Committee, contested the privatization reforms (Venkata Ratnam, 2006, p. 43). The reversal of the Government's decision to privatize some large companies demonstrated the ability of politically affiliated unions to resist the Government's reforms when they united across party lines (Candland, 1996).

There were about 226 protests against privatization; as well as strikes, these included demonstrations, marches, rallies, sit-ins and road blocks. Most of the protests were mobilized by the left-wing trade unions, with

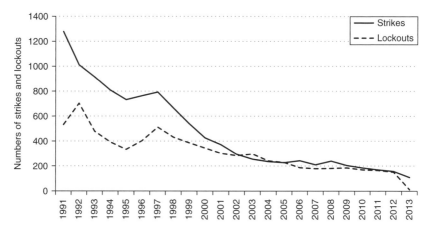

Source: Data from Kumar (1964), Das (1999), Ghosh (2004) and Labour Bureau, Government of India.

Figure 2.5   Numbers of strikes and lockouts in India, 1991–2013

37 campaigns led by CITU and AITUC, and three by BMS and INTUC (Uba, 2008). Although it appears that all the major trade unions, irrespective of their ideological orientations, took part in the protests, there were differences. INTUC avoided mobilization when the Congress Party was in power, while the left-wing unions did not participate in protests against the communist CPI-M Government in West Bengal, though they did take part in protests against the central Government (Uba, 2008). Similarly, despite fragmentation, trade unions have been fairly successful in stalling the changes in labour laws, which tried to introduce greater 'flexibility' in the labour market (Hensman, 2010).

Since 1991, strike action has declined substantially (see Figure 2.5). The re-enactment of the Essential Services Maintenance Act by the Government in 1992, which curbed the right to strike in essential services such as power, communications, transport, health, and so on, was a contributory factor, as were two key legal rulings by the Supreme Court: the 'no work, no pay' judgment of 1990 (Kochar, 1990), and the 2003 judgment that government employees do not have a legal and moral right to strike, which was accompanied by the dismissal of 6074 workers (Pratap, 2011).

None of these developments led to an increase in unionization among wage workers, for a number of reasons. First, since the economic reforms there has been a tendency towards shifting production to ancillary units or less-developed areas where labour is cheap and unions are almost completely absent, and towards subcontracting and outsourcing (Chakravarty, 2010; Banaji, 2000; Davala, 1994). A small survey of 101 firms producing auto components in different regions of the country revealed that only 6 per cent of the firms reported having unions, and the workers were dissuaded from forming a union (Unni and Rani, 2008).

Second, employers have been offering existing union members incentives to leave and non-members incentives not to join. A study by Badigannavar and Kelly (2012) involving 447 workplace union representatives of INTUC, the second largest trade union federation, which is affiliated to the Congress Party in Maharashtra,[20] showed a high level of employer-sponsored action to break legitimate unions in the private sector, and many instances of management actively offering incentives to workers to dissuade them from joining a genuine union (Table 2.9). Similarly, in the automobile sector there are instances of management paying 'compensation' to leading unionists to quit (John, 2012, p. 20) and in some companies management also asked workers to sign an undertaking not to join the new union (Sen, 2011).

Third, it has been reported that there is a growing tendency towards victimization and dismissal of union members. Badigannavar and Kelly (2012) show that over 60 per cent of the union representatives in private manufacturing and services, and almost half of those in public services, reported victimization of union representatives by management. Over half of all the union representatives surveyed reported that workers were dismissed during strikes in the private manufacturing and services sectors (Table 2.9). In the automobile sector in the National Capital Region (NCR), workers were reluctant to form a union as they feared that the labour commissioner's office, to which they had no direct access themselves, would inform employers of their intention and that the potential union leaders would be dismissed (Bose and Pratap, 2012, p. 58). The use of such unfair methods, and an aggressive and autocratic management style, has led to deterioration in labour–management relations in a number of enterprises since the reforms (see Box 2.1).

Alongside the decline in union presence, there has also been a weakening of the bargaining power of the unions, which as noted above have increasingly resorted to cooperative or concession bargaining since the economic reforms. Two reasons may be advanced for this. The first has to do with the state of the unions themselves: only a small proportion of workers are unionized, and the union movement is highly fragmented and difficult to mobilize for dialogue and consultation (Mathur, 1993).

A second reason may lie in the unions' pursuit of redress through litigation, having found the judiciary to be sympathetic to promoting workers' rights (Sundar, 2011). However, since the economic reforms a number of judicial decisions (such as the Supreme Court judgments of 1990 and 2003

Table 2.9   Unfair labour practices reported by union representatives (% of employers in sample)

Unfair labour practice	Public services	Private manufacturing	Private services
Management offered incentives to workers to leave the union	33	57	41
Employer sponsored a union to break legitimate unions	32	43	40
Victimization of union representatives	47	69	62
Workers dismissed during strikes	19	59	53
Illegal lockouts	12	35	32
Illegal breaks in employment of workers to avoid permanent contracts	47	72	61

Source: Badigannavar and Kelly (2012, table 1).

referred to earlier in this section) have gone against the workers and have weakened their position, forcing them to resort to cooperation.

Their reduced bargaining power has led some of the unions, such as BMS and INTUC, to adopt a strategy of cooperation and collaboration, rather than one of confrontation and conflict (Datt, 2008), and to fight for the rights of contractual workers rather than opposing their use altogether. In the PSUs, unions bargain directly with their principal employer, while in the private sector, agreements are often negotiated with the contractor. In the course of negotiating collective agreements, topics covered include regularization and continuity of employment, regular negotiation of wages, social security provision and working conditions (Sundar, 2011). In a number of cases, the unions have been able to regularize contract workers.

Nevertheless, contractual workers still face several problems. The Supreme Court's ruling in 2006 that casual and temporary workers do not have a right to claim permanent employment as they were recruited 'through the back door' (*Secretary, State of Karnataka & Ors* v. *Uma Devi & Ors*, cited in Sundar, 2011) was a major setback. Also, employers often avoid regularization through illegal breaks in employment (that is, dismissal and rehiring); this is one of the unfair labour practices identified by Badigannavar and Kelly (2012), who found that about 72 per cent of employers in private manufacturing and 61 per cent in private services use it to avoid giving workers permanent status (Table 2.9).

Hill (2009) notes that the trade unions have also been looking in new directions, seeking strategic coalitions with civil society organizations and workers in the unorganized sector. The extent of these efforts varies from state to state, depending in part on the different states' policies. In Kerala, Maharashtra, Tamil Nadu and West Bengal, labour welfare funds have been set up; these are tripartite bodies including representatives of workers, employers and the state Government to provide a forum for effective social dialogue in the informal sector. Maharashtra has tripartite boards for head-load workers and security guards; other similar tripartite structures exist in Andhra Pradesh, Gujarat, Madhya Pradesh and Tamil Nadu. Kerala has a number of welfare boards, some of which are specific to occupations (tailors, auto rickshaw drivers, head-loaders, construction workers) while others are sector-specific (for *beedi* workers,[21] cashew workers, agricultural workers, and so on) (NCEUS, 2007). Through these channels, some categories of informal workers have been able to negotiate with the Government to secure legal rights for economic benefits. The National Centre for Labour (NCL), a lead organization for informal labour established in 1995, and the New Trade Union Initiative (NTUI), a non-party-affiliated union established in 2002, also reflect a shift in union strategy to take into consideration the larger issues facing both formal and informal workers in the prevailing economic climate (Hill, 2009).

West Bengal has introduced a number of schemes to benefit informal workers both generally and in specific areas, such as transport, *beedi* manufacturing and construction (Agarwala, 2013). A number of unions (CITU, AITUC and INTUC) have formed a Joint Action Committee (JAC) in the state to address issues pertaining to workers in certain occupations (for example, *beedi* and brick making); it holds meetings every two months and raises awareness campaigns. In the brick-kiln industry the JAC has helped brick workers to unionize; it has also ensured implementation of minimum wages and provision of other welfare benefits (Sen, 2012). However, in the case of *beedi* workers, where the notified wage rate varies between INR142 and INR160, the unions in West Bengal signed bilateral agreements (*beedi* merchant associations and the union federation) to pay just 50 per cent (not exceeding INR80) of the statutory minimum wages, as the wages are much lower in neighbouring states (INR55 in Orissa) (Sen, 2012), to ensure that work does not move to other states where wages are low. Other unions, including BMS and INTUC, have also started to address some of the issues of the unorganized workers.

2.4.2 New Workers' Organizations

Since the mid-1970s informal workers have been organizing themselves into co-operatives, non-governmental organizations (NGOs) and unions, and have been putting their demands to the state for both work and welfare rights (Agarwala, 2013; Harriss-White, 2010). The state has seen these organizations not as a threat but rather as 'low-cost substitutes for the state directed development administration' (Harriss-White, 2010, p. 177).[22] This subsection briefly examines some of the initiatives taken by these different forms of organization over recent decades with the aim of improving the welfare of the workers.

SEWA, the Self Employed Women's Association,[23] emerged during the textile mills crisis in 1972 in Gujarat, when it fought for the rights of seasonal migrant women *badli* workers (that is, contract and casual) who were neglected by both the union (the Textile Labour Association, the single largest textile union in Ahmedabad) and the Government (Blaxall, 2004). A decade later, when about 40 per cent of the textile mills in Ahmedabad were closed down in 1982 (Patel, 1986), a number of women of the displaced textile workers became self-employed in order to run their livelihoods. SEWA, as an independent workers' association, set out to organize these workers and promote their rights.

Since then, SEWA has organized home-based workers, street vendors and hawkers, construction workers and rural producers into groups, to make them aware of their rights and to help them claim health care, child care, maternity protection, life insurance and other forms of social provision. For example, though *beedi* workers were protected and regulated by law under the Factories Act (Jhabvala and Tate, 1996), employers seeking to reduce costs often outsourced the work to be done at home, predominantly by women, thereby depriving them of any entitlements. SEWA began to organize these *beedi* homeworkers in 1979, when they were earning INR8 per 1000 cigarettes rolled, which was about half the minimum wage. After a struggle of more than ten years, during which SEWA organized worker rallies, sit-in protests and strikes, and filed four cases in various courts, an agreement was finally reached with the employers whereby the *beedi* homeworkers were paid the minimum wage (Jhabvala and Tate, 1996).

SEWA continues to negotiate through collective bargaining to increase the wages of the *beedi* workers in western India, mainly in Gujarat and Rajasthan[24] (Sinha, 2013). Similar efforts were also made by Navayuga Beedi Karmika Sangam, a *beedi* homeworkers' union in Hyderabad in southern India, which organized strikes, demonstrations and agitation to publicize the plight of these workers. By 1995, the union had obtained minimum wages for the workers, along with welfare cards which entitled them to maternity benefits and schooling for their children (Hensman, 2001). Other such groups include the Labour Education and Research Network (LEARN) and its subsidiary LEARN Mahila Kamgar Sanghatana (LMKS), which operates in Mumbai in one of Asia's biggest slums, Dharavi. These groups create awareness among workers about their rights, provide training in vocational skill development and/or engage in wage negotiations and collective bargaining, depending upon the requirements of the community (Mathew, 2010). The Chennai-based Working Women's Forum (WWF) is another such proactive organization. Focusing on the rights of women workers in trade and manufacturing, it helps to provide services to its members such as training in entrepreneurship, child care, education, family planning and credit.

Roychowdhury (2003b) argues that the struggles to achieve welfare provision for the poor in recent years have been 'waged by groups and organizations that are new to the politics of welfare', which address issues ranging from 'class, community, occupation, to neighborhood' (p. 5278). She calls these groups 'new trade unions', and argues that they work very differently as they focus on rights and often 'challenge dominant development practices' (p. 5278), in contrast to the NGOs, which are project-based and externally funded.

The wastepickers' trade union (Kagad Kach Patra Kashtakari Panchayat), based in Pune, is one such 'new union'. It has changed the popular perception that wastepickers, who do not have a clear-cut employer–employee relationship, were 'simply people who rummaged in the waste', arguing that 'their members were performing valuable service in the waste economy, collecting and trading recyclable commodities', in a manner that was far more efficient than any of the available alternatives (Kabeer et al., 2013, p. 254). After a great deal of effort, the union achieved a partnership between itself as service provider, the government authority (the municipal corporation) and the consumers, which has yielded substantial social, economic and environmental rewards, and has ensured the right to livelihood and access to benefits such as health insurance for the workers (Sankaran and Madhav, 2011). Bonner and Spooner (2011) also note that in Pune, 'unions of informal workers (street vendors, waste pickers, domestic workers, head-loaders, auto-rickshaw and tempo drivers, and construction workers) form a city-wide Manual Labourers' Association'. This association in fact operates as a trade union federation of informal economy workers and is 'recognized by the municipal authorities as a bargaining counterpart' (p. 93).

Similarly, the NCL represents the interests of workers in the informal sector, undertaking collective bargaining for better wages or social security provisions. The NCL has also been quite successful in organizing slum dwellers in Bangalore city, through its constituent organization Karnataka Kollageri Nivasigela Sangathana (KKNS). The KKNS fights for 'land rights for slum dwellers' and lobbies the state Government for the provision of 'basic amenities such as street lighting . . . sanitation, housing [and] schools' in slum areas (Roychowdhury, 2003b, p. 5282).

The issue of street vendors, one of the most vulnerable groups, comprising about 10 million self-employed workers, was taken up by the National Association for Street Vendors in India (NASVI), a network formed in 1998, with the support of NGOs, community-based organizations, social activists and academics. The network made an effort to ensure their security and the protection of their livelihoods in the face of continuous harassment from municipal officials and police. After 15 years of struggle, heated debate about legal protection and negotiations with the Government, the Street Vendors Bill was finally passed into law on 5 March 2014 (Bhowmik, 2014), marking a significant step towards allowing workers the right to have access to designated space to earn a livelihood without being under the constant threat of eviction and extortion,[25] and to improve their incomes by gaining legal status.

A number of international networks and movements have also been engaged in improving the work and welfare rights of Indian workers. The most well known are HomeNet South Asia, StreetNet International, Building and Wood Workers International (BWI) and the International Domestic Workers Network (IDWN). BWI has supported projects in Odisha (formerly Orissa) and Gujarat to organize kendu and sal leaf-pickers, led by state-wide affiliated unions of informal leaf-pickers. Its support led to the 'recognition of their status as workers, adoption of identity cards, wage increases, and health and safety improvements' (Bonner and Spooner, 2011, p. 101).

Agarwala (2013) argues that there has been a shift in the strategy of informal workers' organizations from a focus on gaining work-related benefits from the employer towards seeking welfare benefits from the state on the basis of citizenship rights,[26] making use of the competitive populism by which political parties seek to gain the votes of the poor, and their supporters, in electoral contests. The shift is largely motivated by the realization that laws providing for minimum wages and working conditions are not well implemented and often enforced. Examining the *beedi* and construction sectors in Maharashtra, Tamil Nadu and West Bengal, the author found that welfare benefits were the highest in Tamil Nadu, followed by Maharashtra and West Bengal; by contrast, work benefits were highest in West Bengal, and much lower in Tamil Nadu and Maharashtra.

These empirical evidences are quite interesting given the fact that Tamil Nadu is one of the most progressive states and has put in place a number of workplace benefits through legislation: the Manual Workers Act in 1982, the first state to give legal protection to informal workers through regulation of working conditions, provision of welfare benefits and establishment of welfare boards for informal workers. Minimum wages are fixed for about 90 per cent of the employment categories in the state (Agarwala, 2013). The Tamil Nadu Manual Workers Social Security and Welfare Boards came into being in 1999 and nine informal sector welfare boards were formed in 2000. Despite these efforts Tamil Nadu has not been able to ensure work-based benefits for its informal workers, only welfare-based benefits. The state government has offered direct welfare benefits in the form of 'food, housing grants, pensions, unemployment doles, agricultural loan forgiveness [and] mid-day meal schemes' to the poor (p. 92). Agarwala argues that the informal workers organizations were able to frame and articulate to seek their demands without threatening the liberal economic structures, as a result creating a new social contract between state and people (Agarwala, 2013). This assertion is distressing, as there is a clear shift in the agenda from workers' rights to citizen's rights, and from the central issue of income poverty and inequality (Roychowdhury, 2015).

2.4.3   Other Initiatives

Past decades have also seen some attempts by academics, social activists and international bodies to improve the livelihoods of the poor or those in the informal sector. One such initiative was the MGNREGA, the first version of which was conceptualized and drafted by academics and social activists. The programme was introduced in 200 districts in 2005/06, and it was extended to the entire country, covering 619 districts, in 2009/10. Another was the adoption by the International Labour Organization (ILO) of the Domestic Workers Convention, 2011 (No. 189), which calls for minimum wage provisions to be extended to cover domestic workers and the provision of basic social security.

The MGNREGA and minimum wages
The MGNREGA seeks to provide a guarantee of up to 100 days of employment opportunities per year per household in rural areas, to all those who are available and willing to work (GOI, 2008). It provides the legal entitlement to work and to be paid at minimum rates; it also stipulates that men and women be paid same wages, which was a significant policy change from earlier employment guarantee schemes. Another important aspect was the inclusion of the right to information and social audits as integral provisions of the Act (Rani and Belser, 2012b). The impact of the MGNREGA has varied depending upon the commitment of the local administration. In many states, workers did receive minimum wages; where this provision was violated, there were widespread protests and civil society played a highly active role through social audits to ensure that the system was properly implemented. Compliance with

minimum wages in rural parts of India where the programme operates increased from 26.4 per cent in 2004/05 to 49.8 per cent in 2009/10. A high proportion of female workers have benefited from the programme, and the strategy has effectively redistributed resources to low-paid workers (Rani et al., 2013).

Apart from providing a minimum level of support for low-income households, the MGNREGA has also helped to reduce the gender wage gap prevailing in rural India and to empower women. Several studies have shown that in some states where women gained work through the MGNREGA, they were able to push up average female wages, thus narrowing the pay gap (Dasgupta and Sudarshan, 2011; Sudarshan et al., 2010). It also created awareness among workers about their basic entitlements, improving their capacity to conduct wage negotiations, as for example in rural areas of Rajasthan and Tamil Nadu (Menon, 2008; Jeyarajan, 2011). As a result, there was a knock-on effect, with agricultural wages rising in several states (Jeyarajan, 2011; Nair et al., 2009). Thus, the Act provided new possibilities for mobilizing workers to ensure proper implementation of the programme, minimum wages and guaranteed certain days of employment.

Domestic workers and minimum wages
Another arena in which social movements and trade unions have been quite successful in protecting the rights and welfare of workers is domestic work. The national domestic workers' movement started in 1985 in Mumbai; extended its operations to Patna, Chennai and Varanasi; and later spread to Andhra Pradesh, Karnataka, Kerala, Madhya Pradesh, Jharkhand and the north-east. There are also networks and federations emerging to address issues related to domestic workers. One such federation is the Maharashtra Rajya Ghar Kamgar Kriti Samiti (Maharashtra State Domestic Workers' Committee), which was formed in 2011, and is a platform for domestic worker unions affiliated to AITUC, BMS, CITU, INTUC, the NTUI and Sarva Shramik Mahasangh. The committee aims to address issues related to wages, working conditions and social security (Neetha, 2013).

The ILO's minimum wage fixing Conventions, Nos 26 (1928) and 131 (1970), do not exclude domestic workers, and it remains at the discretion of the ratifying states to include them within their schedules. To protect domestic workers, Tamil Nadu included them in the Manual Workers Act 1982 and created a separate board for them. Maharashtra drew up a Domestic Workers' Welfare Board Act in 2008; domestic workers are covered by the Janashree Yojana, which provides accident and death coverage and funds schooling for two children, and also by the national health insurance scheme (Menon, 2012).

Extensive campaigning by unions and other organizations, and pressure exerted on political leaders and bureaucrats, led to the inclusion of domestic workers in the schedules of employment in four states (Andhra Pradesh, Bihar, Karnataka and Rajasthan) between 2007 and 2009, and much more recently in Kerala (Gothoskar, 2013). Even so, in 2009/10 only 14.7 per cent of domestic workers in India were covered by minimum wage legislation. Of the small proportion of the country's workers so covered, only 36.8 per cent actually received those minimum wages; more in urban (43.7 per cent) than in rural (18.6 per cent) areas (Oelz and Rani, 2015). Pressure from unions and other groups to extend the coverage of minimum wage provisions, and to have domestic work recognized in schedules of employment, continues.

ILO Convention No. 189 and its supplementing Recommendation No. 201 give further impetus to efforts to address the issues relating to domestic workers, with regard to both minimum wages and working conditions. Though India has not yet ratified the Convention, there is pressure to do so from unions and grass-roots organizations.[27] However, a major obstacle has been the lack of value attached to domestic work socially, which is reflected in the fixing of minimum wages: 'all the state governments . . . decide on wage rates for domestic workers that are lower than other occupations' (Gothoskar, 2013, p. 83; see also Oelz and Rani, 2015). And, as noted above, even these low minimum wages are paid to only a small proportion of those entitled to it.

2.5   CONCLUSIONS

This chapter has noted some major setbacks in the development of industrial relations in India. First, all attempts to amend labour legislation in the decades following independence were blocked. The industrial truce resolution in 1947 could have paved a way towards a labour-inclusive developmental state and laid the foundations for an enduring institutional infrastructure. Had such efforts been supported, they could have led to a much more vibrant industrial relations system. However, the intervention of the state in industrial disputes through adjudication placed limits on the development of voluntary collective bargaining. Second, the close proximity of the labour movement to political parties led to the demobilization of labour, and compromised the interests and rights of workers (Chibber, 2005). Third, the gap between the institutional and legal framework for organizational rights and the practice at the workplace level hampered the development of industrial relations (Ford and Gillan, 2016).

As a result of this baulked development, the role of the Indian IR system in inclusive development is limited, its effectiveness hampered by the exclusion of a large proportion of the workforce. Even in the organized, formal sector where unionization rates are comparatively high, unions have tended to pursue the 'interests' of the few rather than fighting for the 'rights' of all. This trend is also fostered by the change in bargaining strategy from centralized to decentralized bargaining, often at the enterprise or plant level. There has been some effort by unions in the past decade to regain influence by organizing informal sector workers and fighting to improve the conditions of contractual workers; these are positive steps, but the unions need to engage with the issues of concern to these groups much more deeply than they have done so far.

In recent years, many new forms of organization have emerged to try to secure basic rights for the various groups of informal workers. These new organizations, along with seeking to secure specific rights, also generate 'mutual recognition and respect that produces individual self-confidence, self-respect and self-esteem amongst these workers' through their training and education programmes (Hill, 2010, p. 116). Some of these organizations, such as SEWA, have also succeeded in improving livelihoods 'through helping to increase income (cooperatives, skills development), [providing] social protection (health insurance, child care) [and] financial services (SEWA Bank)' (Bonner and Spooner, 2011, p. 90), and negotiating wages through collective bargaining.

These new forms of organizations represent a new model of organizing workers, which combines the creation and promotion of employment. They help informal workers to access their work and welfare rights and also empower women in the process. However, these efforts alone are not sufficient; there is a need for effective, and properly enforced, legislation to protect these workers. The question of labour welfare cannot be shifted from the workplace, so that workers' rights are ensured and they do not rely on piecemeal welfare rights. To be more inclusive, the organizational basis for collective labour relations needs to be strengthened, drawing on new networks and sources of power, including those in the unorganized or informal sector. The MGNREGA and the Street Vendors Bill are promising cases, and similar efforts could bring the large informal workforce within the country's legislative framework, so that their work and welfare rights are assured wherever they may work. To conclude, Sen (2015) argues that the idea of social justice cannot be relegated to an ideal institution, as there is no perfect institution, though it can be improved, but more importantly, 'we have to make sure, with cooperation from all sections of the society, that these institutions work vigorously and well' (p. 197).

NOTES

1. Bhattacherjee (2001) provides a very clear account of the evolution of industrial relations from 1947 to the 2000s, over four time periods. We adopt this periodization here.
2. The Trade Unions Act 1926 and the Industrial Employment (Standing Orders) Act 1946.
3. These were the Trade Disputes Act 1929 (providing for government intervention in ensuring industrial harmony), the Bombay Trade Disputes Act 1938 (imposing restrictions on employers' rights to dismiss employees), and Rule 81-A of the Defence of India Rules (providing speedy dispute settlement through compulsory reference to conciliation or adjudication, with strikes or lockouts prohibited pending resolution).
4. These included the Workmen's Compensation Act 1936 and the Payment of Wages Act 1936; a Committee on Fair Wages was set up in 1946, which led to the Minimum Wages Act 1948, the Factories Act 1948, the Mines Act 1952 and the Plantation Labour Act 1951.
5. The resolution included developing a system of mutual discussion and resorting to the existing statutory and other machinery in a just and peaceful manner, and closer cooperation between workers and employers in all matters concerning industrial production, determination of fair wages and conditions of labour, and fair remuneration of capital through central, regional and unit production committees and work committtes (Punekar, 1966, p. 29).
6. The trade union movement seems to have suffered from political unionism, rivalry, multiplicity of unions, unsound finances, low membership and lack of welfare services (Punekar, 1966), issues that continue to plague the union movement even today.
7. Wages were set by central and industrial wage boards, or for public sector enterprises by the Bureau of Public Enterprises (Jackson, 1972, p. 191).
8. These included the Employees' Provident Fund Act 1948 (requiring compulsory monthly contributions from employers in factories with more than 50 workers), the Employees' State Insurance Act 1948 (specifying joint contributions to cover illness, injury, maternity and disability) and the Gratuity Act 1952 (providing for lump sum payments on superannuation).
9. An amendment to the Trade Unions Act 1926 in 1947 included collective bargaining and recognition of bargaining agents; and a more comprehensive Industrial Relations Bill was placed before Parliament in 1950.
10. Labour falls under the concurrent jurisdiction of both state and central Government.
11. A survey of 30 enterprises included the following sectors: pharmaceutical, automobile, consumer goods, textiles and engineering.
12. AITUC, established in 1920, was the first national federation of trade unions in India, comprising of communists, the Congress and other independent trade unionists. Ideological and political differences led to the formation of splinter unions, which was reunited into AITUC in 1935 due to the Great Depression and the rising prices which affected the working class. The Congress Party decided to form its own union just before independence, as AITUC was under the control of the communists and subsequently there were further splits (Bhowmik, 2006). This trend actually led to linking unions to political parties and weakening of the trade union movement.
13. This was earlier called the United Trade Union Centre (Lenin Sarani) (UTUC-LS).
14. SEWA was recognized as a national federation in 2006, with a membership of 500 000 workers. A mission from the International Confederation of Free Trade Unions headed by General Secretary Guy Ryder and composed of eight prominent union leaders had two day-long discussions with SEWA in 2005, and they supported the proposal to the Government.
15. To qualify as a CTUO, a federation must have a membership of at least 500 000 and cover at least four states and four industries (Datt, 2008).
16. These are the Minimum Wages Act, 1948; the Payment of Wages Act, 1936; the Payment of Bonus Act, 1965; and the Equal Remuneration Act, 1976.
17. A note of caution: there is much debate in India about poverty rates, which vary widely

depending upon the level and method chosen. In this chapter, Planning Commission estimates are used.

18. This means that as households become wealthier or increase their incomes, women in such households move out from low-productive and subsistence employment and become inactive.

19. The employment figures have been computed by the authors from the raw data of the Employment–Unemployment Survey for 2011/12.

20. Maharashtra is defined as a pro-worker state by Besley and Burgess (2004) and as having extensive labour law provisions by Deakin and Sarkar (2011), implying that it would favour the protection of workers' rights.

21. *Beedi*: traditional rolling of cigarettes using tobacco leaves.

22. This area of activity, often called a 'third sector' between state and market, is not unique to India but is prevalent in many developing and emerging economies.

23. SEWA was initially part of the Textile Labour Association (TLA) and in 1982 after increasing conflicts SEWA was asked to leave TLA. Since the 1980s a number of international trade unions and federations have provided support, and the International Union of Food, Agricultural, Hotel, Restaurant, Catering, Tobacco and Allied Workers' Association (IUF) was the first international federation to appreciate the relevance of SEWA for the informal economy workers. Subsequently, after a few years SEWA became a member of the International Textile, Garment and Leather Workers' Federation (ITGLWF) and along with these two global federations was in the forefront of passing the Home Workers Convention in the ILO in 1996 (SEWA, 2006).

24. In 2013, they managed to get a 15 per cent wage increase in Gujarat, and 12 per cent in Rajasthan.

25. A city study conducted in Ahmedabad in 1997–98 revealed that about INR285 million had been collected by the local municipal authorities from street vendors in fees, of which 33 per cent was collected legally and the rest was taken in the form of bribes. Even the INR93 million collected legally did not yield any facilities or services; indeed, the street vendors were frequently harassed and their goods confiscated, which were released after the payment of fines (Rani and Unni, 2000).

26. These welfare benefits include identity cards, health care, education scholarships, social security benefits, child care services, and compensation for injuries and sexual abuse (Agarwala, 2013). This argument is also put forward by other researchers (Vijayabaskar, 2011).

27. An inter-ministerial task force was established and a draft national policy for domestic workers was formulated which suggested mechanisms for fixing minimum wages, regulating placement agencies and other matters (Menon, 2012). A number of meetings were organized with government officials at state level to make them understand the urgent need for ratification of Convention No. 189, if decent work for domestic workers is to be achieved.

REFERENCES

Agarwala, R.N. 2013. *Informal Labour, Formal Politics, and Dignified Discontent in India*. New York: Cambridge University Press.

Ahn, P-S. 2010. *The Growth and Decline of Political Unionism in India: The Need for a Paradigm Shift*. Bangkok: ILO Decent Work Team for East and South-East Asia and the Pacific.

Badigannavar, V. and Kelly, J. 2012. 'Do labour laws protect labour in India? Union experiences of workplace employment regulations in Maharashtra India', *Industrial Law Journal*, **41**(4), pp. 439–70. doi:10.1093/indlaw/dws038.

Banaji, J. 2000. 'India: Workers' rights in a new economic order', Working Paper No. 55, November. Oxford: Queen Elizabeth House, University of Oxford.

Banerjee, D. 2005. 'Trend of factor incomes distribution in Indian factories', *Indian Journal of Labour Economics*, **48**(2), pp. 297–310.

Belser, P. and Rani, U. 2010. *Extending the Coverage of Minimum Wages in India: Simulations from Household Data*, Conditions of Work and Employment Series No. 26. Geneva: ILO.

Besley, T. and Burgess, R. 2004. 'Can labour regulation hinder economic performance? Evidence from India', *Quarterly Journal of Economics*, **119**(1), pp. 91–134.

Bhasker, V.V. 2013. 'Indian auto component industry: A decade of growth and way forward', *Research Journal of Management Sciences*, **2**(3), pp. 19–27.

Bhattacherjee, D. 2000. 'Globalising economy, localising labour', *Economic and Political Weekly*, **35**(42), pp. 3758–64.

Bhattacherjee, D. 2001. 'The evolution of Indian industrial relations: A comparative perspective', *Industrial Relations Journal*, **32**(3), pp. 244–63.

Bhowmik, S.K. 2006. 'Sociology of work in India', in Rehberg, K-S. (ed.), *Soziale Ungleichheit, kulturelle Unterschiede: Verhandlungen des 32*. Kongresses der Deutschen Gesellschaft für Soziologie in München.

Bhowmik, S.K. 2014. 'Street vendors in India get legal protection', *Global Labour Column*, No. 174.

Blaxall, J. 2004. *India's Self-Employed Women's Association (SEWA): Empowerment through Mobilization of Poor Women on a Large Scale*. Washington, DC: World Bank.

Bonner, C. and Spooner, D. 2011. 'Organizing in the informal economy: A challenge for trade unions', *Internationale Politik und Gesellschaft*, **2**, pp. 87–105.

Bose, A.J.C. and Pratap, S. 2012. 'Worker voices in an auto production chain: Notes from the pits of a low road', *Economic and Political Weekly*, **47**(33), pp. 46–59.

Candland, C. 1996. 'Labor institutions and industrial restructuring in India', IRIS-India Working Paper No. 26. College Park, MD: University of Maryland, Centre for Institutional Reform and the Informal Sector.

Chakravarty, D. 2010. 'Trade unions and business firms: Unorganised manufacturing in West Bengal', *Economic and Political Weekly*, **45**(6), pp. 45–52.

Chandrasekhar, C.P. and Ghosh, J. 2002. *The Market that Failed: A Decade of Liberal Economic Reforms in India*. New Delhi: Left Word Books.

Chibber, V. 2005. 'From class compromise to class accommodation: Labor's incorporation into the Indian political economy', in Katzenstein, M. and Ray, R. (eds), *Social Movements and Poverty in India*. Lanham, MD: Rowman & Littlefield.

Das, D.K. 2003. 'Manufacturing productivity under varying trade regimes: India in the 1980s and 1990s', Working Paper No. 107. New Delhi: Indian Council for Research on International Economic Relations.

Das, H. 1999. 'Trade union activism: Avoidable or inevitable', *Indian Journal of Industrial Relations*, **35**(2), pp. 224–36.

Das, K.S.L. 2011. 'Foreign management and Indian workers' struggle', *Labour File*. http:/www.labourfile.org/PrtintDocument.aspx?ID=712.

Das, K.S.L. and George, S. 2006. 'Labour practices and working conditions in TNCs: The case of Toyota Kirloskar in India', in Chang, D. (ed.), *Labour in Globalising Asian Corporations: A Portrait of Struggle*. Hong Kong: Asian Monitoring Resource Centre.

Das, S. 2010. *Managing People at Work: Employment Relations in Globalizing India*. New Delhi: SAGE.

Dasgupta, P. and Goldar, B. 2005. 'Female labour supply in rural India: An econometric analysis', Working Paper No. 265. New Delhi: Institute of Economic Growth. http://iegindia.org/workpap/wp265.pdf (accessed 7 December 2015).

Dasgupta, S. and Sudarshan, R. 2011. 'Issues in labour market inequality and women's participation in India's National Rural Employment Guarantee Programme', Working Paper No. 98, Policy Integration Department. Geneva: ILO.

Dasgupta, S. and Verick, S.S. (ed.) 2016. *Transformation of Women at Work in Asia: An Unfinished Development Agenda*. New Delhi and Geneva: SAGE Publications and ILO.

Datt, R. 2008. 'Regional and industrial spread of trade unions in India', *Indian Journal of Labour Economics*, **51**(4), pp. 993–99.

Davala, S. 1994. 'New economic policy and trade union response', *Economic and Political Weekly*, **29**(8), pp. 406–8.

Dayal, S. 1980. *Industrial Relations System in India: A Study of Vital Issues*. New Delhi: Sterling Publishers.

Deakin, S. and Sarkar, P. 2011. 'Indian labour law and its impact on unemployment 1970–2006: A leximetric study', Working Paper No. 428. Cambridge: Centre for Business Research, University of Cambridge.

Debroy, B. and Kaushik, P. 2005. *Reforming the Labour Market*. New Delhi: Academic Publishers.

Deshpande, L., Sharma, A.N., Karan, A. and Sarkar, S. 2004. *Liberalization and Labour: Labour Flexibility in Indian Manufacturing*. New Delhi: Institute for Human Development.

Ford, M. and Gillan, M. 2016. 'Employment relations and the state in Southeast Asia', *Journal of Industrial Relations*, **58**(2), pp. 167–82.

Ghosh, B. 2008. 'Economic reforms and trade unionism in India: A macro view', *Indian Journal of Industrial Relations*, **43**(3), pp. 355–84.

Ghosh, S. 2004. 'Dispute incidence in manufacturing and co-movements in economic activity: Evidence from India', *Indian Economic Review*, **39**(2), pp. 349–69.

Gothoskar, S. 2013. 'The plight of domestic workers: Confluence of gender, class and caste hierarchies', *Economic and Political Weekly*, **48**(22), pp. 63–75.

Government of India (GOI). 2008. *The National Employment Guarantee Act 2005 Operational Guidelines*. New Delhi: Ministry of Rural Development.

Government of India (GOI). 2015. *Report on the Working of the Minimum Wages Act, 1948 for the Year 2013*. Chandigarh: Ministry of Labour and Employment, Labour Bureau.

Harriss-White, B. 2010. 'Work and well-being in informal economies: The regulative roles of institutions of identity and the State', *World Development*, **38**(2), pp. 170–83.

Hensman, R. 2001. 'The impact of globalisation on employment in India and responses from the formal and informal sectors'. http://www.iisg.nl/clara/publi cat/clara15.pdf (accessed 8 July 2014).

Hensman, R. 2010. 'Labour and globalization: Union responses in India', in Bowles, P. and Harriss, J. (eds), *Globalization and Labour in China and India*. Houndmills, UK: Palgrave Macmillan.

Hill, E. 2009. 'The Indian industrial relations system: Struggling to address the dynamics of a globalizing economy', *Journal of Industrial Relations*, **51**(3), pp. 395–410. doi:10.1177/0022185609104305.

Hill, E. 2010. *Worker Identity, Agency and Economic Development: Women's Empowerment in the Indian Informal Economy*. New York: Routledge.

Himanshu. 2005. 'Wages in rural India: Sources, trends and comparability', *Indian Journal of Labour Economics*, **48**(2), pp. 375–406.

India Labour and Employment Report (ILER). 2014. *India Labour and Employment Report 2014: Workers in the Era of Globalization*. New Delhi: Institute for Human Development and Academic Publishers.

Jackson, D. 1972. 'Wage policy and industrial relations in India', *Economic Journal*, **82**(325), pp. 183–94.

Jagannathan, S. 2015. 'Minimum wage fixation and wage setting practices at local/ enterprise level in Mahrashtra' (unpublished).

Jeyarajan, J. 2011. 'Women and pro-poor policies in rural Tamil Nadu: An examination of practices and responses', *Economic and Political Weekly*, **46**(43), pp. 64–74.

Jhabvala, R. and Tate, J. 1996. 'Out of the shadows: Homebased workers organize for international recognition', SEEDS Working Paper No. 18, Series on the homeworkers in the informal economy. Geneva: ILO.

John, M. 2012. 'Workers' discontent and form of trade union politics', *Economic and Political Weekly*, **47**(1), pp. 19–22.

Jose A.V. 2016. 'Real wages in rural India', in Kannan, K.P., Mamgain, R.P. and Rustagi, P. (eds), *Labour and Development in Honour of Professor T.S. Papola*. New Delhi: Academic Foundation.

Kabeer, N., Milward, K. and Sudarshan, R. 2013. 'Organising women workers in the informal economy', *Gender and Development*, **21**(2), pp. 249–63.

Kannan, K.P. and Raveendran, G. 2009. 'Jobless growth in India's organised manufacturing', *Economic and Political Weekly*, **44**(10), pp. 80–91.

Kannappan, S. 1966. 'The many facets of Government influence on industrial relations in India', in Ross, A.M. (ed.), *Industrial Relations and Economic Development*. London: Macmillan.

Kapsos, S., Bourmpoula, E. and Silberman, A. 2014. 'Why is female labour force participation declining so sharply in India?', Research Paper Series No. 10, Geneva: ILO.

Kochar, R.J. 1990. 'Right to strike: Has Supreme Court moved backward?', *Economic and Political Weekly*, **25**(29), pp. 1564–66.

Krishnan, T.N. 2010. 'Technological change and employment relations in India', *Indian Journal of Industrial Relations*, **45**(3), pp. 367–80.

Kumar, P. 1964. 'Strikes in India: An analysis', *Economic Weekly*, **16**(41), pp. 1603–7.

Mathew, T.K. 2010. 'Role of social movements in organising the unorganised sector workers: A case study of LEARN, Dharavi', thesis submitted to Tata Institute of Social Sciences, Mumbai.

Mathur, A.N. 1992. 'Employment security and industrial restructuring in India: Separating facts from folklore. The exit policy controversy', *Indian Journal of Labour Economics*, **18**(4), pp. 227–33.

Mathur, A.N. 1993. 'The experience of consultation during structural adjustment in India (1990–92)', *International Labour Review*, **132**(3), pp. 331–45.

Mazumdar, D. and Sarkar, S. 2008. *Globalization, Labour Markets and Inequality in India*. London: Routledge.

Menon, M. 2012. 'Ground realities for domestic workers', *Hindu*, 13 January.

http://www.thehindu.com/todays-paper/tp-national/tp-newdelhi/ground-realiti es-for-domestic-workers/article2797533.ece (accessed 7 December 2015).

Menon, S.V. 2008. 'Right to Information Act and NREGS: Reflections on Rajasthan', Munich Personal RePEc Archives (MPRA) Paper No. 7351.

Nair, K.N., Sreedharan, T.P. and Anoopkumar, M. 2009. 'A study of National Rural Employment Guarantee Programme in three grama panchayats of Kasargod district', Working Paper No. 413. Trivandrum: Centre for Development Studies.

National Commission for Enterprises in the Unorganised Sector (NCEUS). 2007. *Report on Conditions of Work and Promotion of Livelihoods in the Unorganised Sector*. New Delhi: Government of India.

Nayar, B.R. 2006. 'When did the "Hindu" rate of growth end?', *Economic and Political Weekly*, **41**(19), pp. 1885–90.

Neetha, N. 2013. 'Minimum wages for domestic work: Mirroring devalued house-work', *Economic and Political Weekly*, **48**(43), pp. 77–84.

Nouroz, H. 2001. *Protection in Indian Manufacturing: An Empirical Study*. New Delhi: Macmillan India.

Oelz, M. and Rani, U. 2015. 'Domestic work, wages and gender equality: Lessons from developing countries', Working Paper No. 5. Geneva: ILO Gender, Equality and Diversity Branch.

Oommen, T.K. 2009. 'Indian labour movement: Colonial era to the global age', *Economic and Political Weekly*, **44**(52), pp. 81–9.

Patel, S. 1986. 'Contract labour in Ahmedabad textile industry', *Economic and Political Weekly*, **21**(41), pp. 1813–20.

Prasad, K.V.E. 1994. 'Trends in employment', in Ramaswamy, E.A. (ed.), *Countdown: Essays for Trade Unionists*. New Delhi: Friedrich-Ebert Stiftung.

Pratap, S. 2011. 'Shrinking spaces for collective bargaining in India', Working Paper (CWE).

Punekar, S.D. 1966. 'Aspects of state intervention in Industrial relations in India: An evaluation', in Ross, A.M. (ed.), *Industrial Relations and Economic Development*. London: Macmillan.

Ramaswamy, E.A. 1988. *Worker Consciousness and Trade Union Response*. New Delhi: Oxford University Press.

Rani, U. and Belser, P. 2012a. 'Low pay among wage earners and the self-employed in India', *International Labour Review*, **151**(3), pp. 221–42. doi:10.11 11/j.1564-913X.2012.00146.x.

Rani, U. and Belser, P. 2012b. 'The effectiveness of minimum wages in developing countries: The case of India', *International Journal of Labour Research*, **4**(1), pp. 45–66.

Rani, U. and Furrer, M. (2016). 'Decomposing income inequality into factor income components: Evidence from selected G20 countries', ILO Research Paper Series No.15. Geneva: ILO.

Rani, U., Furrer, M., Oelz, M. and Setareh, R. 2013. 'Minimum wage coverage and compliance in developing countries', *International Labour Review*, **152**(3/4), pp. 381–410.

Rani, U. and Unni, J. 2000. *Urban Informal Sector: Size and Income Generation Processes in Gujarat, Part II*. New Delhi: National Council of Applied Economic Research.

Rao, M.A.M. 1980. 'India's industrial relations policy', in Mongia, J.N. (ed.), *Readings in Indian Labour and Social Welfare*. New Delhi: Atma Ram & Sons.

Reddy, D.N. 2016. 'Wage fixation prices in Andhra Pradesh' (unpublished).

Roychowdhury, S. 2003a. 'Public sector restructuring and democracy: The State, labour and trade unions in India', *Journal of Development Studies*, **39**(3), pp. 29–50.

Roychowdhury, S. 2003b. 'Old classes and new spaces: Urban poverty, unorganised labour, new unions', *Economic and Political Weekly*, **37**(50), pp. 5277–84.

Roychowdhury, S. 2015. 'Bringing class back in: Informality in Bangalore', *Socialist Register*, **51**, pp. 73–92.

Roychowdhury, S. 2016. 'Mapping and assessment of social dialogue and labour administration frameworks at state level: Karnataka State', unpublished draft report, International Labour Office, New Delhi.

Sankaran, K. and Madhav, R. 2011. 'Gender equality and social dialogue in India', Working Paper 1/2011. Geneva: ILO Industrial and Employment Relations Department and Bureau for Gender Equality.

Sarkar, S. and Mehta, B.S. (2010). 'Income inequality in India: Pre- and post-reforms period', *Economic and Political Weekly*, **45**(37), pp. 45–55.

Self-employment Women's Association (SEWA). 2006. 'SEWA joins the ICFTU', July. www.sewa.org/july_2006.asp (accessed 18 April 2017).

Sen, A.K. 2015. *The Country of First Boys and Other Essays.* New Delhi: Oxford University Press.

Sen, R. 2011. 'Industrial relations at Maruti-Suzuki', *Indian Journal of Industrial Relations*, **47**(2), pp. 191–205.

Sen, R. 2012. 'Employee participation in India', Dialogue Working Paper No. 40. Geneva: ILO.

Sheth, N.R. 1993. 'Our trade unions: An overview', *Economic and Political Weekly*, **28**(6), pp. 231–36.

Shrouti, A. and Nandkumar, G. 1994. *New Economic Policy, Changing Management Strategies: Impact on Workers and Trade Unions.* New Delhi: Friedrich-Ebert Stiftung.

Sinha, S. 2013. 'Supporting women home-based workers: The approach of the Self-employed Women's Association in India', WIEGO Policy Brief (Urban Policies) No. 13 (Women in Informal Employment Globalizing and Organizing).

Srivastava, R. (2016). *Structural Change and non-standard employment in India*, Conditions of Work and Employment Series No. 68. Geneva: ILO.

Sudarshan, R.M., Bhattacharya, R. and Fernandez, G. 2010. 'Women's participation in the NREGS: Some observations from fieldwork in Himachal Pradesh, Kerala and Rajasthan', *IDS Bulletin*, **41**(4), pp. 77–81.

Sundar, K.R.S. 2008. *Impact of Labour Regulations on Industrial Development and Employment in Maharashtra: A Study of Maharashtra.* New Delhi and Geneva: Institute for Studies in Industrial Development and International Institute for Labour Studies.

Sundar, K.R.S. 2011. 'Non-regular workers in India: Social dialogue and organizational and bargaining strategies and practices', Dialogue Working Paper No. 30. Geneva: ILO.

Sundaram, K. and Tendulkar, S.D. 2006. 'Changing structure of Indian workforce, quality of employment and real earnings, 1983–2000', paper presented at international seminar on 'India: Meeting the Employment Challenge, Conference on Labour and Employment Issues in India', Institute for Human Development/World Bank, New Delhi, 27–29 July.

Uba, K. 2008. 'Labor union resistance to economic liberalization in India: What

can national and state level patterns of protests against privatization tell us?',
Asian Survey, **48**(5), pp. 860–84.

Unni, J. and Rani, U. 2008. *Flexibility of Labour in Globalizing India: The Challenge of Skills and Technology*. New Delhi: Tulika Publishers.

Varshney, A. 2001. 'Mass politics or elite politics? India's economic reforms in comparative perspective', in Sachs, J.D., Varshney, A. and Bajpai, N. (eds), *India in the Era of Economic Reforms*. New Delhi: Oxford University Press.

Venkata Ratnam, C.S. 2001. 'Country case study: India', Industrial Relations and Increasing Globalization in Selected Countries, Reference Series No. 6. Singapore: International Confederation of Free Trade Unions, Asia and Pacific Research Organisation.

Venkata Ratnam, C.S. 2003. *Negotiated Change: Collective Bargaining, Liberalization and Restructuring in India*. New Delhi: SAGE/Response Books.

Venkata Ratnam, C.S. 2006. *Industrial Relations*. New Delhi: Oxford University Press.

Vijayabaskar, M. 2011. 'Global crises, welfare provision and coping strategies of labour in Tiruppur', *Economic and Political Weekly*, **46**(22), pp. 38–46.

Webster, E., Joynt, K. and Sefalafala, T. 2016. 'Informalization and decent work: Labour's challenge', *Progress in Development Studies*, **16**(2), pp. 203–18.

Witt, M.A. and Redding, G. 2013. 'Asian business systems: Institutional comparison, clusters and implications for varieties of capitalism and business systems theory', *Socio-economic Review*, **11**(2), pp. 265–300.

3. Industrial relations and inclusive development in South Africa: A dream deferred?

Susan Hayter and Nicolas Pons-Vignon

3.1 INTRODUCTION

The election of the first democratic government in South Africa in 1994 marked the end of apartheid and centuries of racial exclusion and oppression. Organized labour had been a key agent in the struggle for liberation. The transition to a political democracy was accompanied by a new vision for labour policy, forged through a process of tripartite social dialogue. It created a number of new labour market institutions, including in the area of industrial relations. A state-of-the-art tripartite institution was established to facilitate ongoing consultation on public policy, and allow the negotiation of social pacts between organized labour, business and the government on key development issues. Support for sectoral bargaining councils was reinforced so that these could set wage floors in different sectors and assure workers a fair share of productivity gains. These would also build consensus around training and industrial policy needs and promote stability. Initiatives were created to stimulate greater workplace cooperation, facilitate productive transformation and the achievement of 'world-class manufacturing'.

This chapter examines the role that these industrial relations institutions played in forging a more inclusive development path.[1] Section 3.2 provides a historical account of the evolution of industrial relations institutions. Section 3.3 examines the broader context in terms of patterns of growth and trends in the labour market. It describes a labour market characterized by low labour force participation, high levels of unemployment, and high and increasing inequality. Section 3.4 assesses the degree to which industrial relations institutions have helped to reconcile economic and social goals at a policy level, address wage inequality and facilitate stable and productive labour relations. Section 3.5 concludes that while these new industrial relations institutions extended labour protection to millions of workers who had previously been excluded, they provide a patchwork of innovative institutions. Work in conditions of poverty and insecurity, together with a lack of broader economic and social transformation, is placing strains on this institutional patchwork and causing it to tear at the seams. Rather than weaken and deregulate the protection of workers at the core, there is a need to expand and reinforce both protective and participative standards so that these cover those in the informal economy, and on the periphery of labour markets..

3.2   THE EVOLUTION OF INDUSTRIAL RELATIONS: FROM STATE-SPONSORED EXCLUSION TO DEMOCRATIC INCLUSION

To understand the evolution of industrial relations institutions in South Africa it is important to understand the system's antecedents: that is, the processes of control over work relations on which South African capitalism was founded. The Union of South Africa was formed in 1910 as a dominion of the British Empire.[2] It united British and Afrikaner interests but denied political franchise to the African majority.[3] A series of laws laid the foundations for a racial division of labour that would remain a persistent and intractable feature of labour market inequality over a century later.[4] These laws aimed at ensuring an abundant supply of disenfranchised, low-wage, low-skilled migrant black labour, particularly for the mines (Bonner et al., 1993; Webster, 1999).

Scholars concerned with the historical development of institutions theorize about 'contingent events' or 'critical junctures' at which a particular institutional path is taken. The policy choices made during these critical junctures in history close off alternative options, and lead to the establishment of institutions and self-reinforcing path-dependent processes that are difficult to alter (Capoccia and Kelemen, 2007). The evolution of the South African industrial relations system can similarly be explained by a number of watershed events, or critical junctures, each revealing fundamental contradictions within the system and leading to a realignment of institutions.

The first of these watershed events was the Rand strike and rebellion of March 1922, which grew out of major strikes on the Witwatersrand goldfields by white workers demanding protection from the rising numbers of low-paid, low-skilled African workers who they felt threatened their job security and pay (Webster, 1978). This crisis in labour relations led to the adoption of South Africa's first comprehensive labour law.

The Industrial Conciliation Act No. 11 of 1924 laid the cornerstone for a dual system of industrial relations that protected white workers and excluded black African workers. The Act provided for the voluntary establishment of permanent collective bargaining institutions known as 'industrial councils' on the basis of an agreement between an employers' organization and a registered trade union or unions.[5] African workers and indentured Indian workers were excluded from the definition of 'employee' and thus from joining registered trade unions and participating in these industrial councils (Du Toit et al., 2015). A separate dispensation was established for public servants, whose wages and working conditions were unilaterally determined by a Public Services Commission.

The adoption of a comprehensive policy on apartheid by the newly elected National Party Government in 1948 reinforced this dual system of industrial relations.[6] White supervisors were able to exercise absolute authority over black African workers at the workplace. The termination of employment was only regulated by the terms of the contract and notice periods contained therein. No legal standard existed to measure the fairness or otherwise of an employer's decision to terminate employment (van Niekerk, 2002). When black workers demanded higher wages and threatened to disrupt production, they were either summarily dismissed, or businesses turned to the State to maintain industrial order (Lapping, 1986; Bonner et al., 1993). This was to have longer-term consequences as low trust and adversarial relations became deeply entrenched in South African workplaces. A few independent unions emerged, such as the South African Congress of Trade Unions (SACTU), however, they were crushed in successive waves of state repression (Baskin, 1991).

This dual system of industrial relations became increasingly institutionalized. The number of industrial councils grew from 46 in 1936 to 94 in 1970 (Godfrey et al., 2010). However, the internal contradictions of a system that excluded the majority of African workers precipitated what was to be the second watershed event in the evolution of the industrial relations system. In 1973, a strike by black workers at a brick and tile factory in Durban soon spread to other centres and industries. In the first three months of that year, around 69 000 workers were on strike.

Unions intensified their efforts and organized workers factory by factory. They used this strong organizational power to negotiate and sign recognition agreements with firms which established the right to negotiate wages and working conditions (at the plant level), as well as procedures to deal with grievances, dismissals and retrenchment. These agreements curbed the power of management, who were no longer able to unilaterally dismiss workers.[7] Membership of unregistered independent unions rose dramatically over the following years, despite the hostile environment (Baskin, 1991; Maree, 1987).

Rising instability in enterprises and industries led to the establishment in 1977 of the Wiehahn Commission to investigate industrial relations, which recommended an end to the dual system of industrial relations. The Industrial Conciliation Act was amended to allow for the registration and recognition of black trade unions.[8] However, the intention was not to permit freedom of association, but rather to control the emerging unions and limit their political activities by incorporating them into existing institutions, particularly industrial councils (Du Toit et al., 2015). Established registered unions, particularly craft unions, did not want to give up their privileged position and resisted these changes. At the same time, the new independent unions were wary of co-option and there was considerable contestation over the reconfiguration of industrial relations institutions.[9]

3.2.1   Formation of Trade Union Federations

In 1979, major independent unions came together to form the Federation of South African Trade Unions (FOSATU). This marked an important step toward the consolidation of the power of organized labour. A second was the formation of the Council of Unions of South Africa (CUSA) in 1980. When political repression reached new levels in the mid-1980s with two successive declarations of a state of emergency, both federations moved to the forefront of the political struggle, forging links with political, civic and students' organizations and participating in mass 'stay-aways' (a form of political protest action similar to a general strike).

Unity talks led to the amalgamation of 33 unions including FOSATU affiliates. The Congress of South African Trade Unions (COSATU) was launched in 1985 (Baskin, 1991). The Congress adopted a number of resolutions, including the principle of 'one union, one industry' based on the concept of broad-based industrial unionism. A year later CUSA merged with the Azanian Confederation of Trade Unions (AZACTU) to create the National Council of Trade Unions (NACTU).

Shortly after the formation of COSATU, its new union leadership met exiled leaders of the African National Congress (ANC). With the unbanning of political groups in 1990, COSATU officially entered into a 'tripartite' alliance with the ANC and the South African Communist Party (SACP). At the first meeting of the alliance national coordinating committee, the ANC, SACP and COSATU agreed that the alliance did not mean that there would be agreement on all policy matters. There was also discussion of the need to develop a culture of political pluralism within the alliance and to guarantee the independence of the union movement in the longer term (Baskin, 1991, pp. 433–7).[10]

3.2.2 A Unified Employers' Organization

One of the precursors to a unified employer organization was the South African Consultative Committee on Labour Affairs (SACCOLA), which originated in the South African Employers' Committee on International Labour Affairs that had been established to participate in the International Labour Organization (ILO) – until South Africa's withdrawal from that organization in 1964. It continued to be a member of the International Organization of Employers (IOE) until its expulsion in 1983. SACCOLA offered a platform on labour issues for predominantly white employers' associations, the South African Chamber of Business and large employers, and did not function as a mandated representative body (Bendix, 2007). When consultations began on the political transition in the early 1990s, some business interests questioned SACCOLA's right to speak on behalf of South African employers (Bendix, 2007). A concerted effort was made to form a unified and representative employers' organization. With the assistance of the IOE, discussions were held between SACCOLA and two organizations representing black businesses: the National Federated Chamber of Commerce (NAFCOC) and the Foundation for African Business and Consumer Services (FABCOS) for small businesses. This led to the creation of a lead employers' organization, Business South Africa (BSA), in April 1994. BSA brought together 18 different organizations, placing it on a par with organized labour in consultations on economic and social policy.

3.2.3 Towards Corporatist Policy Concertation

In the late 1980s, the Government attempted to introduce far-reaching amendments to labour law and curtail trade union activities, COSATU and NACTU opposed these amendments and organized a three-day national stay-away in 1988. Despite this opposition the Labour Relations Amendment Act (LRA) came into force on 1 September 1988. SACCOLA, COSATU and NACTU met in 1989 and 1990 to discuss the growing crisis. They reached an agreement to return to the previous dispensation, which the Government had little option but to recognize. This was formalized as the Laboria Minute of 14 September 1990. This marked the beginning of the third watershed event in the evolution of industrial relations institutions in South Africa. The Minute included agreement that any new labour legislation would be the subject of consultation and consensus with the social partners prior to its submission to Parliament. This laid the foundation for policy concertation,[11] understood as making policy by means of agreement between government and representatives of employer associations and trade unions, and the establishment of corporatist institutions.[12]

A similar development took place in respect of macroeconomic policy. COSATU rejected the introduction of a new value added tax (VAT) and its application to basic foodstuffs, and led a two-day general strike, which turned out to be a much larger protest than the anti-LRA stay-away in 1988. In 1992 COSATU and major business organizations agreed to establish the National Economic Forum (NEF). Government agreed to participate. The goal of the NEF was to negotiate policy with regard to 'issues of economic growth, social equity and democratic participation in decision making' (Du Toit et al., 2015). This suggested that macroeconomic policy might also be the subject of policy concertation post-1994 in a new democratic dispensation.

3.2.4   The New Labour Law and Regulatory Framework

The unbanning of the ANC and other organizations, the lifting of emergency restrictions, and the release of Nelson Mandela in February 1990. This marked the beginning of the political transition that culminated in the first democratic elections in 1994. The newly elected ANC Government set out a wide-ranging vision for a new industrial relations system characterized by corporatist policy-making and constitutionally guaranteed organizational and collective bargaining rights.

Whereas many other countries were deregulating labour markets to achieve greater flexibility in the 1990s, the vision of the new Government in South Africa was one of 'regulated flexibility'. It sought to achieve this by establishing a regulatory framework within which to negotiate flexibility (functional, wage and numerical) and protect workers' rights. This vision is clearly articulated in the Presidential Comprehensive Labour Market Commission's 1996 report: 'Extensively bureaucratic regulation is inimical to flexibility while an over-reliance on market forces is incompatible with labour market security and may result in increased inequality. Voice regulation provides the best means of charting a course that avoids both of these undesirable outcomes' (PCLMC, 1996, p. 3).

One of the first Acts of the post-democratic Government was the National Economic Development and Labour Council (NEDLAC) Act No. 35 of 1994, establishing a corporatist institution for policy-making.[13] The draft Labour Relations Bill was one of the first pieces of legislation to be submitted to NEDLAC for discussion, and was the subject of intense tripartite negotiations and agreement. The Labour Relations Act (LRA) No. 66 of 1995 comprised of the following principal elements:[14]

- Inclusive labour regulation. The Act repealed separate legislation for the agricultural, educational and public service sectors. It includes all workers within its scope (e.g. domestic and agricultural workers), with the exception of the defence force and national intelligence services.

- Employers' organizations and trade unions. The Act protects the right to organize. Workers and employers may register a trade union or employers' organization, provided certain basic criteria are met. While not compulsory, registration enables unions to access other organizational rights necessary for collective bargaining.
- Collective bargaining. The Act promotes collective bargaining. A number of statutory rights are conferred upon trade unions that are sufficiently representative (either on their own or acting together), such as the right to access an employer's premises for union-related purposes, and the right to hold meetings and ballots. One or more unions representing a majority of workers may acquire additional rights, such as the right to information for bargaining purposes. Collective bargaining can take place at all levels.[15] Collective agreements are legally binding and enforceable. The right to strike is protected, provided certain procedural requirements are met.
- Bargaining councils. The Act makes provision for the establishment of permanent institutions for collective bargaining at the sectoral level (replacing industrial councils). NEDLAC is responsible for demarcating the sector and geographical area for which an application is made to register or amalgamate a bargaining council. The Registrar of Labour Relations in the Department of Labour then determines whether parties to a bargaining council are considered sufficiently representative and ensures that 'adequate provision is made in the constitution for the representation of small and medium businesses'.
- Extension of collective agreements. The Minister of Labour may extend collective agreements reached in bargaining councils to all workers and enterprises falling within its scope, if the parties to the agreement are considered sufficiently representative.[16] Bargaining councils have procedures by which non-parties may apply for exemption from part or all of the collective agreement.
- Statutory councils. Parties not yet sufficiently representative may apply to the Registrar to establish a statutory council, provided that a union (or more than one union) has at least 30 per cent membership, or members of the employer's organization employ at least 30 per cent of employees in a sector or area. This serves as a stepping stone to the establishment of a bargaining council.
- Employee participation. The Act also makes provision for the establishment of statutory workplace forums to encourage consultation,

participation and joint decision-making in workplaces with more than 100 employees.[17]

- Fair employment practices: The Act codifies rules on unfair dismissal and establishes employee rights such as consultation procedures and employment protection in respect of the transfer of undertakings.
- Dispute resolution institutions: The Act established a new state-funded independent dispute resolution body, the Commission for Conciliation, Mediation and Arbitration (CCMA), and recognizes private procedures for dispute resolution. It also established a labour court with the same status as a high court.

The LRA was supplemented by three other statutes:

- The Basic Conditions of Employment Act (BCEA) 1997, established an Employment Conditions Commission (ECC) to advise the Minister of Labour on a number of matters. These include sectoral determinations, which set minimum terms and conditions of employment, including minimum wages, in respect of a sector or area, and are made by the Minister of Labour after considering reports and recommendations made by the ECC. As is discussed later in the paper, twenty years later, in November 2017, Cabinet approved a National Minimum Wage Bill and repealed the sections of the BCEA concerning the ECC and sectoral determinations.
- The Skills Development Act 1998, aims to address the skills shortage in the country and improve the skills of the workforce. It established a new financial and institutional framework for training and skills development through Sector Education and Training Authorities (SETAs).
- The Employment Equity Act 1998, which seeks to promote equal opportunities in the workplace and eliminate discriminatory employment practices.

3.2.5   The Actors in the New Industrial Relations System

Registered trade union membership increased in the period following the transition to democracy (see Table 3.1). The most prominent feature of this increase was the rapid growth of industrial unions representing black lower-skilled workers (Macun, 1997). There has been some variation across sectors, with significant growth in the public, mining and electricity sectors and a decline in the manufacturing and finance sectors (Macun, 2014). Trade union density – that is, the proportion of employees who belong to a trade union – is estimated to be around 28.2 per cent.[18]

Table 3.1   Registered trade unions and membership, 1995–2016

Year	No. of registered trade unions	Total no. of trade union members (000)
1995	248	2691
1996	334	3016
1997	417	3413
1998	463	3801
1999	497	3359
2000	537	3552
2001	488	3939
2002	513	3278
2003	533	4069
2004	390	3135
2005	367	3135
2006	357	3049
2007	317	3220
2008	285	3299
2009	244	3239
2010	222	3058
2011	218	3193
2012	208	3028
2013	203	3250
2014	196	3556
2015	190	3557
2016	191	3926

Source: Department of Labour.

Three union federations emerged as major actors: COSATU, the Federation of Unions of South Africa (FEDUSA) and NACTU. COSATU remains the largest federation and its share of union membership has increased relative to the other major federations. The expulsion of its largest affiliate, the National Union of Metalworkers of South Africa (NUMSA) in 2014 changed the trade union landscape. In April, 2017 a new independent federation was launched, the South African Federation of Trade Unions (SAFTU) which includes the Association of Mining and Construction Union (AMCU), NUMSA and other former COSATU unions such as the Food and Allied Workers Union (FAWU) and a large number of unaffiliated unions, including many representing informal workers. It has become the second largest federation in South Africa, after COSATU. The third-largest federation, FEDUSA, is made up of unions whose members are predominantly semi-skilled and skilled workers. The next federation, NACTU, has contracted dramatically in membership terms since 1994.

As for the employers, 155 employers' organizations were registered with the Department of Labour as of April 2017 (see Table 3.2). Membership of registered employers' organizations grew steadily. However, the constellation of associations changed as organized employer interests continued to grapple with issues of transformation and differences in the size (and interests) of employer members. NAFCOC and FABCOS withdrew from BSA in the mid-1990s and formed the Black Business Council (BBC), a confederation of black professional and business associations. In 2003, BSA and the BBC merged into a single organization, Business Unity South Africa (BUSA). Divisions within organized business came to the fore again

Table 3.2   Registered employers' organizations and membership, 1995–2016

Year	No. of registered employers' organizations	Registered employers' organizations membership (000)
1995	188	n/a
1996	196	n/a
1997	258	n/a
1998	241	n/a
1999	260	n/a
2000	252	47
2001	265	39
2002	270	45
2003	268	41
2004	239	43
2005	229	39
2006	213	51
2007	201	58
2008	180	49
2009	167	43
2010	164	53
2011	166	56
2012	165	56
2013	164	56
2014	164	71
2015	157	64
2016	155	64

Source: Department of Labour.

in 2011, at which point a number of organizations suspended their membership in BUSA and reconstituted the BBC. Despite these differences, the BBC and BUSA continued to cooperate in representing organized business interests at NEDLAC. In May 2017, apparent differences between the two umbrella bodies brought an end to this cooperation.[19]

3.2.6 New Institutions of Corporatism, Collective Bargaining and Dispute Resolution

The industrial relations system now consists of a number of innovative institutions. The first of these is a corporatist institution, NEDLAC, which is composed of four chambers: Trade and Industry, Public Finance and Monetary Policy, Labour Market and Development. Mandated representatives from the Government, organized labour and organized business have equal representation in the first three chambers. The fourth chamber includes civil society groupings to give a voice to community interests and groups that may otherwise be marginalized, such as disabled people and youth. The aims of NEDLAC are to:

- promote the goals of economic growth, participation in economic decision-making and social equity;
- seek to reach consensus and conclude agreements (social compacts) on matters pertaining to social and economic policy;
- consider all proposed labour legislation relating to labour market policy before it is introduced in Parliament;
- consider all significant changes to social and economic policy before it is implemented or introduced in Parliament; and
- encourage and promote the formulation of coordinated policy on social and economic matters.

The second innovative institution are the bargaining councils, which dramatically expanded coverage by collective agreements. In 1992, 735 533 employees were covered by industrial council agreements. As of April 2017, there are 38 bargaining councils in the private sector, 6 government and local government bargaining councils, and 3 statutory councils covering an estimated 2.6 million employees.[20] During the intervening years, a number of smaller councils were consolidated, and a new Public Sector Coordinating Bargaining Council (PSCBC) was established for the public service covering the three tiers of government (national, provincial and local). Around 1.3 million workers in public services now bargain collectively over wages and other working conditions, and their unions represent a significant proportion of the membership in COSATU. While a few statutory councils have been established, only one has made the next step and graduated to become a bargaining council.[21]

Collective bargaining also takes place outside the bargaining council system. This is for example the case in one of South Africa's core sectors: mining companies belonging to the Chamber of Mines negotiate a multi-employer agreement; while those mining platinum and diamonds, and new mining companies, bargain at an enterprise level. In automobile manufacturing, collective bargaining is carried out in a National Bargaining Forum (NBF) consisting of the Automobile Manufacturers Employers' Organization (AMEO) comprising the seven automobile manufacturers[22] and NUMSA. Single-employer bargaining is more typical in the retail sector and among state-owned enterprises. An estimated 30 per cent of employees are covered by collective bargaining agreements.

Outside of these collective bargaining arrangements, at least until 2017, wages and working conditions are determined through sectoral determinations covering 3.5 million employees across a range of sectors including agriculture, forestry, contract cleaning, civil engineering, private security, domestic work, and wholesale and retail.

The third innovative institution is the CCMA, which provides dispute prevention as well as dispute resolution services, including mediation, conciliation and arbitration. All disputes regarding unfair dismissals, organizational rights, the interpretation of collective agreements and some unfair labour practices, as well as interest disputes arising from collective bargaining, are referred to the CCMA in the first instance. Parties to a collective agreement and bargaining councils can also establish their own private dispute resolution system, which may be accredited by the CCMA. A labour court with the same status as a high court adjudicates labour disputes; appeals are made to the Labour Appeal Court.

3.2.7 Continuity and Discontinuity in the Development of Industrial Relations Institutions

The new regulatory framework introduced in 1995 marked a distinct departure from a previous trajectory of exclusion that denied the majority of black African workers the most basic workers' rights, towards a democratic, inclusive and participatory industrial relations system (Webster, 2013). Millions of workers previously excluded from the system, especially in the public sector, domestic work and agriculture, could now enjoy the same rights as other workers including the right to collective bargaining. A new institutional pathway for industrial relations was forged through the involvement of organized employers and labour in the design of labour market policy under the auspices of NEDLAC; the negotiation of wages and working conditions at industry-level bargaining councils; and the enhancement of workplace participation through workplace forums.

Interestingly, while there was a clear break with the previous trajectory, there was also considerable institutional continuity, particularly in respect of the structure of the collective bargaining system which in the case of bargaining councils remained relatively centralized at industry level. This institution has been a consistent feature of South African labour law since 1924. The changes introduced ensured the inclusion of all unions considered sufficiently representative, and the expansion of functions, including, for example, the provision of dispute resolution services. The persistence of this institution despite the shop-floor organizing and bargaining strategies of the independent unions in the 1970s and 1980s can be attributed to two factors. First, in the interests of stability, employers refused to engage in dual-level (industry and enterprise) bargaining. Second, the establishment of national trade unions in most sectors of the economy permitted unions to consolidate their influence by focusing on centralized bargaining.

3.3 GROWTH, EMPLOYMENT AND DISTRIBUTION: A CONSTRAINED CONTEXT

The context within which the new industrial relations institutions developed has been characterized by low growth, high levels of income inequality and high structural unemployment.

3.3.1 Economic Growth and Development

Economic development in South Africa occurred around a minerals–energy complex (MEC; see Fine and Rustomjee, 1996) including the mining of gold, platinum and coal, and the development of related industries, from metals to electricity and petrochemicals. The vast majority of the coal produced was used to meet the country's energy needs (not least for purposes of gold mining), through its conversion to both electricity (over 50 per cent) and oil (over 30 per cent). The growth of manufacturing was centred on primary production linked to the MEC, such as metal fabrication directly following from iron-ore processing (Fine and Rustomjee, 1996).

While South Africa's economy has seen some recovery since the democratic transition, hopes of strong economic growth and structural transformation have not been realized. With the exception of sectors that have been beneficiaries of industrial policy, such as automobiles and components, manufacturing has continued to decline as a proportion of gross domestic product (GDP) since 1993. It remains dominated by sectors with strong linkages to the MEC, including minerals beneficiation (iron, steel and aluminium) and the conversion of coal into oil and chemical by-products. The liberalization of capital controls and financial markets did not bring much-needed investment into industry. Instead, investment and capital formation have been increasingly concentrated in the financial services sector (Mohamed, 2010). Prominent companies have moved their primary listing offshore. The trajectory of development has been one of deindustrialization, with a shift from dependence on mining to services. The share of mining in output has halved since 1994, while that of manufacturing has remained stagnant. By the standards of a developing economy, growth has been low, particularly since the global economic recession in 2008 (see Figure 3.1).

3.3.2 Employment

Unemployment remained very high despite periods of economic growth. At the beginning of the democratic transition, unemployment stood at around 30 per cent, and the share of employment in the manufacturing sector had been steadily declining. For the fourth quarter of 2016 unemployment is estimated to be at 26.5 per cent, increasing to 30.9 per cent when workers who have abandoned the search for work are included (see Table 3.3). Unemployment rates are highest for the black population and for women. In reality, the 'non-searching' are no less committed to finding work than the 'searching'. The prohibitive costs of job search suggest that the broader unemployment rate provides a better reflection of unemployment (Posel et al., 2013).

The apartheid spatial economy remains largely unchanged, increasing the cost and burden of job search for those who can least afford it. Only 43.5 per cent of a working-age population of 35.9 million people are employed. This labour absorption rate is extremely low compared with Brazil (60 per cent), China (70 per cent) and India (55 per cent). Given the high levels of unemployment and the low absorption rate, employment in the informal economy[23] is notably smaller than other countries in this volume (Brazil, China and India). The reasons for this include historical impediments to the establishment of micro-enterprises of black workers in the informal economy, such as restrictive regulations and the repressive enforcement thereof, and a legacy of spatial and racial segregation (see, e.g., Kingdon and Knight, 2004).

Despite this dismal picture, around 3.4 million jobs have been created

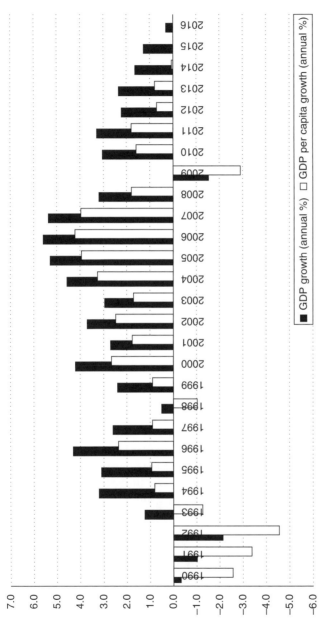

Note: GDP growth for 2016 estimated by Statistics South Africa.

Source: World Bank, World Development Indicators.

Figure 3.1 GDP growth in South Africa, 1990–2016 (%)

Table 3.3   Labour market indicators, 2016

Indicator	No. (000)/rate (%)	Women	Men
Working-age population	36 905	18 679	18 226
Labour force	21 849	9883	11 966
Employed	16 069	7031	9037
Formal (non-agricultural)	11 156	4754	6402
Informal (non-agricultural)	2695	977	1718
Agricultural	919	305	614
Private households	1299	995	304
Unemployed	5781	2852	2929
Not economically active	15 055	8796	6260
Discouraged jobseekers	2292	1289	1003
Other	12 763	7506	5257
Labour absorption rate	43.5	37.6	49.6
Unemployment rate	26.5	28.9	24.5
Black	30.0		
Coloured	22.0		
Indian/Asian	11.1		
White	6.6		
Labour force participation rate	59.2	52.9	65.7

Source: Statistics South Africa, Quarterly Labour Force Survey, 2016, 4th quarter.

since 1995. Sectoral employment trends show that employment remained relatively stable in mining but declined in agriculture and manufacturing (see Figure 3.2). Two-thirds of the new jobs were created in construction, wholesale and retail trade, financial services and the services sector. Studies show that a large proportion of these new jobs, particularly those in financial services (which includes temporary employment services, contract cleaning and security services), are of a more contingent nature (Tregenna, 2008; Reddy, 2012). Bhorat et al. (2013), using industrial classification data, estimate that employment in sectors characterized by fixed-term labour contracting ('other financial and business services') grew by 8.3 per cent between 1999 and 2011, surpassing economy-wide employment growth of 2.1 per cent for the same period.

A number of case studies provide evidence of widespread restructuring across a range of sectors and changes in work arrangements, including outsourcing to contractors and further subcontracting (homework), use of temporary labour (ranging from agency hire to work gangs or 'bakkie brigades'), and the increased use of temporary and part-time contracts

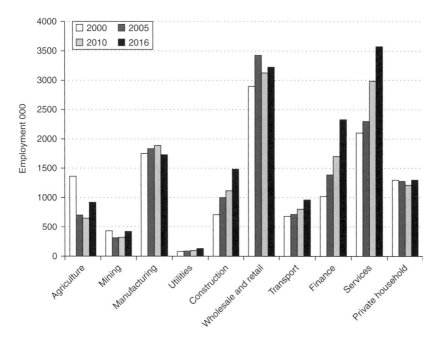

Sources: 2000, 2005: Statistics South Africa, Labour Force Survey (LFS), revised, 2009 (Sep.); 2010, 2016: Statistics South Africa, Quarterly Labour Force Survey (QLFS), 4th quarter.

Figure 3.2   Employment by sector, 2000, 2005, 2010 and 2016

(for a range of case studies, see Bezuidenhout and Kenny, 1998; Pons-Vignon and Anseeuw, 2009; Crush et al., 2010; Webster and von Holdt, 2005). This restructuring and reorganization of work has drawn new lines of exclusion between those at the core – earning regular wages, and now enjoying representational rights and labour protection – and non-core workers, subject to job and income insecurity, or surviving on the periphery of unemployment and informal subsistence activities (Webster, 2013).

3.3.3   Income

Despite the transition from apartheid, the distribution of the gains from growth remain highly skewed. Studies using different measures all conclude that aggregate income inequality has increased since 1994 (Yu, 2010; Bhorat et al., 2009; van der Berg, 2014). The Gini coefficient,[24] estimated at around 0.66, is one of the highest in the world (Leibbrandt et al., 2010; Finn, 2015; and see Table 3.4). Most studies find this to be the result of an increase in the share of income going to the top decile of the earnings distribution (Leibbrandt et al., 2010; Bhorat et al., 2009). While income disparities continue to show the racial imprint of apartheid, there has been a significant increase of within-race inequality for all racial groups, the greatest being within the black African group (Leibbrandt et al., 2010).

Table 3.4   Gini coefficients, 1993, 2000, 2008, 2012

Year	Gini coefficient
1993	0.66
2000	0.68
2008	0.70
2012	0.66

Sources: Leibbrandt et al. (2010) and Finn (2015).

Decompositions of the Gini coefficient by income source show that the most important contributor to overall inequality is income from the labour market. This is driven by an increase in wage inequality in the top of the wage distribution (the D9/D5 decile ratio) and fifth deciles (see Table 3.5), and the zero income of the unemployed (Leibbrandt and Woolard, 2001; Bhorat et al., 2009; Leibbrandt et al., 2010; Rani and Furrer, 2016). While non-contributory state transfers, in particular old-age grants and child support grants, contribute to reducing income inequality, these tend only to benefit the lowest three deciles, which are also those where households with the highest numbers of unemployed are to be found (Rani and Furrer, 2016).

A number of studies find that the mean for wage earners has increased

Table 3.5   Wage inequality: decile ratios, 2000, 2005, 2010, 2011

Year	D9/D1	D5/D1	D9/D5
2000	18.44	4.61	4.00
2005	14.24	3.33	4.27
2010	15.65	3.46	4.52
2011	15.00	3.25	4.62

Source: Authors' own calculation based on Post-Apartheid Labour Market (PALM) series.

in real terms since 1994 (Burger and Yu, 2007; Yu, 2010; Wittenberg, 2014; and see Figure 3.3). This has led a number of economists to blame wage-setting institutions for the high levels of unemployment (see, e.g., Klein, 2012). However, claims that wage growth has resulted in high unemployment are at odds with recent studies that show that the growth in real wages has been matched by increasing labour productivity (Wittenberg, 2014; Burger, 2016; and see Figure 3.3).[25]

What is perhaps of greater concern is the fact that these increases in real wages have not been sufficient to address inequality and poverty. Wage inequality, particularly between the median and top earners, has increased. Those in the top decile are estimated to earn around 15 times as much as workers in the bottom decile (see Table 3.5). While wages continue to make up the largest component of household income (Finn, 2015), access to wage income (and a wage earner) does not guarantee a decent standard of living. Half of those who live with a wage earner are in households that fall below the poverty line.[26] Moreover, an estimated 60 per cent of African workers and 56 per cent of Coloured workers are low-wage workers (Finn, 2015). For most workers, the struggle to earn a decent wage is at the very core of their efforts to improve incomes and escape poverty. The following section examines the role of that the new industrial relations institutions played in forging an inclusive pattern of development in a context of low growth, high unemployment and growing inequality.

3.4   POST-APARTHEID INDUSTRIAL RELATIONS: A CONTESTED PATH

The new orientation in labour market policy introduced in the mid-1990s intended to create industrial relations institutions that would contribute to growth and equity. Tripartite policy concertation would provide the tools to reconcile economic and social goals. By supporting the development of industry-wide collective bargaining institutions, industrial relations actors in a given sector would 'regulate flexibility' and negotiate fair wages. The codification of unfair labour practices together with the right to establish workplace forums, would prevent arbitrary dismissal, transform workplace practices and enhance productivity. The new labour dispute system would help to institutionalize labour conflict and resolve labour disputes. What role, if any, have these institutions played in shaping the country's development path?

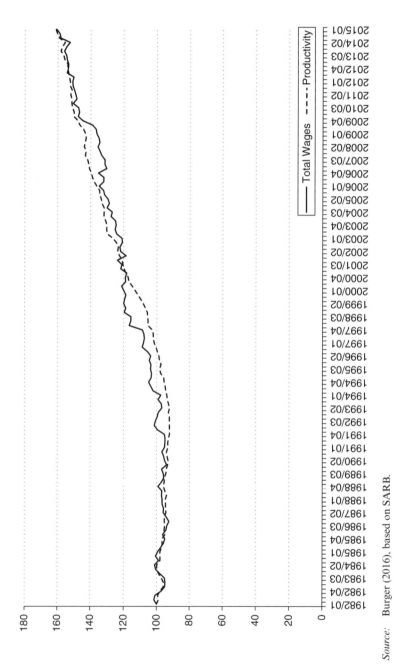

Source: Burger (2016), based on SARB.

Figure 3.3   Real wages and productivity indexes, 1982–2015

3.4.1   Tripartism: Concertation, Consultation or Unilateralism?

Since 1994, NEDLAC has contributed significantly to the negotiation of a shared vision on labour market policy, to the restructuring of the labour market and to establishing broad-based support among the social partners for trade and competition policy (Webster and Sikwebu, 2010; Webster and Joynt, 2013). Tripartism clearly involved a process of 'policy concertation' on labour market policy, as described by authors such as Compston (2002). NEDLAC works on the basis of consensus. Tripartite partners work to reach agreement. Where agreement cannot be reached, this is given over to Parliament to resolve. However, some authors argue that the effectiveness of this corporatist institution in balancing economic and social goals has been hampered by a lack of consultation on fiscal and monetary policy, and a seeming inconsistency between corporatist labour market policies and orthodox macroeconomic policy (Nattrass, 2013).

Prior to the 1994 elections, the ANC had campaigned on a blue-print socio-economic policy framework called the Reconstruction and Development Programme (RDP), which had been formulated with the support of COSATU, the SACP and civil society organizations. The RDP suggested a strong developmental state that would manage the path of economic development. COSATU viewed the RDP as providing the terms that the new government would use to implement economic policy. Soon after the democratic transition, the General Secretary of COSATU was appointed as Minister responsible for the RDP, a decision that appeared to cement this shared vision. However, the new Government faced an immediate challenge. The economy had contracted between 1990 and 1993, and it was keen to establish its credentials as a fiscally responsible administration committed to maintaining macroeconomic stability and creating an investor-friendly environment (Blumfeld, 1997).

In a very early departure from policy concertation, in 1996 the Government unilaterally adopted a set of orthodox economic policies under a new rubric of Growth, Employment and Redistribution (GEAR). This focused on the immediate reduction of budget deficits and, in 2000, the adoption of a framework based on inflation targeting. It gave primacy to economic growth as the means by which to meet social imperatives. The introduction of the Accelerated and Shared Growth Initiative for South Africa in 2006 (ASGISA) modified the conservative fiscal stance embodied in GEAR by placing greater emphasis on the role of infrastructure development in job creation. Nevertheless, both GEAR and ASGISA shifted the focus of macroeconomic policy away from the explicitly redistributive goals set out in the RDP (Gelb, 2010).

In the 2000s, labour market policy continued to be the subject of policy concertation in NEDLAC. In the context of a rapid increase in insecure forms of employment, COSATU called for a ban on labour broking. The triangular nature of the relationship between the labour broker, employee and client raised important challenges to labour protections that are premised on a direct employment relationship. The process of amending the LRA started in July 2009 when a set of proposed amendments were submitted to NEDLAC for discussion. After extensive negotiations in NEDLAC, agreement was reached and the LRA was amended in 2014, and four new sections were introduced regulating temporary employment services including by setting, in principle, a limit of three months for temporary employment through a labour broker.

Rising inequality and protracted and violent strike action provoked another significant tripartite reflection on the effectiveness of labour market policy culminating in the adoption of the Ekurhuleni Declaration on wage inequality and labour market stability at the NEDLAC Labour Relations Indaba in November 2014.[27] It took three years, and the establishment of an Advisory Panel on the national minimum wage for an agreement to be reached. In February 2017 NEDLAC announced a Declaration on Wage Inequality and Labour Market Stability.[28] The Declaration includes tripartite agreement to the introduction of a new national minimum wage (by no later than 1 May 2018) and an accord on collective bargaining and industrial action.[29] This marks perhaps the most important development in labour market policy since the 1990s. It is notably another labour market policy emerging from a process of policy concertation between government, organized business and labour with inputs from civil society.

These achievements in forging consensus on labour market policy and trade and industrial policy in NEDLAC coincided with the strengthening within the Ministry of Finance of a National Treasury 'responsible for managing South Africa's national government finances'. Some authors argue that by exercising fiscal restraint over government activities, this policy portfolio has secured a stronghold on policy-making across all areas of state intervention, insisting these be subject to the overall macro-economic model (Segatti and Pons-Vignon, 2013).

Policy documents emanating from the newly established Economic Development Department, and those of the Department of Trade and Industry, suggest an important role for the state in building consensus on policy packages to address developmental challenges and stimulate employment creation.[30] A number of accords have been concluded by government, organized labour, organized business and representatives of the community and youth constituencies. These include a National

Skills Accord (2011), a Local Procurement Accord (2011) and a Youth Employment Accord (2013).

Agreement has not always been reached in NEDLAC. In the same year that the Youth Employment Accord was reached, NEDLAC could not agree on a proposal for a youth wage subsidy, resulting in the submission of an employment tax incentive bill directly to Parliament. The proposal for a youth wage subsidy had been the subject of heated debates between the National Treasury and COSATU, which opposed the wage subsidy on the grounds of its potential to displace existing workers. Organized labour objected to the tabling of the draft Employment Tax Incentive Bill before Parliament. Given the ramifications for its mandate, NEDLAC sought legal opinion on the failure of the Government to submit the proposal to its Labour Chamber (given its implications for labour market policy).[31] The Employment Tax Incentive Act No. 26 of 2013 was signed into law.[32]

While NEDLAC remains an important forum for reaching consensus on labour market policy, contestation over economic policy continues outside formal corporatist institutions for interest representation. There is thus space for NEDLAC to play a greater role in reconciling economic and social goals and creating the conditions for government, organized labour, business and civil society to coalesce around a common development agenda.

3.4.2 Collective Bargaining: Regulating Flexibility?

What role has collective bargaining played in reducing wage inequality and addressing the rise in insecure forms of employment? For the purposes of this study, an analysis was conducted of the content of more than 200 collective agreements in the LRS AWARDS database for the period 2011–13, the year before the LRA amendments were introduced on temporary employment services, fixed-term and part-time employment in 2014.[33]

For 2013, in the private sector, the highest average base wage was achieved through enterprise agreements and the second-highest through bargaining council agreements. The wage floor established by all types of collective agreements was higher than the average minimum wage established through sectoral determinations (see Figure 3.4). At first glance, this suggests a coordinated wage policy: sectoral determinations set the minimum wage in sectors with no collective agreements; sectoral collective bargaining sets the minimum wage in other sectors; and both sectoral collective agreements and enterprise-level agreements contribute to, and ensure the fair distribution of, the productivity gains.

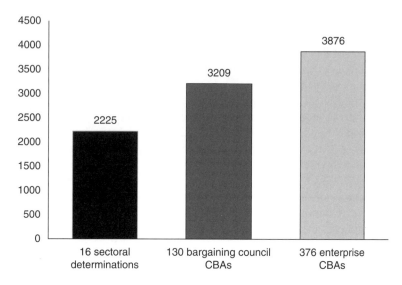

Source: LRS AWARDS database, 2014.

Figure 3.4   Institutional wage determination, 2013

Analysis of the content of collective agreements (see Table 3.6) shows that this is not the case. The demands of unions centred on a percentage increase that reflected the cost of living. There is little information exchanged on economic factors affecting the sector. The numerical literacy of workers is low, and unions need to deliver a bargain that workers can understand. Collective agreements thus tend to benchmark the consumer price index with across-the-board percentage increases. There are three difficulties with this approach. First, inflation is backward-looking and does not reflect prices or developments in the coming year. Second, with low wages for some categories of workers, across-the-board percentage increases tend to exacerbate wage gaps over time (for example, a 10 per cent increase on 2000 rand is far less than a 10 per cent increase on 8000 rand). Unions have managed to collapse lower grades, resulting in larger increases for workers at the bottom of the wage structure, thereby no doubt contributing to the compression of the bottom half of the wage distribution. However, this is likely to be limited to those covered by collective agreements. Third, this limits the use that other policy tools – such as a national minimum wage – can play in facilitating an inclusive and coordinated wage policy.

Issues of productivity and performance are very weakly embedded in collective bargaining. Some bargaining council agreements, such as

Table 3.6 Typical content of bargaining agreements

	Smaller enterprises	Larger enterprises and bargaining councils
Definitions	Preamble Scope of the agreement	Preamble Scope of the agreement
Duration of agreement	More likely to be single year	More likely to be multi-year, although trade unions are increasingly resisting and attempting to return to single-year agreements
Wages	Increase expressed as %, generally across the board	Increase expressed as %; generally across the board, although there are instances of staggered increases applied to broad categories (low, middle and higher grades)
	Increases less frequently linked to inflation	Increases often linked to consumer price index using a formula including a factor of e.g. 1–2%
	Base wage relatively common	Sometimes base wage for different grades; tendency to eliminate particular grades as a means of raising base wages and closing gaps Allowances for shift work
Other conditions of employment	References to 'status quo' without definition	Clauses relating to short time more prevalent after 2009 Maternity leave Occupational health and safety Sick leave Range of responses to labour broking and casual, contract or temporary workers, varying from consultative to strong regulatory responses; sometimes outright bans (see Table 3.7) Family responsibility leave Compassionate leave Provident fund Medical aid
Employment relations		Shop stewards' leave Full and final settlement Peace clause

Source: Labour Research Services.

the National Textile Bargaining Council Agreement, explicitly provide for attendance-linked incentives (0.75 per cent per week paid quarterly); others include framework clauses that seek to facilitate further 'productivity bargaining' at the enterprise level.[34] Some of these are complemented by detailed guidelines for productivity negotiations in annexes to the agreement.[35] The degree to which these arrangements are related to a fairer distribution of productivity gains remains an open question (Godfrey et al., 2017).

The role of unions in generating real wage gains for workers and reducing inequality is supported by the empirical literature. Studies of union wage effects find a union wage mark-up (Moll, 1993; Butcher and Rouse, 2001; Banerjee et al., 2008).[36] Whereas the union mark-up increased during the 1990s, there is evidence to suggest that it declined between 2000 and 2010 (Hofmeyr and Lucas, 2001; Ntuli and Kwenda, 2014). Bhorat et al. (2012) examining data for 2005 find a union wage mark-up of around 6 per cent, significantly lower than that estimated in previous studies.

There is also evidence for a wage mark-up associated with coverage by bargaining council agreements. A study by Butcher and Rouse (2001) examining data for 1995 found that African workers covered by an industrial council agreement – even if they were not union members – earned more than workers outside the system.[37] Examining data for 2005, Bhorat et al. (2012) estimated coverage by a bargaining council to generate an average mark-up of 3 per cent in the private sector and 15 per cent in the public sector.

In respect of the wage distribution, most studies find that these institutions compress the distribution of wages and reduce wage inequality (Schultz and Mwabu, 1998; Butcher and Rouse, 2001; Bhorat et al., 2009; Bhorat et al., 2012). By improving real wages for workers, particularly for those at the bottom of the wage distribution, unions and bargaining councils appear to have offset some of the effects of structural discrimination in labour markets.

The analysis of collective agreements in the period prior to the amendments to the Labour Relations Act in 2014, which regulated temporary agency work, shows that collective bargaining played an important role in balancing flexibility and security. Many sectoral agreements contain clauses on labour broking, subcontracting and temporary employment services (TES), examples of which are given in Table 3.7. These fall into one or more of the following categories:

- regulating flexibility by limiting or setting terms for the proportion of production that is subcontracted or the proportion of temporary workers that may be hired;

- improving employment security by regularizing temporary workers; and
- ensuring parity for workers with different contracts in respect of pay, training and benefits.

Bargaining council agreements have also been effective in limiting the potential effects of TES and/or outsourcing on wages by including measures to ensure the application of collective agreements to all workers and enterprises. These include provisions on the application of the collective agreement to all TES and labour brokers, provisions requiring the registration of TES/labour brokers with the bargaining council, and the policy-based extension of collective agreements by the Minister of Labour. The amendments to the LRA in 2014 codified some of these practices (for example, time limits on the use of temporary employment contracts) and reinforced this policy-based extension of collective agreements. Section 32(5A) of the Act now requires the Minister to take into account the composition of the workforce (including TES, fixed-term, contract and other non-standard employees) when deciding whether a bargaining council that has requested the extension of its collective agreement is sufficiently representative.

Is this framework for 'regulated flexibility' being applied at the expense of enterprises and employment? Are the sectoral bargaining arrangements creating 'rigidities' and preventing the development of small and medium-sized enterprises? Godfrey et al. (2006a) show that while bargaining councils cover just under one-third of all employees, only 4.6 per cent of this coverage is the result of the extension to non-parties (that is, employees in enterprises that are not members of employers' organizations belonging to the Council). Moreover, enterprises and non-parties can apply for exemption from the entire collective agreement or from the application of a particular clause. In 2004 around 78 per cent of applications for full or partial exemption were granted. The largest proportion of applications came from small firms (Godfrey et al., 2006b). Smaller enterprises also report that they benefit from other services offered by some bargaining councils, such as payroll administration, paralegal advice and the dissemination of information on industrial relations developments (Godfrey et al., 2006c).[38] The authors conclude that:

> data on bargaining council coverage shows that any alleged rigidities in the bargaining council system impact on a fairly small proportion of the workforce. This suggests that the level of criticism of the extension mechanism is not warranted. (Godfrey et al., 2006a, p. 749)

Table 3.7   Regulating flexibility: Labour broking and temporary employment services

Agreement	Year	Regulating internal flexibility	Regulating job security	Parity	Application to non-parties
Fishing Bargaining Council Agreement	2013			Temporary employees paid at same rate set out in remuneration schedule (clause 9.6)	Agreement extended (*Government Gazette*, 1 Feb. 2013, No. 36103)
Industrial Chemicals Sector Substantive Agreement	2012–13	Parties to agreement only to engage labour brokers that are compliant with law and applicable CBA (Summary Part A, clause 6)	Issue of job security/labour broking subject of plant-level negotiations (clause 4)		Collective agreement applicable to TES/ labour brokers
National Textile Bargaining Council Agreement	Main agreement 2007, amended 2010, 2012, 2013	Labour brokers limited to non-core activities outlined in agreement for a period of time not exceeding six months (clause 7 of 2013 agreement)	Contract employees to be converted into permanent employees after 12 months (clause 5 of 2012 agreement)	Temporary employees to be paid 80% of the basic hourly wage payable to an employee (clause 27 of 2010 agreement); joint liability for labour brokers for non-compliance with wages and conditions applicable to sector (clause 7 of 2010 agreement)	Agreement extended (*Government Gazette*, 26 Nov. 2010, No. 33782; 6 Jan. 2012, No. 34910; 14 June 2013, No. 36444)

Metal and Engineering Industries Bargaining Council (MEIBC) Agreement	2010, amended Jan. 2013– June 2014	Commitment to minimize use of TES; only engage TES from companies registered and accredited by the MEIBC and compliant with law and CBA (clause 20(1);(2))	Where employer engages worker for period beyond terms in the Limited Duration Contract (model contract provided), worker shall become permanent (clause 20(3)(e))	TES to enjoy existing terms and conditions of employment outlined in main agreement (clause 20(3)(f))	Agreement extended (*Government Gazette*, 12 Apr. 2013, No. 36338)
Furniture Bargaining Council Agreement	2012–14			TES/labour broker to remunerate as per wage schedules in the CBA and all provisions to apply (clause 9.2); joint liability of TES/labour broker and employer for any contravention of terms of CBA (clause 9.2)	Collective agreement applicable to TES/labour brokers
National Bargaining Council for Wood and Paper, Pulp and Paper Wage Agreement	2012–13	Employers only to engage TES/labour brokers that provide proof of compliance with relevant legislation; proof	Use of TES limited to six months, after which position to be filled in terms of recruitment and selection procedure (clause 5)		

Table 3.7 (continued)

Agreement	Year	Regulating internal flexibility	Regulating job security	Parity	Application to non-parties
		of compliance to be made available to union on request (clause 5)			
Motor Industries Bargaining Council (MIBCO) Agreement	2011–13	TES/labour brokers to be registered with MIBCO (clause 3.7(1)); phase out TES in Sector 5 (fuel dealers, service stations) by Feb. 2012 (clause 3.7(5)): no employer to have more than 35% of core workforce consisting of TES by Aug. 2013 (clause 3.7(6))		Workers on fixed-term contracts to enjoy same pay and benefits as permanent employees for duration of contract (clause 3.6(4)): joint liability of client and TES/labour broker for any contravention of terms in CBA and Basic Conditions of Employment Act (clause 3.7(2))	Collective agreement applicable to workers on fixed-term contracts, TES/labour brokers

Note: 1. Temporary employment services.

98

3.4.3   Workplace Cooperation and Dispute Resolution: Stable and Productive Industrial Relations?

What about the new institutions for employee participation in the workplace and for the prevention and resolution of labour disputes? Legislated workplace forums, together with other policy support measures, were introduced to promote 'post-Fordist' cooperative working practices between labour and management. However, by 2011 only 56 statutory workplace forums had been established, although it is not clear how many of these are functional (Du Toit et al., 2015). Attempts at implementing workplace change and increasing worker participation have been limited to a few highly innovative workplaces (Ewert, 1997; Webster and Omar, 2003). It appears to be very difficult to 're-engineer' workplace relations by legislating new institutions for consultation and cooperation.

Case studies of work restructuring across the mining, manufacturing and service sectors show that labour–management relations in the workplace continue to be characterized by authoritarian management practices and high degrees of adversarialism (Webster and Omar, 2003; von Holdt, 2003; Webster and von Holdt, 2005; Hunter, 2000). In the 'co-operation in labour–employer relations' index of the *Global Competitiveness Report 2014–2015* (World Economic Forum, 2014), South Africa ranks (for the third year in a row) 144th out of 144 countries. In some sectors, such as forestry, the restructuring of work arrangements eroded the protection previously afforded by collective labour institutions, resulting in the need for the state to step in to regulate conditions for workers in very vulnerable situations (see Box 3.1).

In respect of dispute resolution, the CCMA has seen a steady increase in its caseload, from 59 222 in the first year of operation (1996/7) to 161 674 in 2011/12. Around 80 per cent of referrals are dismissal cases (Benjamin, 2013). Of the collective interest disputes referred to the CCMA in 2011/12, 61 per cent were resolved. The CCMA has also been engaged in preventative services, intervening and facilitating collective bargaining at the earlier stages of disputes to prevent them from spiralling. It developed specific criteria to ensure that respect for the autonomy of collective bargaining was not compromised by state intervention to prevent labour disputes (Benjamin, 2013).

The industrial relations climate showed signs of improvement in the first ten years after the democratic transition. However, it has deteriorated in recent years. Historical data on strikes are incomplete, and any data prior to 1994 need to be interpreted with caution, given the repression of trade unions described above. Taking these caveats into account, while there appeared to be a degree of stability in the immediate post-apartheid

---

BOX 3.1   THE RESTRUCTURING OF WORK AND EROSION
OF WORK QUALITY: THE CASE OF FORESTRY

Plantation forestry developed in South Africa first to service mining and then to ensure the supply of timber needed for the country's growth. From the 1950s the State supported the emergence of two private pulp and paper companies. Together with the state-owned company, they owned most of the country's plantations. The forestry sector was vertically integrated 'from stump to mill': trees were planted, harvested and processed to produce either paper or sawn timber. This industry was (and remains) highly labour-intensive. For example, most harvesting is done by hand, involving large groups of workers who cut, debark, stack and transport trees.

The industry became unionized in the 1980s. This transformed the paternalistic labour process that had characterized work relations. Unions negotiated substantial pay increases for workers and challenged the authoritarian power exercised by white managers over black workers. However, this balance was short-lived.From the early 1990s, these companies adopted a strategy of outsourcing (in, for example, silviculture and harvesting) in part to avoid unions (Pons-Vignon, 2015). This resulted in a dramatic decline in union membership.

Competition between contractors placed downward pressure on prices, resulting in further subcontracting of the least profitable and most labour-intensive activities (for example, weeding an area after felling), with many of these subcontractors operating informally. The transformation of the industry was dramatic. Whereas formerly all forestry workers had been employed by one of the large grower-producers, by 2012 only 13 per cent were permanent workers, 5 per cent were on fixed term contracts and 82 per cent were employed by subcontractors. Workers in temporary forms of employment, or disguised self-employment, lack access to medical aid, pension or other benefits (Clarke, 2012). Their payment is often entirely task-based. Performance against production targets is recorded by subcontractors. The method for assessing whether targets have been met remains opaque to these workers, generating widespread frustration and mistrust. This system, which allows the employer to unilaterally set and monitor targets, has tipped the balance of power in favour of employers (and subcontractors).

Recognizing the vulnerability of this sector, in 2006 the Department of Labour issued a sectoral determination on wages and working hours. However, levels of compliance remain an open question, given the nature of the payment system and the numbers of informal subcontractors.

Source: Author's research.

---

period, the total number of workdays lost to strikes has shown an upward trend since 2007 (Figure 3.5), as has the rate of strike action (the number of days lost per 1000 employees; see Figure 3.6). The spike in the days lost to strike action in 2010 was the result of a strike wave in the construction industry and two state-owned enterprises – one in rail, ports and pipelines and the other the electricity public utility – prior to the football World Cup, which was hosted by South Africa that year. In 2014, mining industries continued to have the most workers participating in strikes (62.9 per cent of the total number of workers involved in work stoppages). A strike in the platinum mines that year lasted for five months, the longest strike in South Africa's history. A one-month strike in the manufacturing industry in the same year by metalworkers resulted in cuts in production in steel and engineering companies. Motor manufacturers had to shut down production as a result of the disruptions (DOL, 2014a). In 2015, the transport industry recorded the most days lost to strike action as compared to other industries (DOL, 2015).

Industrial relations and labour disputes are also less institutionalized. For example, in 2016, 59 per cent of strikes were unprotected as workers and unions did not comply with legislative procedures before embarking on strike action (DOL, 2016). A number of major strikes took place outside of the legal institutional framework, including the 2012 strike by agricultural workers in the Western Cape, the strike by South African postal workers in 2014, and the outsourced workers' protests at South African universities in 2016 (Dickinson, 2015; Luckett and Mzobe, 2016). The increase in strike action has also been accompanied by rising levels of violence, inter-union rivalry, destruction to property and police brutality, such as that which characterized the security guards' strike in 2006, the public sector strike in 2010, the strike in the state-owned enterprise for rail, ports and pipelines in 2010, and the strike at a platinum mining company in Marikana in 2012 (von Holdt, 2010; Alexander et al., 2012; Benjamin, 2013).

Dissatisfaction with pay remains the single major trigger for strike action, accounting for 82 per cent of workdays lost in 2016 (DOL, 2016). Demands at the bargaining table need to be seen in the context of a broader struggle against deprivation. Twenty years after the democratic transition, South Africa is still confronted by challenges of poverty, inequality and unemployment. Around 7.5 million adults are either unemployed or discouraged jobseekers. The only available channels of social support depend on these individuals living in households with a child, elderly or disabled person. This amplifies dependence on the few employed individuals in the family, who are likely to be earning low wages: 'High dependency ratios in working class communities mean that in the absence of social protection, workers' wages are the main safety net ... even the limited income available to low paid workers is eroded through support for the unemployed' (Coleman, 2013, p. 7). The high levels of industrial action, their length and the fact that over half are unprotected reflect the desperation that workers face, and their

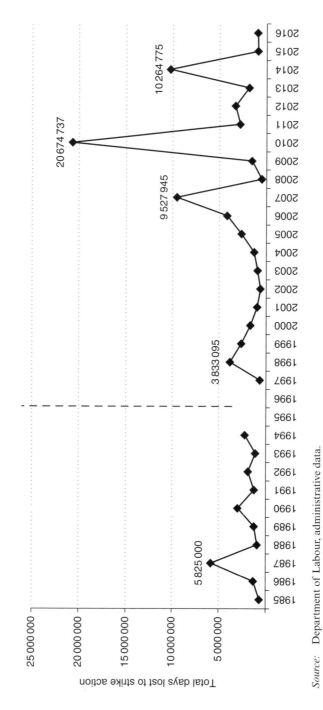

Source: Department of Labour, administrative data.

Figure 3.5   Total workdays lost to strike action, 1985–2016

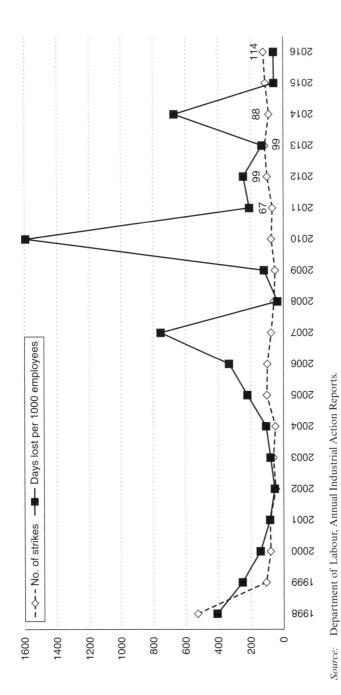

Source: Department of Labour, Annual Industrial Action Reports.

Figure 3.6 Number of strikes and strike rate (days lost per 1000 employees), 1998–2016

own method of resistance as they struggle to secure an income for their families.

The growing dissatisfaction with persistent social inequalities is fuelled by reports of increases in executive compensation. A review of the reports of companies listed on the Johannesburg Stock Exchange for the financial year 2012 showed a dramatic increase in executive salaries (Massie et al., 2014), with the average cash and benefits package of the 50 chief executive officers (CEOs) studied amounting to almost ZAR13.1 million, rising, once the gains on the vesting and exercise of share options are included to almost ZAR49 million. By contrast, the median entry wage for workers in 2012 was ZAR3500 per month, which amounts to just ZAR42 000 per year (LRS, 2013).

The rising discontent in collective labour relations is exacerbated by the representational and organizational challenges facing both labour and business. Paradoxically, while unions gained influence and institutional power beyond the shop floor after the democratic transition, they lost organizational power as a result of the departure of union leaders into politics, government and business. This diminished technical capacity within unions, lead to a hollowing out of union structures as the remaining leadership focusing their limited organizational resources on national issues, at the expense of shop-floor issues (Buhlungu, 2010; von Holdt, 2003). The growing gap between union officials (earning better wages and working in offices) and union members at the workplace also fuelled mistrust and perceptions of corruption (Alexander et al., 2012; Hartford, 2012). During the strikes that took place in the South African Postal Service, the 2013 strikes in agriculture and at a platinum mine in Marikana, and the 2014 strike in the platinum sector, workers shunned established trade unions and sought alternative channels of representation (see, e.g., Dickinson, 2015). The widening of cleavages based on contractual and migrant status undermined collective solidarity, precipitating a backlash by groups of workers, or what Chinguno (2015) describes as 'insurgent unionism'.

There has also been growing tension within the 'tripartite alliance' between the ANC, SACP and COSATU. The intention behind the democratic incorporation of labour into a political alliance was not to co-opt labour into statist politics. COSATU and its constituent unions always retained the right to mobilize and embark on collective action independently of the Government. However, the lack of social transformation exacerbated tension between the interests of a political class and those of the working class. COSATU has been marked by a bitter leadership dispute and intense dissatisfaction among some of its major affiliates with their alliance partner, the ANC. Open confrontation among the leadership of

COSATU, the expulsion of its General Secretary and of NUMSA (the largest affiliate) in 2014, together with the decision by other key affiliates including FAWU to leave COSATU, presented significant challenges to organized labour. As noted earlier in this chapter, a new independent trade union federation, SAFTU, was launched in April 2017, which includes NUMSA, AMCU (which led the five-month strike at the world's largest platinum mines in 2014), FAWU and a number of other non-aligned unions. Whether this will result in the fragmentation of organized labour, or the renewal of an independent and inclusive labour movement remains to be seen. The appointment of a former trade union leader, turned successful business person, as President of South Africa in February 2018 provides some hope that the organizations involved will be able to reconstitute a political alliance, albeit on different terms.

The unified representation of business interests is also a challenging task. This is exacerbated by the slow transformation of top management. A report by the Commission for Employment Equity in 2014 shows that, 16 years after the introduction of the Employment Equity Act, the racial make-up of South Africa's top management remains skewed. The share of whites in top management is 62.7 per cent, double that of all other population groups and more than three times that of black Africans, who represent only represent 19.8 per cent of top management (DOL, 2014b). The urgent need for transformation is also on the agenda of organized business.

The tragic events at Marikana which resulted in the deaths of 34 striking mineworkers and many others during the course of the disputes across a number of platinum mines in 2012 marked the fourth watershed event in industrial relations in South Africa and a critical juncture in industrial relations. Some argue that this reflects a design failure and the 'corporatist' institutions created under the new LRA to forge a compromise between industrial relations actors with competing interests were ill-conceived. Changes in the balance of power on which the agreement on labour market policy was premised in 1995 generated a backlash, and new forms of conflict and solidarity emerged (Chinguno, 2015). Others argue that the issue is not one of flawed institutions; instead, a context of poverty, unemployment and inequality is placing untold strains on the institutionalization of industrial relations (Du Toit et al., 2015).

Like others, this fourth watershed event, together with rising inequality, provoked a realignment of labour market institutions. NEDLAC's Labour Chamber again provided proof positive of its innovative capacity as a corporatist system of interest representation to forge agreements on fundamental labour market challenges with agreement to a Declaration on Wage Inequality and Labour Market Stability. The National Minimum

Wage Bill, Basic Conditions of Employment Amendment Bill and Labour Relations Amendment Bill were approved by Cabinet in November 2017. This marks the most important development in labour market policy since the 1990s.

3.5   CONCLUSION

The fact that South Africa remains one of the most unequal countries in the world more than 20 years after its transition to a democratic society illustrates just how pervasive and corrosive the system of apartheid was. The high degree of adversarialism it reproduced in workplaces became, and remains, a deeply embedded feature of labour–management relations. Rising levels of discontent, evidenced by the increasing level of strikes, reflect a contested path, characterized by growing exclusion and inequality. Many features of the previous dual system of industrial relations remained highly path-dependent.

The regulatory framework introduced after the democratic transition charted a new inclusive trajectory for industrial relations. For the first time, millions of workers in the public sector were able to negotiate over their terms and conditions of employment. Organized employers and unions played a central role in the formulation of national labour market policies and in new statutory institutions which delivered significant protection for workers not otherwise covered by collective bargaining, such as unorganized domestic workers and farm workers.

These institutions delivered immediate improvements and protection for millions of workers. They provided institutional space within which to reach innovative collective agreements in the face of widespread restructuring and rising insecurity in employment. Organized labour was able to use bargaining power to reduce wage inequality for core workers and fight creeping job insecurity. However, this institutional patchwork is straining at the seams.

The lack of a broader economic and social transformation weighs heavily on the bargaining agenda. The fragility of this institution is all too apparent. With no other channel through which to improve incomes and address social injustice and inequality, collective bargaining rounds are the site of bitter struggle. This pressure is compounded by the painful realities of unemployment and poverty. Growing dissatisfaction threatens the stability of production and continued investment in the country's productive capacity, and will hobble future development prospects.

The strike at a platinum mine in Marikana in 2012 that resulted in the deaths of striking mineworkers and many others represents another watershed event in industrial relations. It precipitated tripartite agreement to the reregulation of labour markets, the realignment of labour market institutions and a concerted effort to ensure greater inclusion in labour market policies.

The introduction of a new national minimum wage in 2018 strengthened labour protection and will no doubt improve the conditions of the millions of workers whose income is not sufficient to release them from poverty. However, there is still a need to strengthen participatory standards including consultation and participation in the workplace and collective bargaining if productivity gains are to be realized and distributed more equitably. These are important steps in the direction of an inclusive labour market; however, they will do little for the unemployed or for discouraged workers who are no longer looking for a job. Rather than weaken and deregulate the protection of workers at the core, there is a need to reinforce labour protection as well as institutions for labour participation, while at the same time designing new innovative policy measures that provide income to those on the periphery of labour markets. The institutions of social dialogue required to lay down such an inclusive development path exist.

NOTES

1. Inclusive development is understood as encompassing increases in gross domestic product (GDP) per capita, a reduction in poverty, structural transformation of the economy, employment growth and a decline in inequality.
2. In 1934, following the enactment of the Status of the Union Act, South Africa became a self-governing nation state within the British Empire. In May 1961, following a referendum, South Africa finally became a republic and a sovereign state.
3. South African statistics continue to use the racial categorization inherited from apartheid. 'Black' includes African, Coloured (a mixed-population group, mainly based in Cape Town) and Indians. In this chapter we use all these terms as appropriate.
4. For example, the Mines and Works Act of 1911 reserved skilled mining jobs for whites. The Natives' Land Act of 1913 and the Native Urban Areas Act No. 21 of 1923 controlled the settlement and movement of the local African population. This legislation set aside 7.3 per cent (later increased to 13 per cent under the Native Trust and Land Act of 1936) of the country's total land area as reserves on which to accommodate the 'native' population, controlled the 'influx' of African people into urban areas and restricted their economic activities there (Davenport and Saunders, 2000).
5. These were self-governing institutions within the framework of the Act. They could be registered if the Minister considered the parties sufficiently representative of employers and employees within a given area.
6. A new consolidated Industrial Conciliation Act No. 28 of 1956 entrenched the racial division of labour by prohibiting the registration of unions that had both white and Coloured workers. Existing so-called 'mixed' unions were required to establish separate branches for these groups, and only white members could hold office. The Act also reinforced the system of (skilled) job reservation for white workers (Du Toit et al., 2015).
7. The government had attempted to legislate plant-based liaison and works committees in an effort to restrict union organization by African workers. These 'parallel means' were

largely rejected by African workers, despite amendments that gave these committees the right to negotiate plant-level agreements on wages (Godfrey et al., 2010).

8. Amendments in the Industrial Conciliation Acts 94 of 1979 and 95 of 1980, and the Labour Relations Amendment Acts 57 of 1981, 51 of 1982 and 2 of 1983.
9. For a well-documented account of the debate concerning registration by the new independent unions and associated intellectuals, see Godfrey et al. (2010).
10. Alliance politics were not new and had already been a feature of the broad national liberation movement. The ANC, SACP and SACTU had been in alliance prior to SACTU's collapse in the 1960s (Baskin, 1991).
11. Policy concertation involves the codetermination of public policy by the government, trade unions and employers' organizations. It is distinct from pluralist policy-making within a corporatist institution involving consultation and a system of interest interme-diation. In the latter, trade unions and employers' organizations may have an influence on policy; however, government retains the final decision (Berger and Compston, 2002).
12. The existing National Manpower Commission, an advisory body, was transformed into a forum for negotiating labour market policy.
13. NEDLAC subsumed both the National Manpower Commission, which had been trans-formed into a negotiating forum when NACTU and COSATU agreed to participate, and the National Economic Forum.
14. This section is drawn from Du Toit et al. (2015).
15. For a thorough analysis of the collective bargaining system, see Godfrey et al. (2010).
16. The LRA, 1996 Amendment Act No. 6 of 2014 requires the Minister to consider the com-position of the workforce, in particular the proportion of employees employed through temporary employment services, on fixed-term contracts and in other non-standard forms of employment that may make representativeness thresholds difficult to reach.
17. This provision was complemented by the Workplace Challenge in 1995, a joint initiative of NEDLAC and the Department of Trade and Industry, now managed by Productivity S.A., offering support in developing 'best operating practices' and 'world-class competi-tiveness and workplace relations'.
18. See www.ilo/ilostat and Visser et al. (2015).
19. https://www.cnbcafrica.com/news/financial/2017/05/22/black-business-council-vs-busine ss-unity-south-africa/ (accessed 28 May 2017).
20. Information supplied by the Department of Labour, South Africa, April 2017; and Du Toit et al. (2015).
21. The Amanzi Statutory Council was registered as a bargaining council in 2012 (informa-tion supplied by Department of Labour).
22. BMW (South Africa) (Pty) Ltd, Mercedes-Benz South Africa (Pty) Ltd, Ford Motor Company of Southern Africa (Pty) Ltd, General Motors South Africa (Pty) Ltd, Nissan South Africa (Pty) Ltd, Toyota South Africa Motors (Pty) Ltd and Volkswagen South Africa (Pty) Ltd.
23. This includes undeclared employees and own-account workers working in informal establishments.
24. A standard measure of income inequality of the deviation of the distribution of income among individuals or households within a country from a perfectly equal distribution. A value of 0 represents absolute equality, a value of 100 absolute inequality.
25. Wittenberg (2014) uses the Post-Apartheid Labour Market (PALM) series, which com-bines the three labour market series for the period since 1994 – the October Household Survey (OHS), LFS and QLFS – and employs different statistical methods to address some of the inconsistencies in the data in examining the relationship between wage growth and labour productivity. Burger (2016) uses data provided by the South African Reserve Bank (SARB) for the level of wages and value added. He uses data on the percentage change and applies statistical methods to address breaks in the 'levels' series and create two indexes.
26. Finn (2015) uses the poverty line calculated by Budlender et al. (2015).

27. http://nationalminimumwage.co.za/wp-content/uploads/2015/08/0012indaba_declara tion.pdf (accessed 28 May 2017).
28. http://new.nedlac.org.za/wp-content/uploads/2014/10/Declaration-on-wage-inequality-and-labour-market-stability.pdf (accessed 28 May 2017).
29. http://new.nedlac.org.za/wp-content/uploads/2014/10/Agreement-on-the-Introduction-of-the-national-minimum-wage.pdf and http://new.nedlac.org.za/wp-content/uploads/2 014/10/Accord-stabilising-labour-relations.pdf (accessed 28 May 2017).
30. *A New Growth Path*, released by the Economic Development Minister in December 2010, and the Industrial Policy Action Plans (2013–2016 and 2015/16–2017/18) released by the Department of Trade and Industry.
31. This decision was supported by the overall convenors (labour, government, community and employers) and endorsed by the Management Committee of NEDLAC (MANCO).
32. Implementation of the Act has not been without controversy. During the 2014 collective bargaining round in the metal and engineering sector, NUMSA tabled a demand that employers not make use of the measure during negotiations.
33. The LRS AWARDS database of the Labour Research Services (LRS) tracks the outcomes of collective bargaining. See http://www.lrs.org.za/award/ and Elsley and Mthethwa (2014).
34. The presence of a higher-level agreement is not, however, a prerequisite and productivity bargaining has also taken place at the enterprise level in industries where the national agreement is silent on this point (for example, in the wood and paper sector).
35. For example, the Metal and Engineering Industry Bargaining Council Agreement, 2010, the Chamber of Mines Gold Chamber Agreement, 2011–13, and the National Bargaining Council for the Clothing Industry Memorandum of Understanding on Absenteeism and the Productivity, 2007.
36. Examining data for 1993, Schultz and Mwabu (1998) find a much higher mark-up of 145 per cent for African male workers in the bottom of the decile, and a lower mark-up 19 per cent at the top decile of the wage distribution.
37. Non-union workers covered by an industrial council agreement earned 10 per cent more, and union members 30 per cent more, than those outside the system.
38. Two-thirds of private sector bargaining councils also administer social benefits, including pensions, provident funds, medical aid and disability benefits (Budlender and Sadeck, 2007).

REFERENCES

Alexander, P., Lekgowa, T., Mmpoe, B., Sinwell, L. and Xezwi, B. 2012. *Marikana: A view From the Mountain and a Case to Answer*. Johannesburg: Jacana.

Banerjee, A., Galiani, S., Levinsohn, J., McLaren, Z. and Woolard, I. 2008. 'Why has unemployment risen in the new South Africa?', *Economics of Transition*, **16**(4), pp. 715–40.

Baskin, J. 1991. *Striking Back: A History of COSATU*. Johannesburg: Ravan Press.

Bendix, S. 2007. *Industrial Relations in South Africa* (9th edn). Cape Town: Juta.

Benjamin, P. 2013. 'Assessing South Africa's Commission for Conciliation, Mediation and Arbitration (CCMA)', DIALOGUE Working Paper No. 47. Geneva: ILO.

Berger, S. and Compston, H. 2002. *Policy Concertation and Social Partnership in Western Europe: Lessons for the 21st Century*. New York, USA and Oxford, UK: Berghahn Books.

Bezuidenhout, A. and Kenny, B. 1998. 'Subcontracting in the mining industry', *Innes Labour Brief*, **10**(1), pp. 30–36.

Bhorat, H., Goga, S. and van der Westhuizen, C. 2012. 'Institutional wage effects: Revisiting union and bargaining council wage premia in South Africa', *South African Journal of Economics*, **80**(3), pp. 400–414.

Bhorat, H., Mayet, N., Tian, N. and Tseng, D. 2013. 'The determinants of wage inequality in South Africa', mimeo, ILO Country Case Studies on Inequality. Geneva: ILO.

Bhorat, H., van der Westhuizen, C. and Jacobs, T. 2009. 'Income and non-income inequality in post-apartheid South Africa: What are the drivers and possible policy interventions?', Development Policy Research Unit Working Paper 09/138. Cape Town: University of Cape Town.

Blumfeld, J. 1997. 'From icon to scapegoat: The experience of South Africa's reconstruction and development programme', *Development Policy Review*, **15**(199), pp. 65–91.

Bonner, P., Delius, P. and Posel, D. (eds). 1993. *Apartheid's Genesis 1935–1962*. Johannesburg: Ravan Press and Wits University Press.

Budlender, J., Leibbrandt, M. and Woolard, I. 2015. 'South African poverty lines: A review and two new money-metric thresholds', South African Labour and Development Research Unit Working Paper No. 151. Cape Town: SALDRU University of Cape Town.

Budlender, D. and Sadeck, S. 2007. 'Bargaining council and other benefit schemes', paper prepared for National Treasury of South Africa, June.

Buhlungu, S. 2010. *A Paradox of Victory: COSATU and the Democratic Transformation in South Africa*. Scottsville: University of Kwazulu-Natal Press.

Burger, P. 2016. 'Have real wages fallen behind or increased out of line with productivity? A macroeconomic perspective'. http://www.econ3x3.org/article/have-real-wages-fallen-behind-or-increased-out-line-productivity-macroeconomic-perspec tive (accessed 30 October 2017).

Burger, R. and Yu, D. 2007. 'Wage trends in post-apartheid South Africa: Constructing an earnings series from household survey data', Development Policy Research Unit Working Paper 07/117. Cape Town: University of Cape Town.

Butcher, K.F. and Rouse, C.E. 2001. 'Wage effects of unions and industrial councils in South Africa', *Industrial and Labour Relations Review*, **54**(2), pp. 274–349.

Capoccia, G. and Kelemen, R. 2007. 'The study of critical junctures: Theory, narrative, and counterfactuals in historical institutionalism', *World Politics*, **59**(2), pp. 341–69.

Chinguno, C. 2015. 'The unmaking and remaking of industrial relations: The case of Impala Platinum and the 2012–2013 platinum strike wave', *Review of African Political Economy*, **42**(146), pp. 577–90.

Clarke, J. 2012. 'Showdown over labour looms', *SA Forestry*, August, http://saforest ryonline.co.za/articles/human_resources/showdown_over_labour_looms/.

Coleman, N. 2013. 'Towards new collective bargaining, wage and social protection strategies in South Africa – Learning from the Brazilian experience', GLU Working Paper No. 17.

Compston, H. 2002. 'The strange persistence of policy concertation', in Berger, S. and Compston, H. (eds), *Policy Concertation and Social Partnership in Western Europe: Lessons for the Twenty-first Century*. New York, USA and Oxford, UK: Berghahn Books.

Crush, J., Ulicki, T., Tseane, T. and Jansen van Veuren, E. 2010. 'Undermining labour: The rise of sub-contracting in South African gold mines', *Journal of Southern African Studies*, **27**(1), pp. 5–31.

Davenport, T. and Saunders, S. 2000. *South Africa: A Modern History*. Basingstoke: Palgrave Macmillan.

Department of Labour (DOL). 2014a. *Industrial Action Report: 2014*. Pretoria.

Department of Labour (DOL). 2014b. *14th Commission for Employment Equity Annual Report, 2013–2014*. Pretoria.

Department of Labour (DOL). 2015. *Industrial Action Report: 2015*. Pretoria.

Department of Labour (DOL). 2016. *Industrial Action Report: 2016*. Pretoria.

Dickinson, D. 2015. 'Fighting their own battles: The Mabarete and the end of labour broking in the South African Post Office', SWOP Working Paper No. 2, University of the Witwatersrand.

Du Toit, D., Godfrey, S., Cooper, C., Giles, G., Cohen, T., Conradie, B. and Steenkamp, A. 2015. *Labour Relations Law: A Comprehensive Guide* (6th edn). Durban: Lexis Nexis.

Elsley, T. and Mthethwa, G. 2014. 'Wage Detemination in South Africa since 1994', *Bargaining Indicators 2014: Twenty Years – A Labour Perspective* (Vol. 14, November). Cape Town: Labour Research Services.

Ewert, J. 1997. 'Training for "world-class manufacturing": Rhetoric and reality in the South African engineering industry', *South African Journal of Labour Relations*, **21**(2), pp. 25–41.

Fine, B. and Rustomjee, Z. 1996. *The Political Economy of South Africa*. Johannesburg: Wits University Press.

Finn, A. 2015. 'A national minimum wage in the context of the South African labour market', Working Paper #1, National Minimum Wage Research Initiative, University of the Witwatersrand.

Gelb, S. 2010. 'Macroeconomic policy and development: from crisis to crisis', in Freund, B.H. Witt (ed.), *Development Dilemmas in Post-Apartheid South Africa*. Scottsville: UKZN Press.

Godfrey, S., Maree, J. and Theron, J. 2006a. 'Regulating the labour market: The role of bargaining councils', *Industrial Law Journal*, **27**(April), pp. 713–52.

Godfrey, S., Maree, J. and Theron, J. 2006b. 'Flexibility in bargaining councils: The role of exemptions', *Industrial Law Journal*, **27**(July), pp. 1368–86.

Godfrey, S., Maree, J. and Theron, J. 2006c. 'Conditions of employment and small business: Coverage, compliance and exemptions', Development Policy Research Unit Working Paper No. 06/106. Cape Town: University of Cape Town.

Godfrey, S., Maree, J., Du Toit, D. and Theron, J. 2010. *Collective Bargaining in South Africa: Past, Present and Future?* Cape Town: Juta.

Godfrey, S., Elsley, T. and Tall, M. 2017. 'Sectoral collective bargaining, productivity and competitiveness in South Africa's clothing value chain: manufacturers between a rock and a hard place', Conditions of Work and Employment Series No. 87. Geneva: ILO.

Hartford, G. 2012. 'The mining industry strike wave: What are the causes and what are the solutions?', *GroundUp*, 10 October. http://www.groundup.org.za/article/mining-industry-strike-wave-what-are-causes-and-what-are-solutions/ (accessed 4 April 2016).

Hofmeyer, J. and Lucas, R. 2001. 'The rise in union wage premiums in South Africa', *Labour*, **15**(4), pp. 685–719.

Hunter, M. 2000. 'The post-Fordist high road? A South African case study', *Journal of Contemporary African Studies*, **18**(1), pp. 67–90.

Kingdom, G.G. and Knight, J. 2004. 'Unemployment in South Africa: The nature of the beast', *World Development*, **32**(3), 391–408.

Klein, N. 2012. 'Real wage, labor productivity, and employment trends in South Africa: A closer look', IMF Working Paper No. 12/92. Washington, DC.

Labour Research Service (LRS). 2013. *Bargaining Monitor*, **27**(179), http://www.lrs.org.za/docs/LRS_BM_Strategic%20Bargaining%20in%202013.pdf.

Lapping, B. 1986. *Apartheid: A History*. London: Grafton Books.

Leibbrandt, M. and Woolard, I. 2001. 'The labour market and household income inequality in South Africa: Existing evidence and new panel data', *Journal of International Development*, **13**(6), pp. 671–89.

Leibbrandt, M., Woolard, I., Finn, A. and Argent, J. 2010. 'Trends in South African income distribution and poverty since the fall of apartheid', OECD Social, Employment and Migration Working Papers No. 101. Paris: OECD.

Luckett, T. and Mzobe, D. 2016. 'Outsourcing must fall: The role of workers in the 2015 protest wave at South African universities', *Global Labour Journal*, **7**(1), pp. 94–9.

Macun, I. 1997. 'Does size matter: The Labour Relations Act, majoritarianism and union structure', *Law, Democracy and Development Law Journal*, **1**(1), pp. 69–82.

Macun, I. 2014. 'The state of organised labour: Still living like there's no tomorrow', in Pillay, D., Khadiagala, G.M., Naidoo, P. and Southall, R. (eds), *New South African Review 4: A Fragile Democracy – Twenty Years On*. Johannesburg: Wits University Press.

Maree, J. (ed.). 1987. *The Independent Trade Unions, 1974–1984*. Johannesburg: Raven Press.

Massie, K., Collier, D. and Crotty, D. 2014. *Executive Salaries in South Africa: Who Should Get a Say on Pay?* Johannesburg: Jacana Media.

Mohamed, S. 2010. 'The state of the South African economy', in Pillay, D., Daniel, J., Naidoo, P. and Southall, R. (eds), *New South African Review 1 2010: Development or Decline?* Johannesburg: Wits University Press.

Moll, P. 1993. 'Black South African unions: Relative wage effects in international perspective', *Industrial and Labour Relations Review*, **46**(2), pp. 245–61.

Nattrass, N. 2013. 'The South African variety of capitalism', in Becker, U. (ed.), *The BRICs and Emerging Economies in Comparative Perspective*. London, UK and New York, USA: Routledge.

Ntuli, M. and Kwenda, P. 2014. 'Labour unions and wage inequality among African men', *Development Southern Africa*, **31**(2), pp. 322–46.

Pons-Vignon, N. 2015. 'Caught in the grip of the market: Agricultural and forestry workers in post-apartheid South Africa', in Oya, C. and Pontara, N. (eds), *Rural Wage Employment in Developing Countries: Theory, Evidence and Policy*. London: Routledge.

Pons-Vignon, N. and Anseeuw, W. 2009. 'Great expectations: Working conditions in South Africa since the end of apartheid', *Journal of Southern African Studies*, **35**(4), pp. 883–99.

Posel, D., Casale, D. and Vermaak, C. 2013. 'The unemployed in South Africa: Why are so many not counted?'. http://www.econ3x3.org/article/unemployed-south-africa-why-are-so-many-not-counted (accessed 4 April, 2016).

Presidential Comprehensive Labour Market Commission (PCLMC). 1996. *Report of the Commission to Investigate the Development of a Comprehensive Labour Market Policy 1996*. Pretoria.

Rani, U. and Furrer, M. 2016. 'Decomposing income inequality into factor income components: Evidence from G20 countries', ILO Research Paper No. 15. Geneva: ILO.

Reddy, N. 2012. *Labour Broking and Labour's Share: An Econometric Assessment of the Effects of Triangular Employment on Wages and Benefits*. Cape Town: University of Cape Town.

Schultz, T.P. and Mwabu, G. 1998. 'Labor unions and the distribution of wages and employment in South Africa', *Industrial and Labor Relations Review*, **51**(4), pp. 680–703.

Segatti, A. and Pons-Vignon, N. 2013. 'Stuck in stabilisation? South Africa's post-apartheid macro-economic policy between ideological conversion and technocratic capture', *Review of African Political Economy*, **40**(138), pp. 537–55.

Tregenna, F. 2008. 'Quantifying the outsourcing of jobs from manufacturing to services', *South African Journal of Economics*, **76**(2), pp. 222–38.

van der Berg, S. 2014. 'Inequality, poverty and prospects for redistribution', *Development Southern Africa*, **31**(2), pp. 197–218.

Van Niekerk, A. 2002. 'In search of justification: The origins of the statutory protection of security of employment in South Africa', *Industrial Law Journal*, **25**(5), pp. 853–67.

Visser, J., Hayter, S. and Gammarano, R. 2015. 'Trends in collective bargaining coverage: stability, erosion or decline?', Labour Relations Issue Brief No. 1. Geneva: ILO.

von Holdt, K. 2003. *Transition from Below: Forging Trade Unionism and Workplace Change in South Africa*. Pietermaritzburg: University of Natal Press.

von Holdt, K. 2010. 'Institutionalization, strike violence and local moral orders', *Transformation: Critical Perspectives on Southern Africa*, **72/73**, pp. 127–51.

Webster, E. 1978. *Essays in Southern African Labour History*. Johannesburg: Raven Press.

Webster, E. 1999. 'Defusion of the Molotov cocktail in South African industrial relations: The burden of the past and the challenge of the future', in Kuruvilla, S. and Mundell, B. (eds), *Colonialism, Nationalism and Institutionalisation of Industrial Relations in the Third World*. Stamford, CT: JAI Press.

Webster, E. 2013. 'The promise and the possibility: South Africa's contested industrial relations path', *Transformation: Critical Perspectives on Southern Africa*, **81/82**, pp. 208–35.

Webster, E. and Joynt, K. 2013. 'Rethinking social dialogue: NEDLAC into the future', unpublished report commissioned for ILO.

Webster, E. and Omar, R. 2003. 'Work restructuring in post-apartheid South Africa', *Work and Occupations*, **3**(2), pp. 3–22.

Webster, E. and Sikwebu, D. 2010. 'Tripartism and economic reforms in South Africa', in Fraile, L. (ed.), *Blunting Neoliberalism: Tripartism and Economic Reforms in the Developing World*. Basingstoke, UK and Geneva: Palgrave Macmillan and ILO.

Webster, E. and von Holdt, K. 2005. *Beyond the Apartheid Workplace: Studies in Translation*. Pietermaritzburg: University of Natal Press.

Wittenberg, M. 2014. *Analysis of Employment, Real Wage, and Productivity Trends in South Africa since 1994*, Conditions of Work and Employment Series No. 45. Geneva: International Labour Office.

World Economic Forum. 2014. *Global Competitiveness Report 2014–2015.* Geneva: World Economic Forum.

Yu, D. 2010. 'Poverty and inequality trends in South Africa using different survey data', Department of Economics Working Paper No. 04/2010, Stellenbosch: Stellenbosch University.

4. Industrial relations and inclusive growth in Brazil: The swinging pendulum

Janine Berg* and Eduardo Schneider

4.1 INTRODUCTION

Despite having one of the highest rates of income inequality in the world, Brazil, during the 2000s and early 2010s, experienced inclusive growth with sharp declines in the rates of unemployment and informality, and increases in wages and other income gains that benefited those at the bottom of the income distribution. This remarkable achievement translated into a significant fall in the Gini coefficient for income, a measure of inequality, which fell from a high of 0.6 in 2001 to 0.52 in 2014. This chapter analyses the contribution of the industrial relations system to these improvements. It also addresses the economic recession and political crisis that began in 2014, and seeks to shed light on the evolution of the industrial relations system in the country and the contributions of this system to social and economic policies, in both good and bad times. It considers some of the constituent elements of the system and the inter-relationship with political and economic factors that determine the effects of the system, including whether change is incremental and path-dependent, or discontinuous and transformational.

Brazil's industrial relations system has long been criticized by both workers and employers for its 'state corporatist' character. Yet the institutional support that this system has provided, including the policy of extension, whereby even non-members of workers and employers' unions are covered by collective bargaining agreements, the financing of workers and employers' unions,[1] and the numerous tripartite bodies and fora, have sustained the industrial relations system in the country. Under the favourable political and economic environment of the 2000s and early 2010s, workers' unions were able to use their position to deliver important gains for workers, both directly through collective bargaining negotiations, and also indirectly through their influence in setting national policy, particularly with respect to the minimum wage as well as in pushing for important labour reforms such as domestic workers' rights. Similarly, workers' unions were effective in holding off many of the labour market reforms proposed during the economic crises of the 1990s.

In 2017, however, a new government introduced sweeping labour reforms that alter the foundation of the industrial relations system as well as many basic labour rights. While the implications of this new law are yet to be understood, and there are likely to be further reforms, the law represents a dramatic break from the past. Previously, the industrial and labour relation system did not change, but its effects were dependent on the political and economic swings of the pendulum. The 2017 reform may upend this trajectory.

Like the other countries studied in this volume, Brazil has undergone important transitions in its political and economic model, with democratic rule restored only in the late 1980s. The country thus offers a unique case study of how a relatively static industrial relations system (albeit until 2017) has responded to shifts in political and economic context, providing insights into the importance of the context, but also on how systems adapt snd change.

4.2 THE STRUCTURE, LIMITS AND POTENTIAL OF BRAZIL'S INDUSTRIAL RELATIONS SYSTEM

In order to assess the contribution of industrial relations to inclusive growth in Brazil, it is necessary to understand the structure of the Brazilian industrial relations system as well as its limitations and potential. The system is often described as 'state corporatist', though the influence and involvement of the state has varied according to the political regime in power. Still, the main legislative features of Brazil's current industrial relations system have changed little since they were first instituted in the 1930s, during thc Vargas era.[2]

4.2.1 The Structure of Brazil's Industrial Relations System

When Getúlio Vargas assumed power in 1930, as a civilian leader following a military coup, he embarked on an ambitious agenda to industrialize Brazil by building state industries in key sectors of the economy. Worker disputes had been widespread in the country since the beginning of the 1900s and had come to be referred to as the 'social problem'. In response, the Vargas government sought to implement a system of industrial relations that could contain industrial disputes and support the modernization project (Silva, 2008). To this end, the government put in place a 'state corporatist' industrial relations model, with a view to achieving 'social peace', through state regulation of the affairs of both workers' and employers' unions.

Individual labour rights as well as the laws governing the industrial relations system were codified in the Consolidation of Labour Laws (Consolidação das Leis do Trabalho, CLT) of 1943. The CLT specified the four principal elements of Brazilian industrial relations: (1) the structure; (2) the legal recognition of unions; (3) the union tax; and (4) the system of conflict resolution.

The structure

Perhaps the most enduring feature of Brazilian corporatism is its unique structure, referred to as *unicidade sindical*. Under this structure, a union will represent all workers – union members and non-members alike – of a given occupational category in a specific territory. The origins of this occupational structure date from the beginning of the twentieth century, with the decision of the anarchist Confederation of Brazilian Workers (Confederação Operária Brasileira, COB), to opt for a federative union organization, like that of the French General Confederation of Labour (Confédération générale du travail, CGT), as well as the judgment of Decree 1.637 from 1907 to recognize unions in certain professional categories (Silva, 2008). These institutional features were then carried over into the 1931 decision (Decree 19.770), which regulated the creation and activities of unions in Brazil, including the principal of *unicidade syndical*. Unions were to represent workers 'in identical, similar or connected trades in a specific geographic jurisdiction', usually municipal, but at the discretion of the authorities they could cover an entire state, several states or the nation (Pichler, 2005, p. 67). Employers' organizations were structured similar to workers' organizations with the aim of having parallel representation, and like workers, all businesses within the jurisdiction and covering the 'economic category' were covered by the collective bargaining agreements (known as 'collective conventions' or *convenios colectivos*). Federations and confederations of both workers' and employers' unions could exist, but they were not party to collective bargaining and had no authority over local union activities. Nevertheless, the employers did develop well-organized, pyramid-structured national associations covering five sectors: industry, commerce, banks, transportation and agriculture. In addition to representing employers' interests, these associations were responsible for administering the system of training institutes, known as the Sistema S (S system),[3] financed by a 2.5 per cent payroll tax (Zylberstajn, 2006).

The legal recognition and control of unions

The most evident feature of the state corporatist system was the control the government exercised over union recognition. At the height of authoritarian rule, during the Vargas era of 1930–45 and the military regime of 1964–85, the state controlled union activity by granting or withholding legal recognition of each union (workers' and employers' organizations alike), and approval of its leadership. The requirement that unions obtain legal recognition became established shortly after the creation in 1930 of the Ministry of Labour, Industry and Commerce. Each union had to apply to the Ministry for a licence, and had to state in its statutes that it would 'collaborate with the state in promoting social solidarity' and would refrain from engaging in the activities of political parties (Pichler, 2005, p. 58). Moreover, in cases of contested leadership, the Ministry was empowered to choose who would represent the workers. More radical leaders, and particularly those who were affiliated with the outlawed Communist Party, would not be recognized; in some instances, outside leaders (*pelegos*) were put in their place. Although the government also granted licences to employer unions and had the right to interfere in their affairs, in practice these were largely autonomous (Pichler, 2005).

The union tax

In 1940, compulsory union dues (known as the *imposto sindical* or union tax) were instituted, at a rate of one day's wage. All workers – whether union members or not – were required to pay the union tax, which was deducted by employers from their salaries. Employers were also required to pay a union tax, levied as a proportion of the capital of the firm, regardless of whether they were members of the corresponding employers' association. The Ministry of Labour collected the tax and distributed it among the different levels of the union system. Restrictions were imposed on how unions could use the funds, and the state had the right to survey union finances. Any wrongdoing – such as spending funds on political activities – could result in the replacement of union leadership, the seizure of union headquarters, or withdrawal of a union's licence (Pichler, 2005). The union tax has been criticized for providing incentives for the formation of unions – and emergence of union leaders – more interested in getting access to the funds than in genuinely representing the workers. Moreover, as the unions have guaranteed revenues, there is less incentive to affiliate and organize workers (Lang and Gagnon, 2009; Zylberstajn, 2006; Pichler, 2005).

Conflict resolution

The principal goal of the industrial relations system as established under Vargas was to maintain 'social peace'. As such, disputes that arose in the workplace were to be solved not at the workplace, but by the state. To this end, the government established in 1932 the Joint Committees for Conciliation, with the objective of resolving labour disputes; in 1941 the Labour Courts were created, with normative powers over collective agreements. The courts were empowered to intervene in collective (and individual) wage disputes, which in the context of authoritarian regimes and a national development plan meant that wage disputes were often settled in favour of employers. In 1945, the government instituted an annual schedule of deadlines for collective negotiations (known as the *data-base*), strategically distributed over the months of the year so as to avoid combined mobilizations. One of the peculiarities of the conflict resolution system that remains, to a large extent, to this day is the absence of formal in-plant mechanisms for grievance resolution, such as shop stewards or dispute resolution systems. As a result, routine disputes about workplace grievances are handled through individual legal action within the labour court system. The absence of in-company grievance procedures, coupled with laws that permit employers to fire workers without just cause, has meant that workers have tended to keep problems at work to themselves until they are fired, and then seek remedy in the labour courts (French, 2004; Lang and Gagnon, 2009). Moreover, with no provision for representing workers at the workplace and with disputes resolved by the labour courts, collective bargaining was often distant from the concerns of the union membership, further curtailing its development (Pichler, 2005).

4.2.2 The Evolution of Industrial Relations

While the structure of the industrial relations system changed little over the decades, with bargaining parties and institutions remaining more or less the same, the degree of government interference in union affairs, and the policies pursued in this area, varied significantly between democratic periods and periods of military rule, allowing for outcomes that were more favourable to workers under democratic regimes. Examples include a more permissive attitude to strike action and more positive positions on the minimum wage. The rulings of the labour courts have also been strongly influenced by the political regime.

The Vargas era ended with the return to democracy in 1946 and the passage of a new Constitution that placed the Labour Courts under the judicial branch of the government and provided for increased labour rights, including equal pay for equal work, greater job stability (with compensation for the worker in the event of dismissal), participation in profits, and suspension of the requirement that unions obtain legal recognition by the State. While industrial relations were still constrained by the corporatist system, workers and unions began to use the rights enshrined in the CLT to improve their working conditions, particularly by bringing individual grievances to the labour courts. Unions viewed the assistance that they gave to their members in pursuing individual grievances as a way to build loyalty among their base and increase worker mobilization (French, 2004). John French, in his analysis of industrial relations in Brazil from the 1930s to the 1960s, documents the experience of labour leaders, who carried well-worn copies of the CLT with them and were proud that they 'knew more about the CLT than most lawyers', gaining expertise as they advised hundreds of workers on individual grievance cases (French, 2004, p. 107). French notes the irony of their strategy, given that 'the labour court system's creators conceived and defended it as a replacement rather than another arena for class struggle' (p. 102). Constrained as they were by the state corporatist model of industrial relations, unions came to view the legal system as an avenue for their struggles. Indeed, a 1963 survey of union presidents found that only 17 per cent favoured abolition of the labour courts (Mericle, 1977, cited in French, 2004). French concludes that what arose was a 'juridical consciousness of class ... a consciousness resulting from [the existence] of legal labour rights' (French, 2004, p. 111).

During the period of democracy between 1946 and 1964, workers were also successful in advancing their causes through increasing unionization and renewed strike activity, facilitated by the decline in direct governmental intervention in unions (Silva, 2008). Important gains included family allowances and the right to the annual year-end bonus (*13° salário*). Labour unrest, however, continued to increase, with more than 200 general strikes between 1961 and 1963 alone. In 1963, in a campaign headed by the Confederação Nacional dos Trabalhadores da Indústria (CNTI), 700 000 workers went on strike demanding an end to staggered wage renegotiation dates (*data-base*) and the introduction of a more collective representation of workers across occupational categories. The goal was to increase union strength in negotiations, and ultimately to change the structure of unions and labour relations in Brazil. Their demands, however, were summarily dismissed by the labour courts (Corrêa, 2008). Furthermore, the high level of labour unrest, in an atmosphere of severe economic and political crisis, contributed to the military coup of March 1964 that ushered in a military dictatorship which would hold power until 1985.

The military dictatorship and the rise of 'new unionism'

Under the military dictatorship, the Government resumed its interventionist approach to industrial relations. Massive purges of the labour movement were conducted; union leaders were replaced by army officers and suspected communists were arrested (Lang and Gagnon, 2009).[4] Strikes in sectors deemed essential were prohibited, the minimum legal working age was reduced from 14 to 12 years, the scope for individual dismissal was increased, and the normative powers of the labour courts were reduced. Moreover, legislated wage policy took precedence over wage agreements, further weakening both collective bargaining and individual workers' appeals in the courts.

In addition, the military government reformed the CLT in 1967 by introducing a distinction between two kinds of agreements: a collective convention celebrated between workers' and employers' unions representing particular economic and professional categories with mandatory extension to all workers in the territorial jurisdiction of the unions; and a collective agreement between an individual workers' union and one or more firms.

By the mid-1970s a growing restlessness and desire for greater political freedoms began to take hold, reflected in the emergence of an active civil society in opposition to the military dictatorship. By the late 1970s, the Government was beginning to introduce some political liberalization, including the recognition of opposition parties, and in 1979 a political amnesty was granted to many activists and union leaders. In that same year, with inflation at a high level, the Government permitted workers to negotiate supplementary wage increases in the form of productivity increments in collective agreements (Silva, 2008).

The mid- to late 1970s also marked the rise of 'new unionism' (*novo sindicalismo*), associated with the automotive sector in the ABC region of São Paulo. This movement was critical of the previous generation of union leaders, which it saw as being too distant from the workers. Thus, its focus was on organizing the workplace and building closer relations with workers, bringing about the improvement of wages and working conditions through direct negotiations with employers. An important means to this end (one that remains in use to this day) was the election of union members to the factory Committees for the Prevention of Industrial Accidents (CIPAs). CIPA members benefited from protection against dismissal, and were hence able to serve as de facto in-house union representatives, thereby circumventing an industrial relations system that sought to keep negotiations out of the workplace. In 1981, the first 'official' factory committee was formed in the Ford plant, negotiated through a company-level agreement. Eventually, in 1983, the movement 'defied the corporatist structure' and founded the first central union, the Central Única dos Trabalhadores

(CUT) (Lang and Gagnon, 2009, p. 253). It was affiliated with the Workers' Party (Partido dos Trabalhadores, PT), which was formed in 1980, following the abolition of the two-party political system.

Continued pressure for direct presidential elections eventually forced the appointment, through indirect elections, of a civilian President in 1985. Upon taking office, Jose Sarney reinstituted democracy and lifted state controls over union activities and union leaders. A constituent assembly was called in 1986 to adopt a new Constitution, which was promulgated in October 1988.

The return to democracy and the Constitution of 1988

The Constitution of 1988 introduced some important changes regarding individual and collective workers' rights, while leaving much of the industrial relations system intact. For unions, the most significant change was the end of the state's power to intervene in their internal affairs. Also, unions won the right to establish representatives in the workplace in companies with 200 or more employees; an important step towards facilitating the resolution of grievances at company level, and building stronger ties between workers and their unions. In addition, public sector workers gained the right to strike, and there were relaxations on the restrictions of the right to strike overall.

Nevertheless, the Constitution left the fundamental pillars of the industrial relations system intact, including the principle of *unicidade sindical* (whereby all workers in a particular occupational category and jurisdiction are automatically covered by the respective union), the union tax, as well as the Labour Courts. Leaving the union tax in place, but removing the Ministry's role in approving the formation of new unions, encouraged the creation of new unions, many of which were solely interested in accessing the funds of the union tax (Lang and Gagnon, 2009; Pichler, 2005; Zylberstajn, 2006).

The 1988 Constitution also strengthened individual workers' rights by reducing the working week from 48 to 44 hours, extending maternity leave from 90 to 120 days, instituting paternity leave of five days, increasing overtime pay, adding an additional bonus payment for vacation periods, and raising the penalty for dismissals without just cause from 10 to 40 per cent of funds accrued in the Guarantee Fund for Time of Service (FGTS). Domestic workers were also conceded more rights, though fewer than other workers.[5] In addition, the Constitution established several central pillars of the welfare state, including the creation of a national universal health system (Sistema Único de Saude, SUS) and two important programmes that provide benefits to the elderly poor – the rural pension (Fundo de Assistência ao Trabalhador Rural) and the Continued Benefit Provision (Beneficio de Prestação Continuada, BPC).

4.3 TRADE UNIONS AND LABOUR RELATIONS IN CONTEMPORARY BRAZIL

Despite the return to democracy and the promulgation of the 1988 Constitution, the Brazilian system of industrial relations did not change much in the 1990s and 2000s. Unionization rates fell slightly in the 1990s as a result of deindustrialization, but then recovered throughout the 2000s. In 2015, 19.5 per cent of Brazilian workers were members of a trade union (IBGE, 2015). Overall, Brazil has been able to maintain its rates of unionization and has not witnessed the dramatic declines that have occurred in North America and some European countries (Hayter, 2015). Unionization is strongest in other manufacturing (37 per cent) and in education, health and social services (30.2 per cent), agriculture (28.7 per cent) and public administration (27 per cent); it is weakest in the hospitality and catering sector (11 per cent), construction (9.3 per cent) and domestic services (4.0 per cent) (see Figure 4.1).

Data from the 2015 IBGE (Instituto Brasileiro de Geografia e Estatística/ Brazilian Institute for Geography and Statistics) survey[6] of unionization

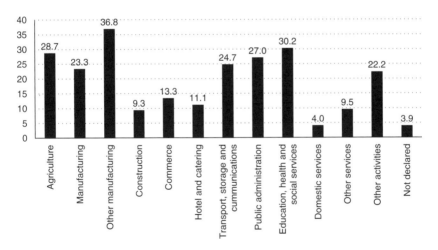

Source: IBGE.

Figure 4.1   *Unionization rates by economic activity in Brazil, 2015 (union membership as % of total employed)*

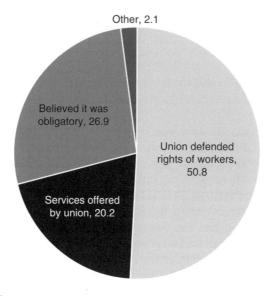

Source: IBGE.

Figure 4.2   Reasons for joining trade union

and labour relations in Brazil provide information on why Brazilian workers have chosen or not to join their trade union. Amongst trade union
members, 51 per cent report that they joined a union because it defended
the rights of workers; an additional 20.2 per cent state that it was because
of the services the union offered (see Figure 4.2). On the other hand, 27
per cent report joining because they believed it was obligatory. Amongst
employees who are not members of their trade union (Figure 4.3), 24 per
cent report that it was because they felt the union did not represent their
interests or they did not believe in the union, and 17 per cent state that the
union did not offer services that were of interest. An additional 26.4 per
cent, however, report that they did not know the union that represented
their occupational category; whereas 12 per cent state that they did not
know how to join.

   That nearly 40 per cent of workers state that they do not know the
union that represents their occupational category, or how to join it,
reflects a disconnect between workers and unions that has been a pervasive feature of Brazil's state corporatist union model. Because of the
union tax and the compulsory coverage of collective bargaining, there
is less incentive for workers to join their union, or for union leaders to
affiliate workers.

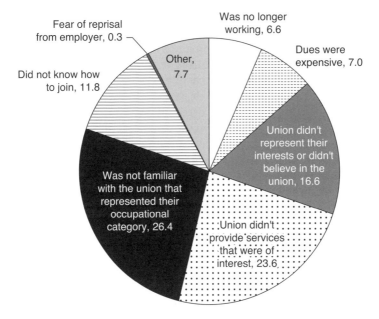

Source: IBGE.

Figure 4.3 Reasons for not joining trade union

Moreover, the removal of ministerial approval for union formation, coupled with access to funds from the union tax, has encouraged an increase in the number of unions in Brazil. Because unions are organized along occupational categories within a given territory, the scope for possible union formation is vast. Indeed, between 1990 and 2013, the number of workers' unions nearly doubled, from 5214 workers' unions to 10192. A similar trend, though not as sharp, occurred with employers' unions, which grew from 3118 in 1990 to 4545 in 2001 (IBGE, 2002, cited in DIEESE, 2011).

Yet, many of these unions have little contact with the workers that they represent. And multiple unions within a firm weakens collective representation at the firm level. As a consequence, workers often have difficulty in having their voice heard, leading to greater workplace dissatisfaction and conflict. The principal exception is those companies that have actively sought to strengthen their connection with the workers who they represent, through in-house union representation, or through union committees (permissible in companies with more than 200 employees) or through the CIPAs (Committees for the Prevention of Industrial Accidents).[7]

Today's Brazilian unions span the range from dynamic and active organizations to 'paper' unions that exist solely to collect funds from the union tax. Most fall somewhere in between. This characterization is supported by the findings of Lang and Gagnon (2009), who undertook case studies of two Brazilian unions with the goal of understanding the influence of the state corporatist structure and labour legislation (the CLT) on union practices, including their degree of autonomy. The authors study the Metalúrgicos do ABC (Metalworkers of São Paulo's ABC region), who are affiliated with the CUT and who were pioneers of the new unionism of the 1970s, as well as the Costureiras for the São Paulo and Osasco Region (Seamstresses), who are affiliated with Força Sindical.

The union, Metalúrgicos do ABC, covers approximately 100 000 metal-workers in 1000 companies, and has a very high union affiliation rate, with 75 per cent of workers belonging to the union. For decades, the union has been active in building closer relationships with its membership, establishing union committees at the workplace, either on a clandestine basis during the military dictatorship, through the CIPAs, or since the 1990s in the Union Committees of Companies (Comitês Sindicais de Empresas, CSEs). Officers of the CSEs sit on the union board for the sector, thereby constituting a channel of representation between the rank-and-file and the union leadership. The union tries to resolve disputes and voice its demands through its committees, avoiding the tribunals whenever possible, and demonstrating its autonomy from the corporatist structure. In those instances where a company does not have a union committee, higher-level unions are called upon to intervene directly in negotiations with the employer. The union negotiates collective conventions that are then supplemented by company-level collective agreements. The researchers found that the union would like more autonomy in respect of whom they represent, but has been blocked by the corporatist structure. For example, in one firm, the union tried to negotiate benefits for the administrative and cleaning staff, but their authority was contested and 'won by smaller unions whose monopoly of representation is guaranteed by *unicidade sindical*' (Lang and Gagnon, 2009, p. 261). Because of their distaste for the union tax, the union goes to court every year to gain an exemption for its members, and has created instead a new 'negotiating fee' that all workers in the base must pay.

The second union studied, the Seamstresses of the São Paulo and Osasco region, is more representative of contemporary Brazilian unionism. The sector is made up of 80 000 formally employed workers in 7500 registered companies, though it is estimated that an additional 100 000 workers are employed informally in the sector, many of them in unregistered firms. The union has attempted to engage more directly with the workers, by setting up factory committees through the 'bank of hours law' or through the CIPA. The union offers courses to CIPA members, as a way to create contact with workers and the union also instructs the committee members to get in touch with unions if there is a grievance that needs resolving.

According to the union, when it does receive complaints from workers, it attempts to initiate direct negotiations with the company, but these attempts are often rebuffed. As a result, sometimes unions organize protests 'at the factory door'. In instances when the union is not able to obtain satisfactory results, or negotiations reach an impasse, the union requests a meeting with company representatives at one of the Labour Ministry's 'round tables', which are mediated by government representatives. Lang and Gagnon (2009) suggest that the frequent recourse to the round tables is indicative of a high degree of dependency on the state. Many provisions of the collective conventions repeat the statutory provisions enshrined in the CLT, and while there are some firm-level collective agreements, these are less common than in the metalworkers' union.

The Seamstresses union is representative of many unions in Brazil that are trying to become more autonomous, but still nonetheless rely heavily on the enduring features of the system. As a result, the problem of lack of worker voice at the firm level persists, as evidenced by the nearly 4 million cases that are filed with the Brazilian labour courts every year (see Figure 4.4). Zylberstajn (2006) explains how small grievances that could normally be solved through dialogue and collective negotiation are instead pushed on to the labour courts, creating a litigious atmosphere among the social partners and 'distorting the vision that social agents have of the role of unions and collective bargaining' (p. 14). The heavy reliance on the courts has also created important backlogs.

Indeed, a 2009 supplement on access to justice in the household survey, the PNAD, found that around 2 per cent of the population had been involved in a conflict involving labour in in the five years preceding the interview. Amongst those in a labour conflict situation, 96 per cent sought out solutions, with 88.2 per cent submitting their case to the labour court, 8.8 per cent to special courts (formerly the small claims court) and 4.0 per cent seeking assistance from their union. Of those who had submitted a case to the courts, less than half (43.1 per cent) had their cases resolved, while 56.9 per cent were still awaiting resolution (ILO, 2013).

Among resolved labour conflicts, the predominant time lapse – between the start and resolution of the conflict – was one year (64.9 per cent of cases). Around one-third of the cases (33.5 per cent) were resolved in one to five years. When considering people who did not seek out resolutions to their labour conflict in the judicial system (12 per cent of the total), the main reason indicated for not doing so was because the problem occurred during a mediation or conciliation (27.5 per cent), or because they were

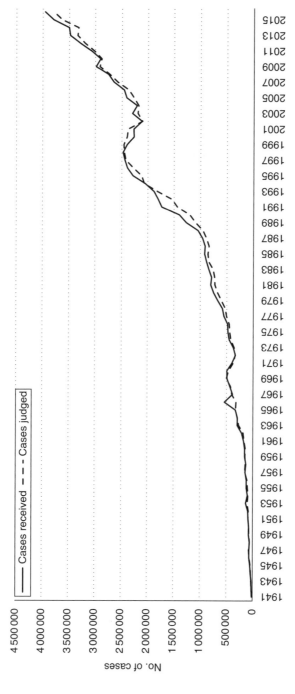

Note: The Justiça do Trabalho is the first level for filing a case. The verdict can be appealed at the regional labour courts or at the Supreme Labour Court.

Source: TST (http://www.tst.jus.br/serie-historica1).

Figure 4.4 Number of cases received and judged at the Labour Courts (Justiça de Trabalho), 1941–2015

of the opinion that the judicial system would take too long to resolve the conflict (15.8 per cent) (ILO, 2013).

4.3.1 Changes in Labour Relations in the 2000s: Results from a Delphi Panel

To better assess the contribution of the industrial relations system to inclusive growth in the 2000s, a group of Brazilian labour experts were asked, using a Delphi Panel, for their assessment of the most significant changes in labour relations in the 2000s, with an emphasis on legal changes.[8] The panel comprised 12 specialists in industrial relations from different backgrounds, both academic (sociologists, economists, lawyers) and professional (union advisers, public administrators and labour lawyers), nine of whom continued on the panel to the end of the exercise.[9] Following the collection of responses from the first round, the experts were asked in the second round to identify the five most important changes in labour relations since 2000, and rank these changes from 1 to 5, with 5 being the most important. The analysis was conducted in 2013, prior to the ensuing economic and political crisis and thus their responses do not consider the 2017 reforms. Table 4.1 presents the results of the experts' assessment, showing the 16 principal changes they identified, ranked by the sum of the points assigned.

Some of the interviewees clearly felt that the measures noted had made very little change to the system of labour relations. The feature that emerged most strongly was continuity and the persistence of the system consolidated in the previous century. In the years from 2000 until the mid-2010s, moreover, deregulatory policies ceased to be pursued, and the environment altered in favour of the workers. Statements by some of the interviewees corroborate this view:

> Another important change was that there ceased to be changes! That is, the succession of measures to flexibilize labour relations ceased. (Frederico)

> As of 2000, in my view, there were no great changes that impacted labour relations in general. The sweeping legislative changes that significantly impacted labour relations in recent times were, in my view, flexibilizations of the workday (banks of hours and others) and of wages (PLR) but this all happened in the 1990s, with repercussions in the 2000s. (Raquel)

> It is my understanding that the principal changes occurred in the labour market and in public policy, but not within the nucleus of the system of labour relations, which continues without significant change. Aside from adding union centrals [*centrais sindicais*] to the group of entities financed through taxes, a normative change that in effect reaffirmed basic features of the system, the most recent relevant change dates back to the beginning of the past decade, when the labour courts ceased to flirt with the neoliberal reforms of the 1990s.

Table 4.1   Principal changes in labour relations in Brazil in the 2000s

Rank	Change identified	Total points awarded[1]
1	Policy for strengthening the minimum wage (Law 12.382/2011)	41
2	Formal recognition of the union confederations and access to union tax revenues (Law 11.648/2008)	15
3	Reduced unemployment[2]	13
4	Legalization of participation in profits and results (PLR) (Law 10.101/2000)	11
5	Extension of rights to domestic workers (EC 72/2013)	11
6	Law of the Individual Micro-Entrepreneur (MEI) providing incentive to formalization (Enabling Law 128/2008)	10
7	Greater formalization[2]	9
8	Defence of social security[2]	6
9	Suspension of work flexibilization measures[2]	5
10	'Ultrativity'[3] of collective norms (TST Ruling 277/2012)	4
11	Expansion of the union agenda to cover development and equality[2]	3
12	Changes in procedure for bringing cases to the labour courts, providing stimulus to negotiation (EC 45/2004)	2
13	Withdrawal of PLC 134/2001, anticipating preference for negotiated over legislated settlements	2
14	Introduction of 'banks of hours' (Law 9.601/1998)	1
15	Introduction of tenure-related benefit to prior dismissal benefit (Law 12.506/2011)	1
16	Social security reform (EC 41/2003)	1

Notes:
1.   There were nine experts assigning points from 1 to 5, for a total of 135 points assigned.
2.   Indicates changes relating to the economic, political or union context.
3.   Refers to the the adherence to collective bargaining agreements, until future collective regulation expressly repeals them. It is a measure that forces parties to the bargaining table, who would otherwise benefit from the expiration of the agreement.

Source: Authors' compilation.

Even that meant no more than yet another pendulum swing of the labour courts, which have gone back and forth since the 1950s. (Carlos)

One of the points raised in the last statement relates to another important finding. As is shown in the literature and reflected in the general understanding of the interviewees, the principal change affecting labour relations in Brazil in the 2000s was one in the political and economic context. Even though the participants were explicitly told in the second round of interviews that the purpose of the survey was to identify institutional changes in labour relations, and not changes in context, the latter were nonetheless indicated. The interviewees' insistence on pointing to these factors underscores their importance. 'Reduced unemployment', 'increased formalization' and the 'suspension of work flexibilization measures' (all in the top ten ranked changes) brought about a new and more favourable environment for labour relations. 'Defence of social security' signalled a break with the neoliberal policies of the 1990s as well as a renewed interest on the part of the state in consolidating and extending the welfare state. 'Expansion of the union agenda' to encompass themes of 'development and equality' came about when the unions were called upon to participate actively in political and economic dialogue, and when previously excluded groups (particularly domestic workers) were brought within the unions' remit. Even 'formal recognition of the union centrals and [their] access to union tax revenues' was intended to make the union movement financially and structurally able to perform this new function.

For the purposes of our assessment of the contribution made by institutional changes to industrial relations and inclusive growth, we discuss the four top-ranked institutional changes. These are: (1) the strengthening of the minimum wage; (2) the formal recognition of the union centrals and their access to union tax revenues; (3) the regulations for participation in profits and results (PLR); and (4) the extension of rights to domestic workers. (Reduced unemployment, the third top-scoring 'change' listed in Table 4.2, is a change in the economic and labour market context, discussed in the previous section.)

Strengthening of the minimum wage
The policy to strengthen the minimum wage, pursued in the 2000s and codified in Law 12.382 of 2011, was ranked overwhelmingly as the most important change with a total score of 41 points, nearly three times as many as the second-highest ranked choice which received just 15 points. The strengthening of the minimum wage improved earnings and income distribution, not only by raising wages at the base of the pyramid, but also by serving as a benchmark in collective bargaining negotiations. Moreover, as many social security benefits are tied to the minimum wage, the increases also benefit those receiving retirement pensions, disability allowances and unemployment benefit.

The Brazilian minimum wage was first instituted in 1940; since then, its value in real terms has fluctuated according to the political regime. During the 1980s, in an attempt to control inflation, the minimum wage lost value, and it was not until 1995 that its purchasing power began to recover. Thereafter, with inflation lower, it followed a more stable trajectory. In 2004, shortly after President Lula came into office, the Brazilian union movement mounted a campaign to increase the minimum wage, which had been a priority in Lula's electoral campaign platform. The Government called for the social partners to discuss the policy, with initial talks focused on the percentage adjustment for 2005 and 2006. Meanwhile, an intense public debate, including representatives of labour, business and retirement pensioners, sought to arrive at a consensus on future adjustments. Finally, in 2007, a policy was launched to restore the value of the minimum wage. This foresaw annual adjustments that would compensate for the previous year's inflation and also incorporate an additional increase equivalent to the rate of growth of GDP in the year before that,[10] so that the minimum wage would reflect the productivity gains of the economy. This rule was followed annually by the Government by executive order even during the 2008 crisis, and was enacted into Law 12.382/2011 during the presidency of Dilma Rousseff.[11] As a result of this policy, the minimum wage grew in real terms by 60 per cent between January 2004 and January 2010, reaching 80 per cent real growth by January 2014.

Furthermore, the Enabling Law (*Lei Complementar*) No. 103 of 2000 allowed Brazilian states to set regional wage floors, in order that a higher remuneration threshold can be set where the cost of living is higher. The first to institute a state-level minimum wage, in 2001, was Rio Grande do Sul. Since that time, other states (São Paulo, Santa Catarina, Paraná and Rio de Janeiro) have also adopted regional minimum wage floors for categories not covered by collective conventions.

Formal recognition of the union centrals (*centrais sindicais*) and access to union tax revenues

This policy, enacted in Law 11.648 of 2008, was the outcome of an extensive national discussion that began in 2003, also on the basis of Lula's campaign platform. In 2003, President Lula established the National Labour Forum (FNT) under the aegis of the Ministry of Labour and Employment. Structured on a tripartite basis, this forum was to discuss and propose legislation for union and labour reform in Brazil, including a possible dismantling of some of the core pillars of the corporatist system, such as *unicidade* and the union tax. In view of the great differences between the policies of union and labour reform, the decision was taken at the outset to split the forum into two groups, one to focus on union reform and the other to address labour reform.

The forum for union reform proceeded in fits and starts. The quest for a project that would enjoy consensus ended up annulling much of its original purpose. Nevertheless, one of the lines of discussion pursued did produce results, chiefly the decision to recognize the legal status of the union centrals and give them access to 10 per cent of union tax revenues. Debate on the bill was complicated but, despite facing strong criticism, it was enacted in 2008 as Law 11.648. Defenders of the bill argued that the union movement, having been weakened in the 1990s, lacked the financial means to engage fully in social dialogue at the national level. Accordingly, the first article of the law reaffirmed the right of the union centrals to 'participate in negotiations at forums, boards of public bodies and other spaces for social dialogue of tripartite composition, at which issues of general interest to workers are under discussion' (Law 11.648/2008, article 1, paragraph II). With this legal recognition, union centrals were able to coordinate with their affiliates on action plans as well as represent workers in the various tripartite forums (Cook and Bazler, 2013).

The same law established eligibility criteria for access of union entities to the funding, based on national and sectoral presence and union affiliation.[12] In 2016, there were eight union centrals that met the criteria to receive funding from the union tax revenues in proportion to their representativeness among the base of affiliated unions (Table 4.2). The CUT, in view of its greater representativeness, receives the largest share of the union tax revenue funding reserved for the centrals (30.4 per cent).

Because the law was the outcome of a process that sought a comprehensive union reform, it is often referred to as union reform, despite being limited to the recognition of the centrals and the modalities for the dispersion of funds. As one interviewee remarks:

Table 4.2   Brazilian union centrals and their representativeness, 2016

Name of union central	Acronym	%
Central Única dos Trabalhadores	CUT	30.40
União Geral dos Trabalhadores	UGT	11.29
Força Sindical	FS	10.08
Central de Trabalhadores e Trabalhadoras do Brasil	CTB	10.08
Central dos Sindicatos Brasileiros	CSB	8.15
Nova Central Sindical de Trabalhadores	NCST	7.45
CONLUTAS	CONLUTAS	2.25
Central Geral dos Trabalhadores do Brasil	CGTB	1.88

Note: Does not add to 100% because not all unions are members of union centrals, and not all centrals meet the criteria necessary to receive the union tax.

Source: *Official Gazette* (*Diário Oficial da União*).

I would not call it union reform, but merely recognition and access to funding for union centrals. However, this measure significantly expanded the protagonism of the centrals, that thenceforth had access to significant funding for the conduct of activities and exertion of pressures, and greater legitimacy for interlocution with the Government and businesses. (Raquel)

Regulations for participation in profits and results (PLR)

In Brazil, the 1946 Constitution conferred on workers the right to a share in company profits or operating results (*Participação nos lucros e resultados*, PLR). This principle was upheld in the 1988 Constitution as 'participation in the profits or results, not linked to remuneration and, exceptionally, participation in management of the company' (article 7, item XI). However, as with so many other constitutional provisions, further regulation was required to bring PLR into effect. This first took the form of an executive order in 1994 (MP 794/1994), which was reissued each year throughout the 1990s and then enacted as Law 10.101 of 2000. PLR is a tool which aims to provide incentives to increase productivity and improve the distribution of rents. PLR payments are not subject to labour taxation and enjoy privileged income tax rates; there is thus a significant financial incentive for both employers and workers to use PLR as a form of compensation, even though the law stipulates that it must not be used as a substitute for workers' pay. Nevertheless, recognizing the risk that PLR payments could be used to replace wages, the law stipulates that they can only be made every six months. Furthermore, PLR cannot be instituted unilaterally by employers and must be negotiated, either by a bipartite committee chosen by management and workers, or through a collective agreement negotiated at sectoral or firm level.

Data from the MEDIADOR system provide information on the prevalence of PLR in collective agreements as well as its characteristics and scope.[13] Of the 47 728 collective agreements deposited and registered in 2012, 9393 (19.7 per cent) made reference to PLR. Upon closer inspection of a sample of the agreements that make reference to PLR, Zylberstajn and Tavares (2013) found that 66 per cent (13 per cent of all agreements) included provisions for negotiation of PLR payments,[14] and that 89 per cent reflected company-level as opposed to sectoral-level agreements, which is understandable given the emphasis on firm performance. Nevertheless, the authors also found that 47 per cent of agreements that mention PLR do not connect bonuses with specific targets, and that in only 4 per cent of the sample is there pure 'profit-sharing'. In those agreements that do establish targets, the most commonly applied criteria are levels of absenteeism (in 32 per cent) and physical production measures (in 17 per cent); safety or accident prevention is a criterion in 12 per cent of the agreements (Zylberstajn and Tavares, 2013).[15]

As of the second half of the 1990s, with inflation stabilizing, the unions began to see PLR as an alternative for securing increases in workers' remuneration beyond the wage gains achieved, and of gaining access to corporate information. As a result, PLR opened up a space for discussions on working environments and conditions, technology, qualifications and other topics, thereby expanding the scope of the union agenda (DIEESE, 2006; Corrêa and Tadeu Lima, 2006). The importance accorded by participants in the Delphi Panel to the legalization of PLR is reflected in the following statements:

> The introduction of PLR negotiations brought about a dramatic change in relations and in work processes. From the direct labour-relations standpoint this was perhaps the principal change. PLR negotiations became the greatest focus of union negotiations, at least from the standpoint of union members linked to large companies – simply in view of the sums negotiated . . . It is this negotiation that has led to the greatest mobilizations and the largest strikes (except in the case of public service) . . . there has been a perceptible loss of importance of wage-reference dates and an increase in the importance of the moment of negotiating PLR. (Frederico)

> There is no doubt that it has had important effects on labour relations, not only because it deals with the participation of workers in the economic results of companies, but also because it has been an important instrument for intensification of labour and increasing of productivity. (Raquel)

Such is the importance of PLR that in 2012 a major portion of the strikes that occurred in Brazil stemmed from demands for PLR agreements. In the manufacturing sector, PLR was the motive behind 37.5 per cent of work stoppages (DIEESE, 2013). Owing to the more favourable economic environment of the 2000s, strikers during this decade were increasingly making active demands, in contrast to the defensive nature of strikes in the 1990s (da Costa et al., 2013).

Extension of rights to domestic workers

Domestic workers have historically been excluded from labour legislation in Brazil, an exception which has contributed to marginalizing an important segment of the labour force. The Consolidation of Labour Laws (CLT) of 1943 specified in article 7 that the rights did not apply to domestic workers. Similarly, the law of 1949 regulating weekly rest periods excluded domestic workers in its article 5. In 1972, for the first time, Law 5.859 entitled domestic workers to 20 days' paid vacation every year, and made contributions to the social security system by both domestic workers and their employers obligatory. The Constitution of 1988 granted even more rights to domestic workers, though these remained more limited than those accorded to other workers.[16] Notably, domestic workers were still excluded from key rights, principally the limitation on working hours.

It is thus significant that in April 2013, the Brazilian Senate promulgated the passage of a constitutional amendment, known as the 'PEC das domésticas' (EC 72/2013) which rectified the disparity, enshrined in the Constitution, between the full rights accorded to most workers and the more limited set of rights assigned to domestic workers. As a result of this amendment, domestic workers would now benefit from all the rights bestowed on other workers, including the 44-hour maximum working week, a 50 per cent overtime pay bonus for extra hours worked, standards of health, hygiene and safety, and protection against discrimination.[17] In addition, domestic work was prohibited for workers under the age of 18. Because domestic work in Brazil has strong gender and race dimensions, the extension of these rights benefits a segment of society that suffers considerable discrimination in the labour market.

Although these advances were legal, unions played a critical role in achieving these gains. The National Federation of Domestic Workers (FENATRAD), is composed of 26 unions and one association, across 15 Brazilian states. FENATRAD is affiliated with the CUT and has received financial, logistical and political support from them, as FENATRAD does not have access to the union tax. FENATRAD and its affiliate unions do not operate as other Brazilian unions, as there is limited collective bargaining for this occupational category.[18] It is highly difficult to organize domestic workers, as their place of work is individual households, though 4 per cent of domestic workers in the sector report being members of a trade union (IBGE, 2015). Nevertheless, FENATRAD has been instrumental in advocating for legal reforms in national policy debates. It has also been active in the international domestic workers' movement, and participated in the International Labour Conference discussions that led to the ratification of the International Labour Organization's (ILO) Domestic Work Convention, 2011 (No. 189).

4.4   INDUSTRIAL RELATIONS AND THE POLITICAL AND ECONOMIC CONTEXT: THE SWINGING PENDULUM

Notwithstanding the 2017 labour reform, the Brazilian industrial relations system remained relatively intact since it was first instituted in the 1930s under Vargas. Nevertheless, the ability of unions to influence outcomes, whether in collective conventions or agreements, or more generally in terms of national economic and social policies, varied tremendously over the decades depending on the political and economic context.

In the 1990s, despite the return to democracy, Brazilian unions were in the difficult position of rebuilding themselves after the period of military rule, while at the same time facing the challenges of deindustrialization brought about through the opening of the economy. Rampant inflation led the government in 1994 to launch the Real Plan, which tied the newly intro-duced currency, the *real* (BRL), to the dollar, in an attempt to achieve price stability. Coupled with financial liberalization, the outcome was a surge in portfolio investment which caused appreciation of the real exchange rate at the same time that domestic companies were being exposed to foreign competition. Domestic industries suffered from the high interest rates needed to attract capital investment and maintain the value of the exchange rate. From 1993 until the currency devaluation of January 1999, imports grew at an average annual rate of 18 per cent, compared with 3 per cent annual export growth; the share of manufacturing in GDP plum-meted from 27 per cent in 1990 to 17 per cent in 2000. The difficulties that businesses experienced reverberated sharply in the labour market. Between 1992 and 1999, unemployment increased from 6.4 per cent to 9.7 per cent, while informality rose from 53.6 per cent to 56.1 per cent (OIT, 2009).

The real value of the minimum wage had declined steadily during the years of military rule, with adjustments often below the rate of inflation. Upon the implementation of the Real Plan the minimum wage fell sharply, and even though it began to rise again very slightly from the middle of the decade, the increases were too small to affect the overall growth of average wages in the labour market, especially in an environment of rising unemployment. The increases in unemployment and informality, along with falling wages, weakened workers' individual and collective bargaining positions. Unions attempted to fight back by increasing strike activity, but these were principally defensive responses to the restructuring, job losses and falling wages that characterized the decade.

The negative economic environment and the dominance of neoliberal orthodoxy in both national and international policy debates also weakened labour's ability to respond to pressure from business and government for labour law reform. Although deregulation in Brazil did not go so far as in neighbouring Argentina, several laws were passed with the aim of making the labour market more flexible. These included the 1994 Law on Cooperatives, which permitted the creation of co-operatives of workers to deliver services to firms bypassing the employment relationship. Though the law was put forward to help landless peasants, it was increasingly used by employers to avoid their legal obligations towards employees. In 1998 the 'bank of hours' was instituted, a working-time arrangement which extended the reference period beyond the previous weekly limit of 44 hours, making working hours more flexible and lowering business costs by permitting the suppression of overtime payments. The measure, however, was restricted to work contracts that were negotiated collectively. Part-time work contracts were also legalized, permitting employment for up to 25 hours per week with reduced labour rights (Marshall, 2004). A policy to facilitate temporary lay-offs was introduced, by which businesses could temporarily suspend labour contracts for up to one year during which time the workers affected would receive unemployment benefits while participating in a training programme. Also significant was the end, with the 1994 Real Plan, of wage indexation to inflation, signalling a policy shift towards determining wages through collective negotiations. The government also authorized Brazilian states to set regional wage floors for categories of workers whose minimum remuneration was not defined in collective contracts (Silva, 2008); and an executive order of 1994 concerning participation in profits and results (PLR) enabled businesses to give biannual bonus payments to workers free from labour taxation, provided that the payments were the outcome of collective negotiations.

Although many of these measures were aimed at increasing labour market flexibility, several were tempered by the requirement, as in the cases of the bank of hours and PLR payments, that their application be the outcome of collective negotiations, thereby enhancing the role of bipartite negotiations in a hitherto highly corporatist industrial relations system. In addition, in 1993, proof of prior negotiation by the parties became a requirement for bringing collective labour disputes before the labour courts. Social dialogue was also strengthened by the establishment in the 1990s of 'sectoral chambers' (*câmaras setorais*) in a number of manufacturing industries that were hard hit by the opening of the economy. A joint initiative of labour and employers to curtail bankruptcies and job losses, the sectoral chambers gained support from both local and federal government, which offered tax reductions and backing for training programmes and infrastructure projects undertaken in support of these industries (Abramo and Leite, 2002). By the end of 2003, there were 23 such chambers in operation, and no fewer than five important agreements had been reached (in the shipbuilding, toys, cosmetics, tractors and machines and, notably, automobile sectors) (Pichler, 2010).

Another development over the decade that helped to strengthen national social dialogue was the creation of space for the participation of workers in institutional forums, such as the Deliberative Council of the Worker Support Fund (Codefat); the Oversight Council of the Time of Service Guarantee Fund (FGTS); and the National Social Security Council (CNPS) (Silva, 2008). The union centrals gained seats on the Administrative Council of the Brazilian National Development Bank (BNDES) and the Work and Employment Enhancement Committee (CVTE). These measures gave workers more of a voice in policy debates and would prove instrumental, when the political and economic environment shifted in the 2000s.

4.4.1   Lula and the Workers' Party: Labour's Resurgence

The 2000s and early 2010s were a propitious time both economically and politically for Brazilian labour, allowing a number of important gains for workers to be realized both directly, through collective bargaining negotiations, and also indirectly, by influencing policy decisions not only in the areas of social provision and wages but more widely in areas such as industrial and fiscal policy.

Labour's increased influence during this period stemmed from a number of sources. To begin with, the election in 2002 of President Lula of the Workers' Party (Partido dos Trabalhadores, PT) meant that labour's concerns were central to the government's agenda. Second, the expansion of tripartite representation in government institutions during the 1990s provided labour with a seat, and thus enhanced voice, in key policy-making forums. This included the Economic and Social Development Council (Conselho de Desenvolvimento Econômico e Social, CDES; also known as Conselhão), a national, multipartite council created in 2003 and incorporating representatives of government, employers, trade unions and civil society to advise on long-term strategic policies for social and economic development. While the CDES has no legal authority, it contributes to the national policy debate and helped to shape government intervention in a wide range of policy areas during this period, including public investment, tax policy, social policy and education policy. Finally, unions were in a stronger financial position to exercise their new role in national policy debates, as a result of the reform providing financing to the union centrals and because the increasing number of formal jobs resulted in greater union tax revenues.

Perhaps the most critical of all the negotiations in which labour participated concerned the adjustments to the minimum wage. The six participating union centrals mobilized popular support for a minimum wage increase and also participated in the national consultations on setting the criteria for subsequent annual increases. As noted above, the Brazilian minimum wage defines the level of remuneration for formal wage employment in both the private and the public sectors, and also serves as a benefit floor for a number of social security policies. Between 2003 and 2010, the minimum wage had increased by 60 per cent in real terms. Besides benefiting workers at the bottom of the wage pyramid, the Brazilian minimum wage serves as a benchmark for wage-setting in collective bargaining, benefiting workers who earn above the minimum wage. Moreover, many social benefits, including unemployment insurance and disability and old-age pensions, are

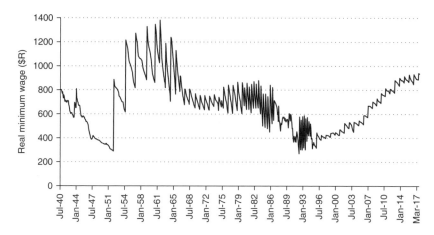

Note: Real minimum wage, $R of March 2017.

Source: IPEADATA.

Figure 4.5   Real value of the Brazilian minimum wage, January 1940–
March 2017

tied to the minimum wage, thus the effect of the increase extended beyond
waged labour and proved to be an important stimulus for the growth of
domestic demand (ILO, 2010; IPEA, 2010). Figure 4.5 shows the fall in the
real value of the minimum wage between 1980 and the mid-1990s, and the
strong recovery that followed through the 2000s and 2010s.

The increase in the minimum wage has been identified in empirical
studies as the most important contributor to the reduction in inequality
in Brazil in the 2000s, with a far greater impact than any of the social programmes, including the Bolsa Família programme (Saboia, 2007; IPEA,
2009). Moreover, as it is directed at workers at the bottom of the wage
distribution, it has done much to lift the earnings of disadvantaged groups.
In 2008, for example, 13.8 per cent of women earned the minimum wage,
compared with only 5.9 per cent of men. For domestic workers – almost
95 per cent of whom are women – the minimum wage was the reference
value for close to half of registered workers (that is, formal workers with a
registered employment contract) and for around 5 per cent of unregistered
workers (Berg, 2011). Within the labour market, the minimum wage
increase helped to compress the wage distribution, for both formal and
informal employees, as can be seen in Figure 4.6, which gives the distribution of earnings in the country during the 2000s.

Another important development was the creation and expansion of

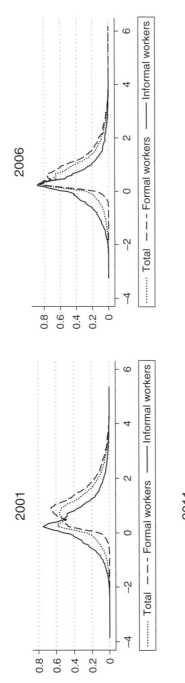

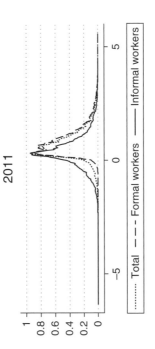

Source: Authors based on PNAD/IBGE.

Figure 4.6 Distribution of labour income, total, informal and formal employees, 2001, 2006 and 2011

a range of social programmes, aimed at reducing poverty as well as inequality, as Brazil has one of the highest levels of income inequality in the world.[19] The government expanded the rural pension programme and the continued benefit provision (BPC), and consolidated and extended the Bolsa Família programme to reach one-quarter of Brazilian families by the end of the decade.[20] The economy also benefited from the Government's launch in 2007 of a comprehensive Growth Acceleration Programme (Programa de Aceleração do Crescimento, PAC), which included a wide range of investments in energy, logistics and social and urban infrastructure, all aimed at ameliorating bottlenecks in production and distribution.

The combination of policies to stimulate domestic demand, coupled with a favourable external environment as a result of a boom in commodity prices, resulted in relatively strong GDP growth, which averaged 4.8 per cent per year between 2003 and 2013, compared with 2.3 per cent between 1995 and 2003. But what distinguishes the period most sharply from others (even from the years 1947–80, when real annual economic growth averaged a remarkable 7.5 per cent), was the inclusiveness of the growth, with growth in household income outpacing growth in GDP.[21] Unemployment fell sharply from over 11 per cent in 2003 to under 5 per cent in 2013. Strong formal job growth, increases in real wages and the expansion of social policies led to the growth of a 'new middle class'. Between 2003 and 2009, 29 million Brazilians joined class C, the statistical middle-income group of the Brazilian population, representing a growth of 34 per cent in this category. In contrast, the two lowest-income classes, classes D and E, shrank by a combined 23 million: a reduction of 29 per cent (Neri, 2010).

The improvement in the labour market, coupled with the minimum wage increases, allowed unions to negotiate more favourable collective bargaining conventions. According to a database on outcomes of collective bargaining negotiations compiled by the Inter-Union Department of Socioeconomic Statistics and Studies (DIEESE), during the second half of the 1990s, only about half of collective bargaining conventions were above the rate of inflation, and average real increases were negative during 1999 and 2001–03. The situation reversed with the favourable economic conditions of the 2000s, with only a minor negative inflection in 2008 owing to the financial crisis (see Figure 4.7). In 2015, however, the negative political and economic situation began to affect collective bargaining outcomes, as the proportion of agreements above the rate of inflation fell from 90 per cent in 2014 to 52 per cent in 2015, with an average real increase of just 0.23 per cent. By 2016, only 19 per cent of collective conventions were above the rate of inflation and 37 per cent were below it, resulting in an average real decrease of 0.52 per cent.

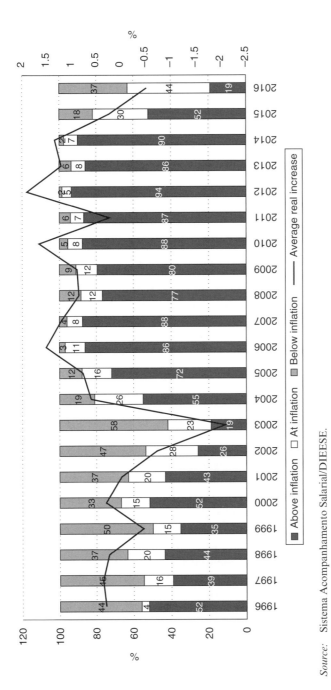

Figure 4.7 Outcomes of collective wage negotiations in Brazil, 1996–2016

4.4.2   The Labour Reform of 2017: Has the Pendulum Broken?

The favourable economic conditions of the early 2010s came to a halt in 2014 as the commodity boom ended and both private and public investment contracted. In 2015, GDP decreased by 3.8 per cent, and by 3.6 per cent in 2016. Unemployment began increasing in early 2015 and by January 2017 it was at 7.5 per cent, compared with 4.5 in January 2014.[22] A political crisis also affected conditions. In 2013, massive protests erupted, originally against an increase in bus transport prices, though later reflecting a general discontent with spending on the FIFA World Cup and the low quality of public services. In 2014, a widespread and ongoing corruption scandal broke out, the 'Lava Jato', that came to include many prominent politicians and business leaders as well as the state-owned oil company, Petrobras. In August 2016, President Dilma Rousseff, Lula's successor, was impeached amid allegations that she shifted funds among government accounts, though most unions regarded it as a *coup d'état*. The corruption scandals continued into 2017, amidst allegations of corruption against Michel Temer of the Partido do Movimento Democrático Brasiliero (PMDB), who assumed the Presidency following the impeachment.

Upon assuming office, the Temer administration signalled its intent to institute wide-ranging reforms, particularly with respect to making the labour code (the CLT), more flexible. There were also important institutional changes. For example, in late 2016, the new government replaced nearly 70 per cent of the members of the CDES, giving greater representation to the business community. The government also replaced the head of the Superior Labour Court, which subsequently shifted its position on some labour matters. For example, in October 2016, the Superior Labour Court suspended its ruling from 2012 (TST 277/2012) on the 'ultrativity' of collective agreements, whereby collective conventions or agreements remain in force until a new collective convention or agreement is negotiated. During a period of economic recession, removing this measure favours employers who would prefer that the more positive collective outcomes of previous periods not remain in force (Corregliano, 2017).

In March 2017, the government was successful – despite widespread protests – in instituting a new law on subcontracting that eased its use. The law gives enterprises wider scope for using temporary and subcontracted workers, lengthens the period for which they can be used, and subsitutes shared liability with subsidiary liability, meaning that workers would only be able to collect debts from the lead firm after exhausting all legal attempts to receive the resources directly from the contracting firm. In addition, the law facilitates the creation of contracting firms, which critics have argued risks increasing disguised employment relationships (DIEESE, 2017).

But the most fundamental change was the passage in July 2017 of Law no. 13.467, which altered 117 articles of the CLT and revoked 21 provisions resulting in a sweeping changes to core pillars of the country's labour law, affecting both individual and collective labour rights. While the full consequences of this reform are yet to be understood, and it is possible that some components will be modified by the legislature or nullified by the courts, the reform drastically alters the industrial relations system that has existed in the country since the 1930s.

Included in the reform is the ability to have enterprise-level agreements between employers and workers prevail over the law, even if the benefits conferred are below what is stipulated in law. Prior to the passage of the reform, the ILO's Committee of Experts on the Application of Conventions and Recommendations (CEACR), published the following observation with respect to the proposal:

> The Committee considers that the introduction of a general possibility of lowering through collective bargaining the protection established for workers in the legislation would have a strong dissuasive effect on the exercise of the right to collective bargaining and could contribute to undermining its legitimacy in the long term. In this respect, the Committee emphasizes that, although isolated legislative provisions concerning specific aspects of working conditions could, in limited circumstances and for specific reasons, provide that they may be set aside through collective bargaining, a provision establishing that provisions of the labour legislation in general may be replaced through collective bargaining would be contrary to the objective of promoting free and voluntary collective bargaining, as set out in the Convention. *The Committee trusts that the scope and the content of Article 4 of the Convention will be fully taken into consideration both during the examination of the Bills referred to above, as well as in the pending judicial proceedings. The Committee requests the Government to provide information on any development in this respect. In this regard, the Committee recalls that the general objection of Conventions No 98, 151 and 154 is to promote collective bargaining.*[23] (Emphasis in the original)

Besides this controversial provision, the labour reform includes other measures that directly affect unions, such as the abolition of the union tax and the introduction of enterprise-level representation at firms with more than 200 employees of three elected workers' representatives who need not be members of a union, but who would participate in collective bargaining negotiations with employers. While the possibility of having firm-level workers' representatives, even if limited to large firms, could have been an advance for addressing some of the disconnect between unions and the rank and file that was a shortcoming of the current system of industrial relations, there is a danger that in circumstances where there are trade union representatives present, these elected representatives will undermine the position and role of unions. This characteristic coupled with the ability for firm-level collective agreements to have precedence over either collective conventions or legislation, risks displacing the role that the current industrial relations system plays in providing labour protection to workers. Moreover, these changes are taking place at the same time as individual labour protections are being rolled back, and their main source of financing, the union tax, is being repealed.

With respect to individual labour rights, the reform introduces on-call (or zero-hour) work contracts (*trabalho intermitente*), whereby a worker could be called in to work with three days' notice but has no guarantee of working hours; it also extends the working day up to 12 hours; and introduces a new category of worker – *trabalhador autônomo* – who can work exclusively for an enterprise, but as a contractor as opposed to an employee; it requires workers who bring cases to the labour courts to be present at hearings and to pay fees if their case is found to be without merit; as well as a series of other reforms. In addition, a reform to the pension system has also been carried out.

Similar to the 1990s, the main unions have adopted a defensive stance, staging a series of national protests against its implementation. The association of labour court magistrates (ANAMATRA) has also voiced its opposition to the new law, stating its incompatibility with international labour standards. Some aspects of the new law may need to be clarified when it comes to their implementation, such as the new category of autonomous worker. What is clear, however, is that distinct from the past where policy changes and labour advances were the reflection of the swings in the political and economic pendulum, the new labour law is far-reaching, and will likely transform the system of industrial relations in Brazil.

4.5   CONCLUSION

Until the reforms of 2017, the corporatist structure of Brazilian unionism had changed little, yet the scope that unions had to operate and the gains delivered to Brazilian workers varied, depending on the political and economic context. The political pendulum swings affected not only union autonomy, activity and influence, but labour laws, minimum wage rates, social policies and the decisions of the labour courts. The pendulum swings also had an important bearing on fiscal and industrial policies that ultimately affected workers.

During the 2000s, as the pendulum shifted with the election of a pro-labour government, Brazilian unionism was able to benefit from its legally institutionalized space as well as step into new policy spaces, to negotiate policies to the benefit of workers. The minimum wage gains have arguably been the most important for workers given their effect on overall wage setting and social benefits, but the union movement also played an important role in influencing the direction of other labour and social policies, as well as putting forth policies to promote inclusive growth. These gains, which resulted in falling unemployment, rising incomes and reduced inequality, in turn helped to further strengthen trade unions' voice and demands.

As a result, collective bargaining outcomes were positive for workers during the decade and trade union demands shifted from the defensive position of the 1990s, where trade unions had managed to thwart many of the efforts to loosen labour protections, to prospective bargaining in the 2000s. Trade unions with higher affiliation rates and a stronger base, and which were actively engaged in direct negotiations with employers, were more effective in delivering gains for their workers. Nevertheless, there are still many trade unions in Brazil that have little or no contact with the workers that they represent and thus are not in a position to provide guidance to workers in their day-to-day work life. As a result, there is still a high dependency on the corporatist structure, as witnessed by the large number of grievances that are filed with the labour courts each year. An important challenge thus remains of strengthening the ties between the trade union leadership and their members on the shopfloor.

In the mid-2010s, the pendulum shifted once again, shrinking labour's space in national debates and weakening their position at the bargaining table. The 2017 reforms, if fully instituted, are likely to result in discontinuous and transformative changes in the industrial relations system that has been a fixture of Brazilian labour relations since the 1930s. While it is still too early to tell what the outcomes of the new labour law will be, unions have adopted a defensive stance and are fighting to hold on to the gains of the earlier period, as well as to maintain the support for collective labour relations. Whether this period is just another swing in the pendulum, or its break, remains to be seen.

NOTES

*   The views expressed in this chapter are my own and do not necessarily represent those of the ILO. I would like to thank José Ribeiro and Adalberto Cardoso for helpful feedback.
1.   In Brazil, employers' organizations are referred to as employers' unions.
2.   Vargas entered power as head of the 'provisional government'. In 1934, he was elected President of the Republic by the constituent assembly. Vargas continued to hold the presidency, but as president-dictator of the Estado Novo (New State), until 1945, when the country had a brief return to democracy.
3.   It is so called because all of the training and service institutes begin with the word 'Serviço' or Service. The five training organizations are SENAI, SENAC, SEBRAE, SENAR and SENAT.

4. For example, in 1965 the militant leadership of the Metalworkers Union of São Paulo (SMSP) was removed; a new leader with ties to the Ministry of Labour and the military Government, Joaquim dos Santos Andrade, became President of the union in an election in which he ran unopposed. He remained in office for the next 22 years (Anner, 2011).
5. Of the 34 rights given to workers, only nine were applicable to domestic workers. Nevertheless, the Constitution did entitle domestic workers to a series of rights that they previously did not have. These included the right to the minimum wage, the '13th month' salary, weekly rest, 30 days paid vacation, maternity leave (16 weeks), advance notice of one month upon dismissal, and retirement pension. Moreover, it gave domestic workers the right to organize (Berg, 2011).
6. Undertaken in cooperation with the ILO and the Ministry of Labour and Employment.
7. However, the existence of these committees differs widely and is particularly low among rural unions. According to the latest union census (from 2001), only 14 per cent of the 6858 urban workers' unions in existence had a union committee within the firm. The existence of a CIPA was much greater – at 46 per cent – but still less than half of urban workers' unions had one. Among the 3911 rural workers' unions in existence in 2001, only 7.6 per cent had a CIPA and just 1.5 per cent had an in-house union committee (DIEESE, 2011).
8. A Delphi Panel is a qualitative research tool that involves questioning a panel of experts with a view to establishing, as objectively as possible, a consensus on a particular issue or problem. It is typically applied in two or more rounds, depending upon the nature of the investigation. In the first round, initial spontaneous responses of each member of the group are collected. For this first round, the following question was asked: 'Please state three principal changes that in your opinion were the most important or had the most significant impact on labour relations in Brazil in the 2000s'. The answers to this question were then shared anonymously with all members of the group, who were then given the opportunity to reassess their own responses, with a view to bringing the various individual responses closer together. It is a participative exercise, with a focus on feedback of information from other members of the group and the possibility of reassessing responses in the light of the additional information so received.
9. The authors acknowledge with thanks the input of the participating experts: Ademir Figueiredo, Carlindo Rodrigues de Oliveira, Carlos Henrique Horn, Cássio da Silva Calvete, Clemente Ganz Lúcio, Frederico Melo, Lilian Arruda Marques, Nelson de Chueri Karam, Raquel Paese and Regina Camargos.
10. For year t, minimum wage increase$_t$ = inflation$_{t-1}$ + GDP growth$_{t-2}$.
11. In 2016, the law came up for renewal and the agreement was extended until 2019.
12. The regulations dictate: (a) affiliation of not less than 100 unions, distributed throughout the five regions of Brazil; (b) affiliation in not less than three regions of the country, with no less than 20 unions in each; (c) affiliation of unions in no less than five sectors of economic activity; and (d) affiliation of unions that represent no less than 7 per cent of the total of unionized employees at the national level (Law 11.648/2008, Article 2, Paragraphs I, II, III and IV).
13. The MEDIADOR system was set up within the Ministry of Labour and Employment in the mid-2000s as a computerized registry of collective bargaining agreements, replacing the old system of physically registering such agreements with the Ministry. Registration of collective bargaining agreements in MEDIADOR has been obligatory since 2007, so that it now constitutes a census of such agreements in Brazil.
14. The other collective agreements contain recommendations for adopting a programme or for specifying principles to follow should the company establish a programme. The authors' analysis is based on a 5 per cent random sample of the agreements that refer to PLR, amounting to 470 cases (Zylberstajn and Tavares, 2013).
15. Some agreements set multiple criteria.
16. For details, see note 5 above.
17. Part of the rights were obtained immediately, whereas others were brought into effect two years later, through the promulgation of Enabling Law (*Lei Complementar*) 150,

of 2015. The passage of this constitutional amendment and the enabling law have put Brazil in a position to ratify the ILO's Domestic Workers Convention, 2011 (No. 189).

18. In 2017, collective agreements were signed covering domestic workers and their employers in Greater São Paulo and the interior of São Paulo State. For more information, see http://www.domesticalegal.com.br/utilidades/sindicatos-do-emprego-domestico/.
19. Poverty is defined here as per capita income below PPP US$1.25 a day. In 1999, 14 per cent of the Brazilian population was below this threshold.
20. Between 2003 and 2010, the number of families benefiting from Bolsa Família more than tripled from 3.6 million to 12.8 million. The BPC doubled during the same period: from 1.7 to 3.4 million beneficiaries (disabled persons and elderly poor).
21. Between 2003 and 2009, real GDP grew on average by 2.9% a year, real household income by 4.7%.
22. Based on data covering the 6 metropolitan areas of Brazil (PME/IBGE). According to the national data, unemployment jumped from 7.2 per cent in the first trimester of 2014 to 13.7 per cent in the first trimester of 2017. Due to a change in methodology of the PNAD, the national data from the early 2000s is not comparable with present figures.
23. Observation (CEACR) – adopted 2016, published 106th ILC session (2017). Available at http://www.ilo.org/dyn/normlex/en/f?p=1000:13100:0::NO:13100:P13100_COMMENT_ID:3300844.

REFERENCES

Abramo, L. and Leite, M. 2002. 'Novas institucionalidades e novas formas de regulação no Mundo do Trabalho', *Pro-posições*, **13**(1), pp. 60–77.

Anner, M. 2011. *Solidarity Transformed: Labor Responses to Globalization and Crisis in Latin America*. Ithaca, NY: Cornell University Press.

Berg, J. 2011. 'Laws or luck: Understanding rising formality in Brazil in the 2000s', in Lee, S. and McCann, D. (eds), *Regulating for Decent Work: New Directions in Labour Market Regulation*. Basingstoke, UK and Geneva: Palgrave Macmillan and ILO.

Cardoso, A. forthcoming. 'Collective bargaining and extension in Brazil', in Hayter, S. and Visser, J. (eds), *Inclusive Labour Protection: The Application and Extension of Collective Agreements*. Geneva: ILO.

Cook, M.L. and Bazler, J. 2013. 'Bringing unions back in: Labour and left governments in Latin America', Working Paper 166, Cornell University School of Industrial and Labor Relations.

Corrêa, D. and Tadeu Lima, G. 2006. 'Participação dos trabalhadores nos lucros e resultados das empresas: Lições da experiência internacional', *Revista Econômia Contemporanea*, **10**(2), pp. 357–88.

Corrêa, L.R. 2008. 'A "greve dos 700 mil": Negociações e conflitos na justiça do trabalho – São Paulo, 1963', *História Social*, **14/15**, 219–36.

Corregliano, Danilo U. 2017. 'Por que agora? Sobre a suspensão da súmula N°277 do TST', *Negociado X Legislado I – Reforma Trabalhista*, pp. 69–72.

da Costa, L., Bellan, A., Linhares, R. and Pagani, V. 2013. 'O movimento recente das greves', *Le monde diplomatique Brasil*, 2 July. http://www.diplomatique.org.br/artigo.php?id=1453 (accessed 2 September 2013).

DIEESE. 2006. 'Participação dos trabalhadores nos lucros e resultados das empresas – 2005'. Estudos e Pesquisas Ano 3, Número 22, Agosto. São Paulo: DIEESE.

DIEESE. 2011. *Anuário dos Trabalhadores, 2010–2011*. São Paulo: DIEESE.

DIEESE. 2013. 'Balanço das Greves em 2012', *Estudios e Pesquisas*, no. 66, Maio. São Paulo: DIEESE.

DIEESE. 2017. 'Impactos da Lei 13.429/2017 (antigo PL 4.302/1998) para os trabalhadores: Contrato de trabalho temporário e terceirização', *Nota Técnica*, no. 175, Abril. São Paulo: DIEESE.

French, J. 2004. *Drowning in Laws: Labor Law and Brazilian Political Culture*. Raleigh, NC: University of North Carolina Press.

Hayter, S. 2015. 'Unions and collective bargaining', in Berg, J. (ed.), *Labour Markets, Institutions and Inequality: Building Social Justice in the 21st Century*. Cheltenham, UK and Northampton, MA, USA and Geneva: Edward Elgar Publishing and ILO.

IBGE. 2015. *PNAD 2015: Aspectos das relações de trabalho e sindicalização*. Rio de Janeiro: IBGE.

ILO. 2010. *Brazil: An Income-Led Growth Strategy*. Geneva: ILO/International Institute of Labour Studies.

ILO. 2013. *Decent Work Country Profile: A Subnational Perspective in Brazil*. Brasilia: ILO Country Office for Brazil.

IPEA. 2009. 'PNAD 2008: Primeiras Análises', Comunicado da Presidência num. 30, 24 de setembro.

IPEA. 2010. 'Efeitos Econômicos do Gasto Social no Brasil', *Perspectivas da Política Social no Brasil*, Livro 8 do Projeto Perspectivas do Desenvolvimento Brasileiro. Brasília.

Lang, K. and Gagnon, M.-J. 2009. 'Brazilian trade unions: In (in)voluntary confinement of the corporatist past', *Relations industrielles/Industrial Relations*, **64**(2), pp. 250–69.

Marshall, A. 2004. 'Labour market policies and regulations in Argentina, Brazil and Mexico: programmes and impacts', Employment Strategy Paper 2004/13.

Neri, M. (ed.). 2010. *A Nova Classe Média: O lado brilhante dos pobres*. Rio de Janeiro: Fundação Getúlio Vargas.

OIT. 2009. *O Perfil do Trabalho Decente no Brasil*. Brasília: OIT.

Pichler, W. 2005. 'Changing industrial relations in Brazil: Developments in collective bargaining in Rio Grande do Sul, 1978–1991', PhD thesis, London School of Economics and Political Science.

Pichler, W. 2010. 'Mudanças nas relações de trabalho: sindicalismo, greves e negociações coletivas entre 1980 e 2008', in Conceição, O.A.C., Grando, M.Z., Teruchkin, S.U. and Faria, L.A.E. (eds), *Três décadas de economia gaúcha. Volume 3: A evolução social*. Porto Alegre: FEE. http://www.fee.tche.br/3-decadas/down loads/volume3/6/walter-pichler.pdf (accessed 8 July 2013).

Saboia, J. 2007. 'Salário minimo e distribução da renda no Brasil no periodo 1995–2005: Fatos e simulações', estudo presentado no 2º seminário de Análisis da PNAD, CGEE/IPEA/MEC/MTE, Brasília, março.

Silva, S. 2008. *Relações Coletivas de Trabalho: configurações institucionais no Brasil contemporâneo*. São Paulo: LTr.

Zylberstajn, H. 2006. 'General developments in industrial relations in Brazil', paper presented at the ILERA World Congress, Lima, Peru, September.

Zylberstajn, H. and Tavares, P. 2013. 'Collective bargaining, wages and productivity in Brazil', paper prepared for the ILO project on Collective Bargaining, Wages and Productivity, December.

5. Industrial relations and inclusive development in China: Connecting institutions and voice

Chang-Hee Lee

5.1 INTRODUCTION: CONNECTING INSTITUTIONS TO VOICE

After three decades of deregulation and decollectivization, China seems to have changed course. Since the early years of the twenty-first century, the state agents of China's industrial relations system have built up formal labour market institutions. Union membership and the coverage of collective contracts have increased. This quantitative expansion of formal institutions coincided with a surge in workers' collective actions, echoing similar developments in Brazil, the Republic of Korea and South Africa since the late 1980s (Silver, 2003; Koo, 2001). Although no official statistics on strikes in China are available, there is a strong indication of a rising wave of collective action, including strikes and demonstrations, by the new generation of the Chinese working class (Elfstrom and Kuruvilla, 2014).

Some observers, following Wright (2000), note that the structural power of China's working class has increased in recent years, in both the labour market and workplace, as a result of a new labour dynamism. The associational power of workers, however, is constrained by the monopoly on representation held by the All China Federation of Trade Unions (ACFTU) (C. Chan, 2009). In a similar vein, it is claimed that the 'appropriated representation' of workers by the ACFTU has caused a 'rupture' between the 'insurgent moment' of the new working class and the 'institutional moment' created by a new orientation in labour market policies. This 'rupture' is one of the key reasons why formal industrial relations institutions are failing to facilitate the 'decommodification' of labour, despite the surge of collective action by workers and institution building by state agents (Friedman, 2011).

This chapter presents an overview of the evolution of labour market institutions in China and sheds light on the evolving relationship between those institutions and the workers' voice. This relationship is one of the most important subjects of comparative industrial relations research, with clear policy implications. The associational and structural power of the working class, manifested through collective bargaining, is one of the key factors shaping income distributions and determining the inclusiveness of economic growth (Hayter, 2011). In the Chinese context, it will affect whether and how the country can achieve its declared objective of rebalancing. Given China's vast potential domestic market – an asset not enjoyed by smaller developing and emerging economies – the bargaining power of Chinese workers, and its institutional accommodation by the state, could be a crucial factor in boosting domestic consumption.

China's transition process can be broadly divided into two periods. The first, between 1978 and 2007, was characterized by the dominance of deregulation and liberalization. This included efforts to build basic labour market institutions, as the old employment and labour relations of the centrally planned economy were dismantled and replaced with individualized employment relations. The second period began in 2008, when China started to make efforts to rebalance its economy and reregulate work. This has been accompanied by a rise in spontaneous collective action by workers. The result has been a process of transformation of labour relations in both the workplace and the broader national context.

The next section of the chapter examines the first period (1978–2007), focusing on the transformation of employment relations and the evolution of new labour market institutions. During this is the period, labour markets (as we know them in market economies) were created in China, beginning in the 1990s with a conscious process of deregulation and restructuring of the old socialist employment system. Section 5.3 moves on to examine recent changes in industrial relations during the second period (2008 to present), characterized by the Government's efforts to rebalance the economy and reregulate work in the face of a global economic crisis, labour shortages and workers' collective actions. Section 5.4 takes a closer look at the transformation of workplace labour relations in two contrasting contexts: the Pearl River Delta and the Yangtze River Delta.

Since the global economic crisis in 2008, the industrial relations policy of the Chinese state, particularly in respect of its wage policies, has been part of the Government's wider efforts to move the economy on to a growth path driven more by domestic consumption. This poses an important question: can China's industrial relations system play a similar role in bringing about a more inclusive and balanced growth model to that played by its counterparts in the developed economies after the Second World War, more than half a century ago? Section 5.5 of this chapter draws on the findings of several quantitative studies examining the effects on labour market performance of new industrial relations practices in areas such as labour law compliance, formalization of employment relations and wage fixing. Finally, the concluding section 5.6 discusses the implications of key findings of the analysis presented here, and raises a number of questions for future research.

5.2 THREE DECADES OF TRANSFORMATION: EMPLOYMENT AND LABOUR RELATIONS IN CHINA, 1978–2007

From the late 1970s onwards China's economy and society made a dual transition – from a traditional agricultural society to a modern industrial society, and from a centrally planned economy to a 'market economy' (Norton, 2006). Before that point, Chinese society had been walled into two completely separate economic and social spaces, the urban and the rural, and the movement of people between the two was severely restricted. With the dual transition, this changed. The proportion of people employed in the primary (agricultural and fisheries) sector declined from 70.5 per cent of the total in 1978 to 34.5 per cent in 2011, while the employment share of the state-owned enterprises (SOEs) was slashed from 60.5 per cent to 19.4 per cent between 1998 and 2010 (World Bank and DRC, 2012, p. 104). The urban employment relations regime underwent institutional change, and rural migrant workers were allowed to move into urban labour markets, albeit with little protection. This movement of rural workers constituted, indeed, one of the links between the two aspects of the dual transition.

5.2.1 Demolishing the Socialist Employment System and Deregulating Labour Markets, 1978–2000

The Chinese road to a market economy
The 14th National Congress of the Chinese Communist Party (CCP) in 1992 is often seen as a decisive moment in China's move towards economic liberalization and dismantling of the socialist employment regime. The 14th Congress, which coined the slogan of 'socialist market economy with Chinese characteristics' – with the emphasis on 'market' – accelerated deregulation and economic liberalization, which had been progressing cautiously through the 1980s.

In the early 1980s, a limited number of localities were able to liberalize their trade and investment policies and try out new employment relations practices in the 'insulated laboratory' of these special economic zones

(SEZs) (Gallagher, 2004, p. 17). This 'segmented deregulation' created competition among local governments seeking to attract investment, further accelerating the trend towards deregulation. The 1980s also saw liberalization of ownership on similar lines, with permission given to enter into joint ventures with foreign firms and the promotion of township village enterprises (TVEs) that enjoyed greater managerial autonomy. At this stage, foreign enterprises played a key role in transferring new labour practices to China, albeit initially only in the SEZs. This in turn prompted the SOEs, facing increased competition from the TVEs and joint venture enterprises, to demand managerial autonomy. Alongside these developments, China began its cautious introduction of an individual labour contract system on a pilot basis in 1986. However, it was only in the late 1990s that such a contract system systematically replaced the 'iron rice bowl' system of lifelong employment in the SOE sector.

It was in this context of increasing managerial autonomy and a nascent individual contract system in the SOEs that the workers' congress system was established.[1] Envisaged as a mechanism for balancing the exercise of managerial power and as a supreme organ for 'democratic management' by all members of the enterprise, the congress was given extensive powers, at least in theory, including the supervision and monitoring of management and even the dismissal of managers it deemed incompetent or unsuitable. Having witnessed the rise of the Solidarity union in Poland, China began to explore internal reform and reorientation of the ACFTU. At its 11th National Congress in 1988, the ACFTU adopted 'tentative plans for trade union reform', which redefined unions' primary role as protecting workers' interests, and proposed direct election of union leadership by the grass-roots membership and the restructuring of unions from the bottom up (Taylor et al., 2003). As such, the 1980s were a period of experimentation which left open many possibilities for political and social reform.

However, the suppression of the Tiananmen Square demonstration in the summer of 1989 closed off a path for negotiation and consultation among various social, economic and political actors that might have shaped the course of transformation (as had happened in the Czech Republic and Hungary, Stark and Bruszt, 1998). The trade union reform agenda was shelved. It was in this context that in 1992 the 14th National Congress of the CCP made a decisive move towards liberalization (Friedman and Lee, 2010).

Replacing the socialist employment regime with contract-based employment relations
In the wake of the 15th CCP National Congress decision on SOE restructuring in 1997, various changes in enterprise ownership were made,

including privatization and the incorporation of private capital. SOE restructuring is believed to have significantly weakened the power of traditional organs such as workers' congresses, enterprise unions and the party organization itself, while greatly enhancing managerial authority. In the process, 38 million workers were laid off. Within the restructured SOEs, the employment system based on the *danwei*[2] was dismantled and replaced by the individual contract system, while workers' entitlements to welfare benefits, including pensions, housing and medical insurance, were radically reduced. Veteran workers of the SOEs were replaced with young, short-term contract workers, leading to a dramatic drop in the seniority of production workers, and the casualization and flexibilization of the workforce. According to a report to the National People's Congress in 2007, only around 50 per cent of enterprises signed contracts with their employees, and 60–70 per cent of those were short-term contracts for under one year (Friedman and Lee, 2010, p. 509). Short-term and insecure contracts became widespread, regardless of the ownership structure of companies (Gallagher, 2004). In 1992, moreover, the CCP had adopted a new wage policy formula which stated that: (1) wage growth should not be higher than productivity growth; and (2) enterprises would have autonomy in fixing wages, albeit under government supervision; effectively giving a free hand to employers in setting wage levels.

The predicament of the hundreds of millions of migrant workers entering urban labour markets was even worse. They were particularly vulnerable to exploitation and discrimination as their rural *hukou*[3] status in effect excluded them from legal protection and social entitlement. Most of them did not have written labour contracts, and non-payment of wages was widespread.

At the same time, it is important to note that the 1990s were also the period in which basic elements of modern labour market institutions were put in place. One of the most important developments in this period was the adoption and implementation of the 1994 labour law. Before this, China's employment relations were regulated by a series of government directives, without a national labour law (Lee, 2009). The 1994 legislation laid down the basic legal framework of employment and labour relations in a new market economy. It also introduced the legal notion of a collective contract (agreement), laying the legal foundation for the ACFTU's bureaucratic push for collective contracts in the early 2000s. During this period, labour dispute and arbitration mechanisms were set up throughout the country, down to district level, while a decentralized minimum wage fixing system was also established.

Through the 1990s, however, the laws, regulations and institutions remained largely ineffective; and for the large numbers of excluded rural migrant workers, largely irrelevant. Violation of the regulations was widespread and widely ignored by local governments, which placed exclusive priority on economic development through attracting investment.

5.2.2   Workplace Labour Relations in the 1990s

The ACFTU was not prepared to deal with the challenges of the new market-based employment relations. With the restructuring of the SOEs and its own governance, some scholars observed that the trade unions at enterprise level lost whatever authority they had had as one element of the 'old three organs' of enterprise governance; namely, party organization, workers' congress and trade unions. Three new organs – shareholders' meetings, the board of directors and board of supervisors – dominated enterprise governance, leaving no effective role for the trade union (Chang, 2005). With the party and management driving the restructuring process, the enterprise union, as a subordinate organization, had to serve the interests of the management. This left workers with no effective voice. There were some isolated cases of SOEs where management and workers maintained, with some modifications, the corporate welfare model (Chan and Unger, 2009; Unger and Chan, 1995), and some SOE workers successfully resisted unilateral SOE restructuring by appealing to the socialist tradition and by effectively using the formal powers given to the workers' congress (Tong, 2005); but these were exceptions to the general rule.

In most enterprises within the burgeoning non-state sector, enterprise unions simply did not exist. ACFTU statistics show that only 0.45 per cent of domestic private enterprises had unions in 1996 (Lee et al., 2014). Even those that did exist were nominal bodies (so-called 'paper' unions) or company unions. Their leaders were more often than not hand-picked by the management, composed mostly of senior and middle management. Rank-and-file workers had virtually no role in the establishment or the operation of these unions (Qiao, 2010). The enterprise union typically functioned as a part and an instrument of the human resources department of the enterprise. They were neither constituted, nor did they function, as an independent association of workers. Indeed, many workers were unaware of the existence of enterprise unions in their workplaces, and of their membership in such unions. Enterprise union leaders acted, at best, as intermediaries between employers and workers (Gallagher, 2004); at worst, they sided with the management when conflicts arose between employers and workers. In some workplaces, trade unions promoted the management agenda of enhancing efficiency by widening wage gaps between different categories of workers (Tong, 2005). In a rare case where enterprise union leaders spoke on behalf of workers, they were the subject of unfair labour practices (Chen, 2007; Friedman, 2011).

The ineffectiveness of enterprise unions contributed to a workplace regime where despotic management could impose disciplinary measures at will, and had complete freedom to hire and fire (Liu, 2009; Zhang, 2008; Metcalf and Li, 2006). Workplace labour relations were thus characterized by uncontested 'flexibility, insecurity and managerial control' (Gallagher, 2004, p. 11; see also Liu, 2009) under a typically Taylorist work organization (Luthje, 2004). The term 'disorganized despotism' (Lee, 1999) succinctly captures the nature of the labour relations regime at the turn of the century, a radical departure from the 'organized dependency' of the socialist employment regime based on the *danwei*.

Towards the end of the 1990s, with SOE restructuring reaching its peak and migrant workers being exposed to the full force of managerial despotism, workers began to take collective action in protest. SOE workers in China's 'rustbelt' protested 'out of desperation' over the reneging by government of its commitment to provide goods for collective consumption, while migrant workers in the 'sunbelt' protested against discrimination over wages and working conditions in newly emerging non-state sectors (Lee, 2007, p. 9). Many of these protests were final acts of dejection 'at the point of collective exit from the factory', by migrant workers who had endured sweatshop conditions in the private sector or SOE workers who had been laid off (Lee, 2007, p. 175). It was in this context of rising labour disputes that the party-state decided to make adjustments to its labour policies in the early 2000s.

5.2.3 Top-Down 'Cloning' of Basic Labour Market Institutions in the Early 2000s

In the early 2000s, Chinese policy-makers attempted to stabilize labour relations in response to the crisis arising from the radical restructuring and deregulation of labour markets. Under the banner of 'building harmonious labour relations', some policy adjustments were made (for example, the reorientation of trade unions' roles, and improvement of minimum wage regulation), and new institutions were established (for example, tripartite consultation mechanisms). Trade union membership and coverage by collective contracts began to increase, accompanied by experimentation with new labour relations practices in some locations.

Revision of trade union law: a reorientation of unions' roles and new forms of unions

The revised trade union law of 2001, while not significantly altering the representative foundations of the unions, represented a reorientation of their basic duties and functions by putting the emphasis on 'safeguarding the legitimate rights and interests of workers' ahead of protecting the 'overall interests of the entire Chinese people' (Lee, 2009). The new law also paved the way for new types of trade union organizations, which could be established across a group of enterprises rather than in just a single company. These changes prepared the ground for the new approach the ACFTU unions were to take up, and for multi-employer bargaining. It also opened a way for ACFTU unions to 'cover', though perhaps not represent, workers in small and medium-sized enterprises, and the informal economy, by setting up general unions with geographical coverage. The successful organization of domestic workers in a number of localities was made possible due to the new forms of trade unions (Hu, 2013).

Enhanced leverage for trade unions and expansion of formal industrial relations institutions

As concern grew over social instability, the Communist Party elevated the political status of local trade union cadres, seeing trade unions as a key pillar of 'social management'. Between the 1990s and the middle of the following decade there was an increase in the numbers of local trade union leaders appointed to senior positions in local legislative bodies and political structures, giving the local unions political leverage with which to promote their agendas (Chen, 2009).

In addition to the political promotion of trade union cadres, local unions gained administrative leverage through a tripartite consultation mechanism introduced in the revised trade union law. Following the establishment of this system in 2001, tripartite structures were cloned in a top-down manner throughout the country, including at the provincial, municipal and district levels, reaching a total number of 26 067 by 2013. The newly created tripartite bodies were not effective in dealing with substantive issues such as wages and working conditions (Qiao, 2011). However, with the support of local governments trade unions were able to use them to promote the spread of new labour relations practices, such as collective contracts (Lee, 2009).

One distinctive feature of developments in Chinese industrial relations in the early 2000s is the quantitative expansion of trade union membership and collective contracts. Of course, there are serious questions about the accuracy and reliability of the official statistics, as well as about what trade union memberships and collective contracts actually mean in the Chinese context. Nevertheless, the figures are indicative of a pre-emptive corporatist strategy on the part of the party-state and the ACFTU, aimed at pacifying and facilitating 'harmonious labour relations' (Lee, 2006). Trade union membership, having fallen to its lowest point of 89 million at the height of SOE restructuring in 1998, rose to 299 million in 2013; and the number of workers covered by collective contracts, which was virtually nil in 1995, reached 267.2 million in 2012. Again, this took place through a process of 'institutional cloning' in a top-down manner, made possible by the enhanced political and institutional leverage of trade unions at all levels.

Local experiments with new practices

In the early 2000s, experiments with industrial relations paved the way for institutional innovations in the late 2000s. New forms of unions, known as union associations or associated unions, were created beyond the confines of individual workplaces and enterprises, at the regional and sectoral level (Liu, 2008; Lee et al., 2014). The formation of these new union associations enabled experiments with regional and sectoral bargaining, which emerged for the first time in Zhejiang province in 2003 (Xu, 2012; Wen, 2011). Some of these experiments were then translated into local regulations. For example in the Jiangsu and Zhejiang provinces, a regulatory foundation was created which allowed for the scaling up these new practices at a later stage. At the same time, local labour non-governmental organizations (NGOs) were set up and corporate social responsibility (CSR) campaigns began to spread. While most of the CSR campaigns were largely cosmetic, offering little more than individual legal assistance, a few did contribute to innovations in labour relations. For example, the direct election of enterprise union leaders was pioneered in one of Reebok's subcontractors with the support of a CSR campaign in 2002 (A. Chan, 2009).

Casualization of employment and rising conflicts

There is no evidence that this quantitative expansion in trade union membership and collective contracts was accompanied by meaningful changes in labour relations at the workplace. Up to the mid-2000s, experimentation was confined to a few localities, and most enterprise unions remained paper unions or company unions. As for the campaign for collective contracts, most enterprise union leaders simply signed off on the template handed out by the upper union or company management. In many cases, these merely replicated the legal minimum conditions, with at best minor modification of fringe benefits (Taylor et al., 2003). The formalistic nature of the collective consultation is well documented (Clarke et al., 2004; Metcalf and Li, 2006).

Through the early part of the 2000s, the informalization and casualization of employment continued to increase. One survey found that 'the share of local resident and migrant workers with a labour contract actually fell from 2001 to 2005, declining from 67 per cent to 65 per cent for local resident workers and from 15 per cent to 12 per cent for migrant workers'

(Gallagher et al., 2013, p. 12). It is also believed that real wage growth for workers – particularly those with low skills – lagged behind productivity growth. The wage share of GDP declined from 52 per cent in 1999 to 40 per cent in 2007 (Lee, 2009, p. 2), while China's Gini coefficient[4] reached its peak in the late 2000s.

At the same time, a tightening of labour markets changed the context for collective action. Starting in 2003, labour shortages began to plague the industrialized provinces of China's coastal areas, and soon spread across the whole country. Large-scale wildcat strikes in the Dalian SEZs in 2005 were a harbinger of the collective activism of the new generation of China's working class. The ACFTU's successful 2006 campaign to organize Wal-Mart workers in a bottom-up manner showed that the Federation was also adopting a new approach to industrial relations challenges (Chan, 2007).

5.3 REBALANCING AND REREGULATING: THE CHALLENGES OF LABOUR RELATIONS SINCE 2008

5.3.1 Aligning Economic Policy and Labour Policy: Rebalancing and Reregulation

In 2008, China celebrated the thirtieth anniversary of its economic reforms, just as the global economic and financial crisis was unfolding. These crisis conditions and awareness of the need to embark on a new phase of development prompted the Chinese Government to shift economic and social policy in new directions. With a decline in demand for China's exports, it became obvious that an export-led growth model could not be sustained. The Prime Minister had famously anticipated this realization in 2006, stating that China's current development model was 'unstable, unbalanced, uncoordinated and ultimately unsustainable'. To rebalance the economy, China began to place priorities on redistributive policies, expanding basic health insurance and pension schemes in both urban and rural areas. The number of people covered by basic pension schemes increased from 102 million in 2010 to 504 million in 2015, while the number of people covered by basic health insurance schemes moved from 195 million to 377 million during the same period.

The transition in the Chinese labour market from surplus to shortage marked a moment known as the 'Lewis turning point' (LTP). By the end of the decade, labour shortages that emerged in the Pearl River Delta in 2003 were widely experienced across China. The ratio of vacancies to jobseekers, which had remained below 0.7 up to 2002, reached 0.9 in 2003 and reached near parity by 2005 (Cai, 2012). At the same time, high levels of employee turnover became a major challenge for employers (Cooke, 2012).

Since 2004, the real wages of migrant workers have risen faster than those of local resident workers. With a tight labour market even for unskilled migrant workers, workers were able to exercise both 'exit' and 'voice'. This manifested in high turnover and growing numbers of collective actions.

The 12th Five-Year Plan (2011–15), drafted in the midst of the global economic crisis, set out to rebalance the economy. The potential economic role of the new labour market institutions began to attract attention as an important tool both for rebalancing of the economy and achieving a 'harmonious society'. For the first time, this Five-Year Plan made an explicit commitment to double citizens' income, increasing minimum wages by at least 13 per cent each year, and promote collective negotiations, including sectoral wage bargaining. The plan significantly modified the wage policy formula set out by the 14th CCP National Congress in 1992. The new formula called for two 'synchronizations' (between citizens' incomes and GDP growth, and between workers' wages and productivity growth), and for wages to be determined jointly by employers and employees (*gongjue*, which literally means 'joint decision' or 'co-determination'). While collective negotiations had previously been promoted as a means to achieve stability, it was now seen as an economic and social means for achieving equitable growth. The ACFTU was quick to recognize this, its top official for the collective bargaining campaign making repeated high-profile comments on collective bargaining as a way in which the trend of the declining wage share of GDP could be reversed and income distribution improved (Zhang, 2014). Indeed, various estimations of China's income inequality measured by Gini coefficients show that the income inequality has started to decline moderately since 2010 (World Bank, 2015; *The Economist*, 2016). This may be explained by a combination of factors, such as labour shortages, redistributive social policy and, the moderating effects of industrial relations institutions, which will be looked at in greater detail below.

Significantly, in 2008 China adopted the labour contract law, which reversed the deregulation agenda of the 1990s. This measure set out to enhance employment protection by encouraging indefinite-term contracts with improved regulation of the termination of employment; to formalize informal employment by strengthening legal sanctions against employers who failed to sign written contracts with employees; and to restore the power balance between workers and employers by making bipartite consultation on certain matters of mutual concern at the workplace mandatory. Most importantly, its provisions applied to rural migrant workers, who had not been covered by the 1994 labour law. The labour contract law brought about significant improvements in actual labour market outcomes. According to one survey, the percentage of local resident workers with labour contracts increased from 65 per cent in 2005 to 71 per cent in 2011, and even more dramatically among migrant workers from a mere 12 per cent to 34 per cent during the same period, reversing the trend of informalization (Gallagher et al., 2013, p. 12). In addition to the labour contract law, the adoption of the labour disputes mediation and arbitration law (2008), employment promotion law (2008) and social insurance law (2010) marked a new era for reregulation and the extension of social protection.

Another noteworthy development was the participation of the All China Federation of Industry and Commerce (ACFIC) in tripartite consultation systems at national as well as decentralized levels, in addition to the China Enterprise Confederation (CEC), which used to enjoy the representational monopoly. The ACFIC is a powerful organization mandated to represent domestic private businesses. In 2008, the ACFIC revised its charter to include labour issues as one of its key mandates, and in 2010 succeeded in getting a seat on the national tripartite consultation mechanism (Lee et al., 2011). The inclusion of the ACFIC in China's industrial relations system adds a new dynamism to industrial relations development, because most local sectoral associations are affiliated to it, which was not the case with the CEC.

5.3.2   The Spread of New Industrial Relations Institutions and Approaches

At this stage, under the influence of the Government's shift towards rebalancing and reregulation, and in the face of rising collective action, new approaches to industrial relations began to take root. What had hitherto been scattered local experiments in labour relations began to spread across China, accompanied by the deepening of labour relations institutions at the workplace.

Greater institutional density of labour relations at the workplace
In close alignment with the Government's new economic and labour policy, the ACFTU successfully lobbied for the adoption of provincial regulations on collective bargaining and/or democratic management in 27 of China's 31 provinces, thereby formalizing the new labour relations practices. At the same time, the ACFTU set an ambitious goal of achieving the so-called 'two universals' (universal union membership and comprehensive collective bargaining coverage). Its institution-building agenda was further extended to include the establishment of workers' congresses and party cell

organizations, previously confined to the traditional SOEs, in non-state enterprises (You, 2014).

According to one study, employers tended to accept unionization of their enterprises as a sign of 'political correctness' as well as a sign of legal compliance; some see unions as a useless bureaucracy rather than a threat (Liu and Li, 2014). This atypical attitude on the part of Chinese employers may be explained by their relationship with the CCP as well as the unique nature of trade unions in China.[5] Additionally, the ACFIC, to which more than 60 per cent of Chinese private entrepreneurs are believed to belong, played an important role in encouraging its members to allow union organization and party cells (Chen and Dickson, 2010; Holbig, 2006).

As a result of these efforts, the 'institutional density' of labour relations – that is, the existence of a set of labour relations institutions at a given workplace – thickened significantly during this period. In 2003, for example, only 22.3 per cent of unionized enterprises had a workers' congress, but by 2012 the proportion had risen to 65.7 per cent. A similar trend is apparent in the spread of collective agreements, particularly wage agreements. Since 2008, the ACFTU has given priority to wage agreements, rather than general collective agreements, resulting in a rapid increase in the numbers of workers and enterprises covered by wage agreements (see Table 5.1).

Table 5.1   Trade unions and collective bargaining in China: summary of published statistics

	2003	2005	2008	2012	2013	2016
Union members (millions)	123.4	150.3	212.2	280.2	299.5	302.9
General collective agreements (millions of people covered)	67.0	97.8	149.5	267.2	287.5	290.5
Collective wage agreements (millions of people covered)	35.8	35.3	51.1	150.3	163.8	169.3
Sectoral agreements (millions of people covered)	n.a.	10.8	15.7	37.6	43.5	43.4
Sectoral wage agreements (millions of people covered)	n.a.	n.a.	3.9	16.2	n.a	n.a
Tripartite consultation bodies[1]	5062	8030	12280	24000	26067	28204
Labour disputes (000s)[2]	226	314	693	641	666	814[3]

Notes:
1. No. of tripartite consultation bodies at all levels.
2. No. of labour disputes referred to labour disputes arbitration councils.
3. 2015.

Sources: ACFTU (various years); National Bureau of Statistics of China (various years).

With the usual caveats about the formalistic nature of these institutions as well as the reliability of the statistics, there has been a deepening of institutional density in labour relations at the workplace since the late 2000s. Lee and Liu (2012) have shown that where multiple layers of labour relations institutions exist, such as trade unions, collective agreements and workers' congresses, among others, they are likely to have positive effects on labour market outcomes; for example, reducing intra-firm wage gaps, workplace conflicts and rates of turnover.

Shifting locus of industrial relations and new approaches by unions and employers

As noted above, the revision of the trade union law in 2001 paved the way for the emergence of new forms of union organizations in small and medium-sized domestic private enterprises in a locality (Liu, 2008), followed by experiments with regional and/or sectoral bargaining in Zhejiang and Jiangsu (Pringle, 2011; Xu, 2012; Lee et al., 2014). ACFTU statistics show a rapid increase in the number of workers covered by sectoral agreements, from 10.8 million in 2005 to 27.9 million in 2011 (Lee et al., 2014). Although this remains a very small proportion of the working population, the number is likely to continue to increase, as the ACFTU is promoting local sectoral wage bargaining.

These changes reflect broader policy and structural changes in the Chinese trade unions, especially with regard to the role of upper-level union organizations in relation to workers and the 'grassroots' unions at workplace level. Up to the early 2000s, the ACFTU remained aloof from labour relations at the enterprise level, giving a free hand to employers at the workplace. However, recently, policies regarding the role of upper-level unions were adjusted to support workers and unions at enterprise level in orderly collective bargaining, again shifting the locus of industrial relations activity beyond enterprise level.

At the same time, employers have developed organizational structures to represent their collective interests in industrial relations arrangements at local and sectoral level. Specifically, it was the indigenous private employers running small and medium-sized enterprises (SMEs) in the specialized industrial clusters of the Yangtze River Delta, particularly in Zhejiang and Jiangsu provinces, who possessed the organizational resources to articulate their collective interests through their local sectoral associations. As will become clear below, there are good reasons why local sectoral collective bargaining emerged in the industrial clusters of local SMEs in the YRD (Lee et al., 2014; Friedman, 2011).

5.3.3 Current Challenges: Workers' Collective Action and the Transformation of Labour Relations in the Workplace

In parallel with the process of institution building, labour relations developments in China's workplaces have also been driven by an increase in labour disputes. The numbers of labour disputes submitted to the country's arbitration systems had already increased rapidly during the 1990s, from 12368 in 1993 to 120191 in 1999. Nearly a decade later, it almost doubled in a single year from 350182 cases in 2007 to 693465 in 2008, largely as a result of the implementation of the labour contract law and the labour disputes mediation and arbitration law. The first of these measures greatly raised workers' awareness of their rights and strengthened legal protection and its enforceability, while the second made it easier to bring disputes to the dispute settlement bodies, free of charge.

While the arbitration cases began to stabilize after 2009, cases of workers' collective action have surged. While there are no official statistics on strikes in China – only an unofficial compilation of reported cases of strike action – we can, nevertheless, gain a rough estimate of the trend from various other sources (*China Labour Bulletin*, 2012; Elfstrom and Kuruvilla, 2014). According to one study based on reported cases of strikes across China, there were on average 3.42 strike cases a month in 2008, increasing to 6.17 in 2010, 18.33 in 2011, and 25.33 in the first three months of 2012 (Elfstrom and Kuruvilla, 2014).

Not only has the number of strikes increased, but their nature has also changed. As Chen and Tang (2013) put it, labour conflicts in the 1990s were mostly predicated on a 'moral economy', involving workers in restructured SOEs who resorted to demonstrations and petitions to protest against unpaid wages and pensions, using pre-reform socialist discourse and subsistence ethics to justify their actions. The Government responded with ad hoc relief and state intervention. In the early and mid-2000s, most labour conflicts were 'rights-based' disputes, in which workers sought arbitration rulings or resorted to collective action against unpaid wages, overtime payments and compensation for industrial injuries. In the later 2000s, workers' collective actions became more 'interest-based', with workers demanding increased pay and better working conditions through strike action. The Government response was a combination of ad hoc mediation, facilitation of negotiations and, much less frequently, state intervention where conflicts threatened to spread beyond a single enterprise (Chen and Tang, 2013).

In this respect, the strike at the Honda Auto Manufacturing Co. in Guangdong province in May 2010 marked a turning point. Not only did it galvanize workers' collective action, as shown in the wave of strikes that followed in its wake (Chan and Hui, 2013), but it also showed many of the new features that have become common in more recent strikes. Wildcat strikes were frequently initiated by younger migrant workers in their twenties, most of whom had grown up in the urban environment. Workers were able to maintain solidarity across different groups, such as student workers and older-generation workers, and also to reach out to the general public, through mobile communications and social media. One of the core demands was re-election and reform of the enterprise union, which had hitherto tended to side with the management (Chan and Hui, 2013; Chang and Brown, 2013).

It was, indeed, in large part the demands of workers that set the Honda strike apart from previous collective actions. Workers demanded not just that wages be improved, but that they be raised to a level equivalent to that paid to final assembly workers, and made consistent across firms in a given sector. When the management responded by offering higher bonuses, workers insisted that the basic wage should be increased, as this offered wage security with accompanying increases in other social benefits. The workers also demanded a seniority allowance in the wage system, along with reform of the promotion system so that migrant production workers might have an opportunity for career advancement in the company.

The Honda workers' demands for wage security, recognition of seniority and reform of the promotion system were similar to those made by Japanese workers in the 1950s (Gordon, 1988; Lee, 1996), Korean workers in the late 1980s (Koo, 2001) and American workers during the New Deal era of the 1930s. Case studies on collective bargaining in electronics enterprises in Guangdong and on sectoral bargaining in Jiangsu province show that workers there put forward similar demands, resulting in better wage security and an increased element of seniority allowance in the pay package (Lee et al., 2014). In other advanced economies, these demands were closely associated with the new labour relations and human resource management practices that characterized to the evolution of internal labour markets during the formative period of industrial relations systems. One of the factors motivating the new working class in these various collective actions was the desire for 'face', 'status' and 'respect' at the workplace (Elfstrom and Kuruvilla, 2014). Japanese blue-collar workers fought for recognition of their status as full members of the enterprise community in the 1950s, at a time when Japanese enterprises operated two separate human resources policies: one for salaried white-collar workers and another for blue-collar workers (Gordon, 1998).

The responses of the Government and the ACFTU to the Honda strike and similar actions also marked a shift in approach. The Guangdong Federation of Trade Unions (GFTU), with the support of the provincial party leadership, intervened to manage the enterprise union elections at Honda, responding to the strikers' demand. After those elections, the Honda union and management, with the GFTU as a worker-friendly mediator, successfully negotiated a wage increase of 37 per cent in 2011, which was even higher than the 34 per cent increase the workers gained through the 2010 strike. This was not an isolated incident. A case study of three electronics enterprises in Guangdong shows that, after wildcat strikes, the local trade union federation organized new elections of enterprise union committees, and instituted annual wage negotiation practices (Lee et al., 2014). This new approach is currently being replicated in many more workplaces in Guangdong, where the GFTU has recently adopted a new election process (Kuruvilla and Zhang, 2016; Wen, 2014).

Most of the union elections introduced by the upper-level trade unions involve a multi-stage process, combining limited direct election and a multi-tier electoral college process. At the lowest level of trade union organization or production units, shop stewards are elected by direct vote of the workers. One level up, at the department level, worker representatives are elected by shop stewards; and those elected worker representatives then vote to elect the members of the trade union executive committee (Wen, 2014; Lee et al., 2014). This new election procedure is a significant improvement on past practice, whereby union leaderships were hand-picked by either the management or the upper-level union, as it involves workers directly in the election process. At the same time, the multi-stage election still allows for intervention by officials of the upper-level union and company management, so that managerial and supervisory employees are still disproportionately represented in enterprise union committees (Chan and Hui, 2013). However, in the three Guangdong electronics companies there were also parallel elections to elect workers' representatives (*gongren daibiao*) specifically to engage in annual wage bargaining. According to a case study (Lee et al., 2014), the elected workers' representatives joined the union representatives (*gonghui daibiao*), that is, the members of the trade union executive committee, for annual wage negotiations with the management. While the local union federation controlled the whole process, these arrangements established better links between the enterprise union committees and workers' representatives at the shop-floor level.

Though impossible to make a generalized observation, an increasing number of cases are being reported of enterprise trade unions taking bold collective action, which was unheard of until a few years ago. Before 2010, it was always workers, not enterprise unions, who took collective action. However, the collective action that took place at the Changde Wal-Mart store in Hunan province in 2013, and at the Pepsi-Cola factories across China in 2014, was organized or at least supported by enterprise unions.

Such cases are often ascribed to courageous individual leaders of the enterprise union involved; however, it is also plausible that union leadership constituted in a more democratic manner is better able to take collective action representing the views of a majority of workers, including managerial and supervisory staff in addition to rank-and-file workers, particularly when the dispute involves relocation and redundancy, as was the case in the Wal-Mart and Pepsi-Cola strikes.

In this respect, the roles of local labour NGOs must be noted. Moving away from providing legal support to individual workers, labour NGOs in southern China have become very active in providing direct support to workers, including during strikes and collective bargaining. The growing influence of the labour NGOs in the collective empowerment of workers has also supported changes in the practices of enterprise unions (Pringle, 2016). Nevertheless, there are limits to representational reforms in a country where there is no legal protection and guarantee of the freedom of association. It remains to be seen whether the development of this 'hybrid representation' is 'a transient stage before mutating into a system based on the principle of freedom of association or a stable feature of Chinese industrial relations' (Lee et al., 2014).

5.4 TWO DIVERGENT PATTERNS OF INDUSTRIAL RELATIONS: THE PEARL RIVER DELTA AND THE YANGTZE RIVER DELTA

So far, this chapter has described the general picture of industrial relations in China. But it is important to bear in mind that there remain significant differences in employment and labour relations between sectors, types of enterprise and localities. Earlier studies of industrial relations emphasized the divergent patterns of industrial relations between state and non-state firms (Chang, 2005; Taylor et al., 2003); while significant differences remain, they may not be as great as they were in the 1990s. Institution building across enterprises with different ownership structures may have reduced the differences, at least in terms of formal labour relations institutions in the workplace (Lee et al., 2014). It is regional diversities that have recently attracted academic attention (Friedman, 2011; Friedman and Kuruvilla, 2015).

In this context, particular attention has been given to the Pearl River Delta (PRD) in Guangdong province and the Yangtze River Delta (YRD) in Jiangsu, Zhejiang and Shanghai provinces; not only because these are the most economically developed regions of China, but also because the two regions display different patterns of industrialization and industrial relations developments. Table 5.2 shows that over the past decade the

Table 5.2 Two distinctive patterns of industrial relations: Pearl River Delta (Guangdong) and Yangtze River Delta (Jiangsu, Zhejiang, Shanghai)

	2005					2008					2011				
	GD	JS	ZJ	SH	N	GD	JS	ZJ	SH	N	GD	JS	ZJ	SH	N
Workers (millions)	50.2	45.1	31.0	8.6	746.5	54.7	47.0	34.9	10.5	755.6	59.6	47.6	36.8	11.0	764.2
Union density (%)	26.6	21.9	25.6	58.7	20.1	32.9	28.9	32.1	65.4	28.1	37.9	36.6	45.4	74.7	33.8
Wage agreement coverage (%)	8.0	11.3	12.0	11.0	4.7	5.8	18.5	15.9	17.2	6.7	8.9	24.2	28.1	22.5	23.5
Firms covered by wage agreement as % of unionized firms	41.8	136.6	80.1	104	17.7	34.3	NA	118	88.9	21.0	63.5	182.6	141	NA	37.0
Firms with workers' congress as % of unionized firms	27.3	48.6	39.2	48.4	18.5	NA	NA	NA	NA	43.1	35.6	55.8	75.8	71.8	52.8

Note: GD: Guangdong; JS: Jiangsu; ZJ: Zhejiang; SH: Shanghai; N: national average.

three provinces of the YRD have almost consistently had higher levels of institutionalization of industrial relations than the PRD in terms of union density, coverage of wage agreements and the proportion of unionized firms that have established workers' congresses (Sun and He, 2012). In some indicators, such as the coverage of wage agreements and workers' congresses, Guangdong has a lower institutionalization rate than the national average. This means that the institutional density of labour relations at the workplace is much higher in the YRD than in Guangdong (Sun and He, 2012).

It is interesting to note that the ratio of firms covered by wage agreements to unionized firms tends to be much higher in the YRD than in Guangdong. This can be explained by different bargaining structures: in Zhejiang and Jiangsu, sectoral bargaining is relatively well developed, while Guangdong collective bargaining usually takes place at enterprise level.

Also noticeable are the differences in prevalence of labour disputes in the two regions. According to one study, there were 22.64 cases of collective labour disputes per 10000 workers in Guangdong in 2005, while the corresponding numbers were 4.08, 3.71 and 12.08 for Zhejiang, Jiangsu and Shanghai, respectively (McCulla, 2010, p. 30). An informal compilation of strike data further reveals that in 2011 the majority of strikes in the manufacturing sector took place in Guangdong province (57 per cent), while the YRD (Jiangsu, Zhejiang and Shanghai) accounted for only 20 per cent in the same year (CLB, 2014, p. 17).

Finally, there is empirical evidence that wages and working conditions are better in the YRD than in Guangdong, even after controlling for relevant factors. One study reports higher social insurance coverage (medical, unemployment and pension), higher proportions of migrant workers with written contracts, fewer incidences of wage arrears and shorter working hours in the YRD than in Guangdong (Liu et al., 2011; Sun and He, 2012). A study of different regional welfare regimes in China concludes that the YRD has a more 'incorporative', 'protective' and 'equitable' social insurance regime for migrant workers than the PRD (Wu, 2008).

In summary, industrial relations in YRD appear to be significantly more institutionalized, less conflict-prone and more worker-friendly than in Guangdong province. What explains these systematic differences between the two foremost regions of economic development in China? Though there is no single definite answer to this question, the discrepancy may be connected with distinctive paths of industrialization and industrial relations arrangements.

Guangdong has been the frontrunner of China's economic reform and opening since the early 1980s, driven mostly by foreign direct investment

(FDI) in the SEZs. In contrast, the YRD's development has been based more on local entrepreneurialism, though there are significant differences between the three provinces: Jiangsu's initial development was driven by TVEs created by local government in the early stages of economic reform, Zhejiang's mostly by local private entrepreneurs, and Shanghai's by a combination of reformed and recombined SOEs. The more indigenous development path of Zhejiang and Jiangu, as opposed to the foreign direct investment (FDI)-driven path of Guangdong, has created different conditions for the development of industrial relations.

In Zhejiang and Jiangsu, local entrepreneurs have developed relatively strong local business associations at geographical and sectoral level, based on their common background and interests. Moreover, 'a close link has developed between the local government and enterprises in Jiangsu, referred to as "local state corporatism"' (Oi, 1995), which has allowed the trade unions to build industrial relations institutions in close coordination with local government and employers (Lee et al., 2014). This has enabled trade unions in the YRD to introduce local regulations designed to promote collective bargaining and workers' congresses, without provoking strong opposition from organized employers. This is perhaps why the institutional density of labour relations at the workplace in the YRD is way above the national average (and above that of Guangdong).

Nor is it a coincidence that new sectoral bargaining practices emerged and spread in Zhejiang and Jiangsu. The first successful model of sectoral bargaining emerged in the woollen sweater manufacturing sector in Xinhe town of Wenling city, Zhejiang province, in 2002. Analyses of some successful cases of sectoral bargaining in Zhejiang and Jiangsu all point to the important roles played by local sectoral employers' associations. In Wenling, for example, employers tried to address the problem of high employee turnover and labour conflicts through coordinated actions among themselves and the development of sectoral bargaining arrangements with local trade unions (Wen, 2011; Clarke and Pringle, 2009; Friedman, 2011; Friedman and Kuruvilla, 2015; Xu, 2012).

Similar developments were observed in Jiangsu province. According to a study on two cases of sectoral bargaining (Lee et al., 2014), after early attempts to agree on sectoral minimum wages and to define average rates of wage growth to address high employee turnover, the local trade union federation and employers' association moved on to fixing sectoral standard wage rates for particular jobs. As sectoral bargaining has continued to evolve, trade unions and employers' associations have also introduced a two-tier bargaining system, whereby once sectoral wage bargaining has been concluded, enterprise unions in larger companies are encouraged to carry out supplementary enterprise-level bargaining with their employers in pursuit of improvements on the sectoral wage agreement. In Jiangsu, trade union federations and employers' associations created an interlocking representational system in which representatives of employers were allotted seats in a 'sectoral workers' congress' in the case of the ceramic sector in Yixing city, or given a senior position within the sectoral union association in the plywood sector in Pizhou city. At the same time, the sectoral union association in Pizhou developed an organizational arrangement in which workers' representatives (*gongren daibiao*) would sit together with union officials (*gonghui guanyuan*) and employers' representatives at the bargaining table. The combination of union official and workers' representative in the bargaining situation is reminiscent of the 'hybrid representation' model of workplace labour relations in Guangdong, discussed above.

A noticeable feature of collective bargaining in Jiangsu is a systematic attempt to align macroeconomic policy goals with wage negotiations. Local governments incorporate key economic and income policy targets into the formulation of non-binding wage guidelines. Then the local tripartite consultation committee will deploy so-called 'wage negotiation councillors', who will guide wage negotiations at the sectoral and enterprise levels in accordance with the non-binding guidelines. It is not known how effective this system has been, but it does show that there is an element of pre-emptive corporatist strategy at work in Jiangsu, through which the state and its agents try to coordinate bargaining outcomes with government economic policy, and also stabilize industrial relations (Lee et al., 2014).

In contrast, it appears that industrial relations in Guangdong are much less institutionalized and coordinated. In Guangdong, there has been no comparable development of strong sectoral associations of local employers, as the province's development was driven by footloose foreign capital. Local unions here faced difficulties in their campaign for multi-employer bargaining, as they could not find interlocutors on the employers' side (Lee et al., 2014; Friedman, 2011). Furthermore, the GFTU faced strong opposition from Hong Kong investors when it tried to introduce provincial regulations to promote collective bargaining (Hui and Chan, 2015). In Guangdong, then, in the absence of a favourable regulatory framework, industrial relations seem to have been evolving more in a direct response to challenges of workers' collective actions at the workplace, with those actions activating labour relations institutions such as workplace unions and collective bargaining. One noteworthy feature of the situation in Guangdong is the role played by independent labour NGOs. Going beyond their earlier focus on providing individual legal assistance to workers with grievances, labour NGOs have also come to the aid of striking workers, supporting them in their negotiations with employers (Pringle, 2016).

5.5 MEASURING THE EFFECTS OF NEW LAWS AND NEW PRACTICES: WHAT DO UNIONS DO IN CHINA?

This section presents the findings of various studies on the effects of changes in laws, policies and institutional arrangements for industrial relations in China on labour market outcomes since the late 2000s.

5.5.1 The Arrival of the Lewis Turning Point

In examining the effects of regulations and institutions, it is important to take into account the profound changes that have occurred in the labour market as a result of demographic transition and rapid industrialization. As noted above, China began to experience labour shortages in early 2003. The aggregate labour force is expected to start to shrink from around 2015 (World Bank and DRC, 2012). According to Cai and Du, the 'Lewis turning point' has already arrived: that is, the unlimited supply of labour from rural areas has run out. In this increasingly tight labour market, workers have gained individual and collective bargaining power, while the wages of migrant workers have increased. According to this study, the urban residence dummy variable accounted for 11 per cent of the wage difference in 2001, 9 per cent of the difference in 2005, and just 5 per cent in 2010, indicating wage convergence between local residents and migrant workers (Cai and Du, 2011).

5.5.2 Effects of the Labour Contract Law

Within this more worker-friendly labour market situation, new laws and regulations introduced in the late 2000s, particularly the labour contract law, helped to improve the protection of workers. Analysis of the China Urban Labour Survey shows that the proportions of local residents and, especially, migrant workers with a labour contract rose sharply between 2005 and 2008 (see section 5.3.1 above); and that, while women were 5–7 per cent less likely to have labour contracts in the early 2000s, the gender differences had largely disappeared by 2010 (Gallagher et al., 2013). For migrant workers, having a labour contract increased the likelihood of pension coverage by 28.2 per cent in 2010, compared to 15.9 per cent in 2005. These findings clearly indicate that implementation of the labour contract law has contributed to the formalization of employment, particularly for migrant workers, even though there remain significant differences between their conditions of work and those of local residents.

5.5.3   Effects of Unionization and New Labour Relations Practices

There is an emerging body of quantitative studies examining the effects of unions and new labour market practices on labour market outcomes. For the purposes of this chapter, seven studies were reviewed which applied the Freeman and Medoff style approach (Freeman and Medoff, 1984). Though there were some common findings, they presented conflicting pictures.

One area where most studies produced a common result was the effect of trade unions on mandatory social insurance schemes. Formerly, non-payment of social insurance by employers was rampant in China. All the studies that covered social insurance schemes reported statistically significantly positive effects of unionization on these schemes (Ge, 2007; Yao et al., 2009; Lu et al., 2010; Yao and Zhong, 2008; Lee and Liu, 2012; Sun and He, 2012). Yao et al. (2009) reported that the presence of a union has the greatest effect on old-age pensions and medical insurance, followed by unemployment insurance and occupational injury insurance. Yao and Zhong (2008) found that pension coverage in unionized companies with collective contracts was 41.3 percentage points higher than in their non-unionized counterparts. Three studies (Yao and Zhong, 2013; Lu et al., 2010; Lee and Liu, 2012) found that unionized companies were much more likely to have written contracts with their employees. The studies showed that union presence enhances compliance and, as a result, has facilitated formalization of employment at Chinese workplaces.

On wages, the findings of the seven studies varied widely. While three (Ge, 2007; Yao and Zhong, 2008; Yao et al., 2009) reported that unionized firms paid higher wages than non-unionized firms, two others found no statistically significant union wage premium (Lu et al., 2010; Lee and Liu, 2012). Some, in fact, even reported negative effects of unions on wages, implying that bargaining is used by employers as a way to suppress wages; these negative effects, however, were not statistically significant (Sun and He, 2012; Huang, 2012).

There are methodological problems with most of these studies, owing to the union monopoly situation, whereby most workers do not have a choice whether or not to join a union: until recently, unionization occurred as the result of a deal between the employer and the trade union federation (Lee and Liu, 2012). This makes it harder to measure union effects separately from firm effects. It also raises a question about the appropriateness of using the union as an independent variable, because we cannot assume that 'trade unions are a voluntary organization of workers, which have institutionalized practice of democracy such as elections and democratic decision-making processes' (Lee and Liu, 2012, p. 211). That is why, for example, Lee and Liu's (2012) study found that the presence of a trade union at the workplace did not itself make a statistically meaningful difference, except in relation to issues of legal compliance.

To address this issue, some studies used additional channels and scales. Yao et al. (2009) introduced a union election variable. Their study showed that where unions had an elected leadership, the already significant effects of unions on mandatory social insurance, wages, shorter working hours, training opportunities and lower employee turnover were even stronger. Lee and Liu (2012) further elaborated the scales to measure the effects of various dimensions of unions at Chinese workplaces by introducing scales for union autonomy (with indicators such as union elections), union organizational strength (union finance and union organization at shop-floor level) and democratic management (collective bargaining and a workers' congress). According to them, what mattered was not whether a union existed or not, but what kind of unions existed. A unionized workplace with collective bargaining practices was associated with lower intra-firm wage differentials, more supplementary benefits, lower employee turnover and fewer labour–management disputes.

The studies by Yao et al. (2009) and Sun and He (2012) reported that the effects of Chinese trade unions were not limited to their members. In particular, Sun and He (2012) showed that the union's presence increased the likelihood that even non-members would have social insurance, and reduced the incidence of forced overtime. They concluded that while Chinese trade unions were not capable of advancing workers' interests, they were capable of defending workers' legal rights, which affected not only members but also non-members. According to him, this was because, as quasi-governmental agencies, Chinese trade unions offered a public service to everybody at the workplace.[6]

There is a need for further research using refined analytical frameworks, tailored to the Chinese context, and based on the most recent data. As Lee and Liu's (2012) study noted, what really makes a difference is not whether a union exists or not, but what kinds of labour relations arrangements and union governance structures exist at the enterprise level. At the same time, with collective bargaining and negotiating with multiple employers becoming more widespread, there is a need to look beyond individual enterprises

Future research will also need to examine the effects of government wage policies, manifested through local minimum wage fixing and non-binding wage guidelines, on unions' bargaining policy and actual wage levels. As noted above, there has been an attempt to coordinate bargaining outcomes with the Government's economic policy parameters, through wage guidelines transmitted by 'wage negotiation councillors'. As Lee and Liu (2012) point out, Chinese industrial relations actors have not only a 'voice face', but also a 'party face', a duality which may be reflected in outcomes.

5.6 CONCLUSIONS

China has gone through a dramatic transformation of the labour market and its institutions since the 1980s. In the 1990s and early 2000s, the aim was to dismantle the socialist employment regime through deregulation and flexibilization. Since 2008, there have been signs that China is changing course, reregulating work, and building and expanding webs of industrial relations institutions from workplace to national level, driven by the state agents of industrial relations. Nevertheless, notwithstanding this 'pre-emptive corporatist strategy' (Lee, 2006), the national system of industrial relations, premised on the representational monopoly, has remained largely unchanged.

This chapter presented evidence of experimentation with 'hybrid representation' in some workplaces in Guangdong and in certain sectors in the YRD, particularly Jiangsu province. Workers' collective action is pushing the boundary of the representational foundation of the system, while the official actors of industrial relations are adjusting their structures and strategies to counter and/or accommodate the challenge. There is no indication so far of whether these two processes – official institution building and workers' voice – will converge to produce a new industrial relations system. Further quantitative and qualitative research is required to document changes at the workplace level and to examine the effects of such changes on labour markets.

NOTES

1. Various versions of the workers' congress have been applied throughout the history of the People's Republic of China from the early 1950s onwards. See Chang (2005).
2. *Danwei* (单位, employing unit) refers to a place of employment during the socialist planned economy. Every aspect of urban citizens' economic, social and political life was linked to the *danwei*, including jobs, housing, child care, clinics, schools, shops and pensions. See Walder (1984).
3. *Hukou* (戶口) refers to a household registration system. People with rural *hukou* face broad discrimination in terms of rights and entitlements when they move to urban areas.
4. A standard measure of income inequality: the higher the score, the greater the level of inequality. There are various estimations of China's Gini coefficients, depending on sources such as China Statistical Bureau, the World Bank and various research institutes.
5. According to a survey in 2006 and 2007, 39 per cent of private entrepreneurs were CCP members and 8.4 per cent had applied to join the party; party members display significantly higher levels of support for the regime than others (Chen and Dickson, 2010).
6. According to Sun and He (2012), this outcome is also related to Chinese unions'

finance. Chinese trade unions' main funding source is not union members' dues, but the employer's contribution of 2 per cent of total payroll. Since the late 2000s, the employer's contribution has been collected through government tax authorities in many localities. Therefore, on the basis of this 'union tax', Chinese trade unions offer a public good to members and non-members alike.

REFERENCES

All China Federation of Trade Unions (ACFTU). Various years. *Annual Report on Chinese Trade Union Statistics*. Beijing.

All China Federation of Trade Unions (ACFTU). 2009. *Guiding Opinion on Active Promotion of Sectoral Collective Wage Consultation*. http://www.110.com/fagui/law_359750.html.

Cai, F. (ed.). 2012. *The China Population and Labour Yearbook*. Beijing: China Academy of Social Sciences.

Cai, F. and Du, Y. 2011. 'Wage increases, wage convergence, and the Lewis turning point in China', *China Economic Review*, **22**(4), pp. 601–10.

Chan, A. 2007. 'Organizing Wal-Mart in China: Two steps forward, one step back for China's unions', *New Labor Forum*, **16**(2), pp. 87–96.

Chan, A. 2009. 'Challenges and possibilities for democratic grassroots union election', *Labor Studies Journal*, **34**(3), pp. 293–317.

Chan, A. and Unger, J. 2009. 'A Chinese enterprise under the reforms: What model of capitalism?', *China Journal*, **62**(July), pp. 1–26.

Chan, C. 2009. 'Strikes and changing workplace relations in a Chinese global factory', *Industrial Relations Journal*, **40**(1), pp. 60–77.

Chan, C. and Hui, E. 2013. 'The dynamics and dilemma of workplace trade union reform in China: The case of the Honda workers' strike', *Journal of Industrial Relations*, **54**(5), pp. 653–68.

Chang, K. 2005. *Laodong guangxixue* (Study of labour relations). Beijing: China Labour and Social Security Publisher.

Chang, K. and Brown, W. 2013. 'The transition from individual to collective labour relations in China', *Industrial Relations Journal*, **44**(2), pp. 102–21.

Chen, F. 2007. 'Individual rights and collective rights: Labor's predicament in China', *Communist and Post-Communist Studies*, **40**(1), pp. 59–79.

Chen, F. 2009. 'Union power in China: Source, operation and constraints', *Modern China*, **35**(6), pp. 662–89.

Chen, F. and Tang, M. 2013. 'Labor conflicts in China: Typologies and their implications', *Asian Survey*, **53**(3), pp. 559–83.

Chen, J. and Dickson, B.J. 2010. *Allies of the State: China's Private Entrepreneurs and Democratic Change*. Cambridge, MA: Harvard University Press.

China Labour Bulletin (CLB). 2012. 'A decade of change: The workers' movement in China 2000–2010', 28 March. http://www.clb.org.hk/en/content/decade-change-workers%C3%A2%E2%82%AC%E2%84%A2-movement-china-2000-2010.

China Labour Bulletin (CLB). 2014. 'Worker protests in China surge after lunar new year', 10 April. http://www.clb.org.hk/en/content/worker-protests-china-surge-after-lunar-new-year.

Clarke, S., Lee, C-H. and Qi, L. 2004. 'Collective consultation and industrial relations in China', *British Journal of Industrial Relations*, **42**(2), pp. 235–54.

Clarke, S. and Pringle, T. 2009. 'Can party-led trade unions represent their members?', *Post-Communist Economics*, **21**(1), pp. 85–101.

Cooke, F.L. 2012. *Human Resource Management in China: New Trends and Practices*. Abingdon: Routledge.

The Economist. 2016. 'Inequality in China – up on the farm', 14 May.

Elfstrom, M. and Kuruvilla, S. 2014. 'The changing nature of labor unrest in China', *Industrial and Labour Relations Review*, **67**(2), pp. 453–80.

Freeman, R. and Medoff, J. 1984. *What Do Unions Do?* New York: Basic Books.

Friedman, E. 2011. 'Rupture and representation: Migrant workers, unions and the State in China', PhD diss., University of California, Berkeley.

Friedman, E. and Kuruvilla, S. 2015. 'Experimentation and decentralization in China's labor relations', *Human Relations*, **68**(2), pp. 181–95.

Friedman, E. and Lee, C.K. 2010. 'Remaking the world of Chinese labour: A 30-year retrospective', *British Journal of Industrial Relations*, **48**(3), pp. 507–33.

Gallagher, M. 2004. 'Time is money, efficiency is life: The transformation of labor relations in China', *Studies in Comparative International Development*, **39**(2), pp. 11–44.

Gallagher, M., Giles, G., Park, A. and Wang, M. 2013. *China's 2008 Labor Contract Law: Implementation and Implications for China's Workers*. Washington, DC: World Bank.

Ge, Y. 2007. 'What do unions do in China?', Working Paper. http://ssrn.com/abstract =1031084.

Gordon, A. 1988. *The Evolution of Labor Relations in Japan: Heavy Industry, 1853–1955*. Cambridge, MA: Harvard University Press.

Gordon, A. 1998. *The Wages of Affluence: Labor and Management in Postwar Japan*. Cambridge, MA: Harvard University Press.

Hayter, S. 2011. *The Role of Collective Bargaining in the Global Economy: Negotiating for Social Justice*. Cheltenham, UK and Geneva: Edward Elgar and ILO.

Holbig, H. 2006. *Fragmented Corporatism: Interest Politics in China's Private Business Sector*. Hamburg: German Institute of Global and Area Studies.

Hu, Dawu. 2013, 'Report – the status of domestic workers and decent work challenges in China', http://www.idwfed.org/en/resources/the-status-of-domestic-workers-in-china-and-decent-work-challenges/@@display-file/attachment_1, accessed 7 April 2017.

Huang, C. 2012. 'Research on the economic effects of collective wage negotiations, based on data from Hangzhou' (in Chinese), Master's thesis, Zhejiang University.

Hui, E. and Chan, C. 2015. 'The politics of labour legislation in southern China: How foreign chambers of commerce and government agencies influence collective bargaining laws', *International Labour Review*, **153**(4), pp. 587–607.

Koo, H. 2001. *Korea Workers: The Cultures and Politics of Class Formation*. Ithaca, NY: Cornell University Press.

Kuruvilla, S. and Zhang, H. 2016. 'Labor unrest and incipient collective bargaining in China', *Management and Organization Review*, **12**(1), pp. 159–87.

Lee, C.-H. 1996. 'The formation of quality circle and industrial relations of the Japanese steel industry' (in Korean), PhD diss., Seoul National University.

Lee, C.-H. 2006. 'Recent industrial relations developments in China and Vietnam', *Journal of Industrial Relations*, **4**(3), pp. 415–29.

Lee, C.-H. 2009. 'Industrial relations and collective bargaining in China', Industrial

Relations and Employment Relations Department Working Paper No. 7. Geneva: ILO.

Lee, C.-H. and Liu, M. 2012. 'Measuring the effects of collective voice', in Hayter, S. (ed.), *The Role of Collective Bargaining in the Global Economy: Negotiating for Social Justice*. Cheltenham, UK and Geneva: Edward Elgar and ILO.

Lee, C.-H., Brown, W. and Wen, X. 2014. 'What sort of collective bargaining is emerging in China?', *British Journal of Industrial Relations*, doi: 10.1111/bjir.12109.

Lee, C.-H., Sheldon, P. and Li, Y. 2011. 'Employers' coordination and employer associations', in Sheldon, P., Kim, S. and Li, Y. (eds), *China's Changing Workplace: Dynamism, Diversity and Disparity*. New York: Routledge.

Lee, C.K. 1999. 'From organized dependence to disorganized despotism: Changing labour regimes in Chinese factories', *China Quarterly*, **157**(Mar.), pp. 44–71.

Lee, C.K. 2007. *Against the Law: Labor Protests in China's Rustbelt and Sunbelt*. Berkeley, CA: University of California Press.

Liu, L., Zheng, G. and Sun, Z. 2011, 'Regional differences in protection of labour rights – Based on survey of migrant workers in YRD and PRD' (in Chinese), *China Social Science Journal*, **17**(4), pp. 107–23.

Liu, M. 2008. 'Union organizing in China: Still a monolithic labor movement?', *Industrial and Labor Relations Review*, **64**(1), pp. 30–56.

Liu, M. 2009. 'Toward labour flexibility with Chinese characteristics? The case of the Chinese construction machinery industry', Working Paper No. 82. Pittsburgh, PA: Industry Studies Association.

Liu, M. and Li, C-Y. 2014. 'Environment pressures, managerial industrial relations ideologies, and unionization in Chinese enterprises', *British Journal of Industrial Relations*, **52**(1), pp. 82–111.

Lu, Y., Tao, Z. and Wang, Y. 2010. 'Union effect on performance and employment relation: Evidence from China', *China Economic Review*, **21**(1), pp. 202–10.

Luthje, B. 2004. 'Global production networks and industrial upgrading in China: The case of electronics contract manufacturing', Working Paper No. 74, Economic Series. Honolulu: East–West Center.

McCulla, E. 2010. 'Labor contention in China: A statistical perspective', unpublished paper. http://www.democracy.uci.edu/files/docs/conferences/grad/McCulla_Labor_Contention_in_China_A_Statistical_Perspective.pdf.

Metcalf, D. and Li, J. 2006. 'Chinese unions: An Alice in Wonderland', in Lewin, D. and Kaufman, B.E. (eds), *Advances in Industrial and Labor Relations* (Vol. 15). Bingley: Emerald Group.

National Bureau of Statistics of China. Various years. *China Statistical Yearbook*, http://www.stats.gov.cn/english/statisticaldata/AnnualData/.

Norton, B. 2006. *The Chinese Economy: Transitions and Growth*. Cambridge, MA: MIT.

Oi, J.C. 1995. 'The role of the local state in China's transitional economy', *China Quarterly*, **144**(Dec.), pp. 1132–49.

Pringle, T. 2011. *Trade Unions in China: The Challenge of Labour Unrest*. Abingdon: Routledge.

Pringle, T. 2016. 'What do labour NGOs in China do?'. https://cpianalysis.org/2016/10/17/what-do-labour-ngos-in-china-do/ (accessed 7 April 2017).

Qiao, J. 2010. 'Between the party-state, employers and workers: Multiple roles of the Chinese trade union during market transition – A survey of 1811 enterprise union chairpersons', in Hishida, M., Kojima, K., Tomoaki, I. and Qiao J., *China's Trade Unions: How Autonomous Are They?* New York: Routledge.

Qiao, J. 2011. 'Tripartite system with Chinese characteristics: A first step towards tripartite consultation and social dialogue', Research and Policy Brief No. 9. Los Angeles, CA: UCLA Institute for Research on Labor and Employment.

Silver, B.J. 2003. *Forces of Labour: Workers' Movements and Globalization since 1870*. Cambridge: Cambridge University Press.

Stark, D. and Bruszt, L. 1998. *Postsocialist Pathways: Transforming Politics and Property in East Central Europe*. Cambridge: Cambridge University Press.

Sun, Z. and He, X. 2012. 'Union building and protection of migrant workers' rights' (in Chinese), *Management World*, **12**, pp. 46–60.

Taylor, B., Chang, K. and Li, Q. 2003. *Industrial Relations in China*. Cheltenham, UK and Northampton, MA, USA: Edward Elgar Publishing.

Tong, X. 2005. 'Labour unions in enterprises: Proactive actors', *Chinese Sociology and Anthropology*, **37**(4), pp. 52–71.

Unger, J. and Chan, A. 1995. 'Corporatism in China: A developmental state in an East Asian context', in McCormick, B. and Unger, J. (eds), *China after Socialism: In the Footsteps of Eastern Europe or East Asia?* Armonk, NY: Sharpe.

Walder, A.G. 1984. *Communist Neo-Traditionalism: Work and Authority in Chinese Industry*. Berkeley, CA: University of California Press.

Wen, X. 2011. 'The internal state mechanism in collective bargaining: Evidence from the collective bargaining in the Wenling sweater industry', *Chinese Journal of Sociology*, **31**(1), pp. 112–30.

Wen, X. 2014. 'Union direct election: Experiences in Guangdong and their lessons' (in Chinese), *Open Times*, **5**, pp. 54–65.

World Bank. 2015. 'Gini index data', http://data.worldbank.org/indicator/SI.POV.GI NI?end=2012&locations=CN&start=2008&view=chart (accessed 7 April 2017).

World Bank and Development Research Center (DRC) of the State Council, People's Republic of China. 2012. *China 2030: Building a Modern, Harmonious and Creative Society*. Washington, DC and Beijing.

Wright, E.O. 2000. 'Working class power, capitalist state interest and class compromise', *American Journal of Sociology*, **105**(4), pp. 957–1002.

Wu, J.M. 2008. 'Comparing three migrant citizenship regimes in globalized China', paper presented at the conference on 'Breaking Down Chinese Walls: The Changing Faces of Labor and Employment in China', Cornell University, 26–28 September.

Xu, X. 2012. 'Assessing the effectiveness of collective bargaining in Zhejiang province' (in Chinese), *Journal of Tianjin Union Management Institute*, **2**, pp. 36–8.

Yao, X., Li, M. and Han, J. 2009. 'Trade unions' role in labor relations: An empirical analysis of Zhejiang province', *Journal of China Institute of Industrial Relations*, **23**(1), pp. 32–8.

Yao, Y. and Zhong, N. 2008. 'Do unions improve workers' welfare: Evidence from 12 Chinese cities' (in Chinese), *World Economic Papers*, **5**, pp. 5–29.

Yao, Y. and Zhong, N. 2013. 'Unions and workers' welfare in Chinese firms' (in Chinese), *Journal of Labor Economics*, **31**(3), pp. 633–67.

You, Z. 2014. *Local Government's Soft-Regulation of Labour Relations: A Case Study of Zhuji County in Zhejiang Province*. Beijing: Social Science Publishing House.

Zhang, J. 2014. 'For establishing collective bargaining as a universal mechanism to protect workers' rights'. http://zgtv.workercn.cn/28411/201401/07/140107082741 098.shtml.

Zhang, L. 2008. 'Lean production and labor controls in the Chinese automobile industry in an age of globalization', *International Labor and Working-Class History*, **73**(Spring), pp. 24–44.

6. Industrial relations in Turkey: Still waiting for a strong and modern system

Aziz Çelik

6.1 INTRODUCTION

Although the roots of its industrial relations system go back to the beginning of the twentieth century, and a significant proportion of the labour market is in waged employment today, Turkey has not yet achieved a strong institutionalized system of industrial relations. Late industrialization and modernization, and the persistence of a largely agricultural economy, delayed the emergence of industrial relations. Moreover, owing to the statist and patrimonial or paternalistic tradition inherited from the Ottoman Empire, Turkish industrial relations have lacked the federalist and corporatist traditions that developed in other parts of the world. Unlike some of the other countries examined in this volume, organized labour in Turkey did not play a significant role during the war of independence at the beginning of the 1920s, and the transition to democracy in the mid-1940s.

The founders of the Turkish republic directed much of their efforts towards creating a modern, secular nation-state. They initiated a comprehensive programme of political, social, economic, legal and cultural reforms over a short period of time (Ahmad, 1995). Specific attention was given to the development of the country's financial system and to industrialization. Their hope was that Turkey would become one of the most prosperous and civilized nations of the world, well placed in the league of the capitalist-democratic Western countries. They embraced a state-led path to industrialization and a paternalistic orientation to social issues. Despite significant progress in a short space of time, this was nonetheless uneven. On the one hand there significant attention was given to industrialization, urbanization and the modernization of the traditional society, on the other, no attention was given to the development of a modern industrial relations system.

The Government in the early republican period had a paternalistic attitide toward labour, and populism and nationalism impeded the emergence of unionism and class consciousness. With a single-party political system and a weak working class, independent workers' organizations did not come into being, and the preconditions for industrial relations were absent. In the absence of private investment in enterprises, the founders of the republic preferred a statist approach to industrialization. Many state-owned factories were established in agriculture, machinery, and textile industries. When trade unions emerged, and industrial relations became institutionalized, this was in the public rather than the private sector. The historical background, institutions, relationships and experiences of these early republican years had long-lasting effects on the Turkish industrial relations system.

In the 1960s, with the industrial workforce and wage employment expanding as urbanization and political democratization developed, new industrial relations institutions were adopted. These included collective bargaining, the right to strike, and employee participation in workplace administration at state-run enterprises. As the institutionalization of industrial relations gained momentum, and with the adoption of Keynesian economic policies and the growth of an industrial workforce, consensus and collaboration between the unions and the Government grew in importance. However, this improvement in industrial relations was interrupted by the coup of 1980, which had enduring effects on industrial relations and dramatically weakened the power of the unions. Indeed, the weakness of industrial relations institutions and traditions in Turkey today is connected to the weakness of democracy in the country.

6.2 HISTORICAL AND CONTEMPORARY BACKGROUND: THE EVOLUTION OF INDUSTRIAL RELATIONS IN TURKEY

The historic process by which industrial relations have been shaped has a lasting legacy for future patterns of industrial relations. This path-dependency is touched on in other chapters in this volume. The trajectory of Turkish industrial relations has been shaped by different factors and dynamics internally and externally.

Under paternalistic rule, there was little room for industrial relations and the participation of social partners. Paternalism and its legacy impeded the institutionalization of industrial relations. While the state recognized and guaranteed substantial individual labour rights in the first labour act in the mid-1930s, it posed heavy restrictions on organized labour. According to the founding fathers of the republic, class conflicts and class contradictions were alien to the structure and the culture of Turkish society, and the duty of state was to regulate irregularities in individual labour relations. Organized labour was considered to represent the antithesis of these values. If there were no classes, there was no need for the institutionalization of collective labour relations.

Both labour and capital were weak in terms of size and institutional capacity in the early republican era. The industrialization of Turkey was initiated by the state in the 1930s, and maintained for decades. Large public enterprises need thousands of workers. The state secured individual labour rights to guarantee the supply of labour in an agricultural society. Severe class conflicts and industrial movements did not occur in the early republican era. Despite all significant changes in the following decades, the legacy of the state tradition had a path-dependent effect.

Contrary to its state tradition, Turkey took some early steps to institutionalize industrial relations in the following decades under the pressures derived from both newly organized labour and international dynamics. Turkey became a member of the International Labour Organization (ILO) in 1932, lifted the ban on trade unions in the mid-1940s, and ratified the ILO Right to Organise and Collective Bargaining Convention, 1949 (No. 98) at the beginning of the 1950s. But it maintained the traditional attitude of unions as merely representing clubs or solidarity associations. The right to strike and collective bargaining were not allowed, and the state ignored unions and restrained them from solving labour issues in the 1950s. The political climate and the tension between the state tradition and newly organized labour transformed the trajectory of Turkish industrial relations, and it began to converge on a Western model. As illustrated below, the institutionalization of industrial relations gained ground for two decades, 1960 to 1980. The emergence of the private sector in the Turkish economy, the dissolution of the agricultural labour force and the proletarianization of labour, and increasing commodification in urban areas, triggered a new era of industrial relations. Turkey's international relations, in particular its desire for European integration, also played a significant role in the trajectory of its industrial relations. At the beginning of the 1960s, Turkey and the European Economic Community signed a treaty which aimed at Turkey's eventual integration to the European Union (EU). As a result of the tension, struggles and interactions between these dynamics, a hybrid industrial relation system was institutionalized in the post-1960 era. The two decades that followed marked an exceptional era in the history of Turkish industrial relations, and one in which it appeared that there might be convergence with a traditional trajectory.

The military regime of 1980 abandoned Keynesian economic policies and deemed industrial relations institutions a burden on the economy, liberalizing the economy and social policy. In the context of the economic transition and liberalization of 1980s, organized labour could not benefit from the legacy of state corporatism to survive, as occured in some countries in Latin America. On the contrary, it suffered from the legacy of a paternalistic state tradition.

While Turkey has returned to democratic governance, the industrial relations regime established after the coup remained. The Justice and Development Party (JDP), which came into power in 2002, has sustained its predecessors' market-driven policies. Unions have lost their role as fundamental players in industrial relations and have become limited, merely symbolic organizations under the heavy influence of the ruling party. The industrial relations regime established in the post-coup era, which continued into the JDP era, included two features: more flexibility in individual labour relations, and authoritarian arrangements in collective labour relations. Union-busting, deunionization, and symbiotic unionism – under which some unions support the government unconditionally in return for unlawful privileges – are accompanied by deregulation and individualization of labour relations under the tag of 'flexibilization' that focuses on the supervision and control of labour. This new industrial relations regime may be called 'authoritarian flexibilization' (Çelik, 2015a). In the light of the general considerations encapsulated above, the evolution of industrial relations in modern Turkey can be divided into six periods.

6.2.1 The Pre-Republican Era, before 1923

The late industrialization of the Ottoman Empire and the late emergence of the working class in its territories delayed the emergence of trade unionism and industrial relations. Following the proclamation of the second constitutional monarchy, there were some early labour movements, and some strikes in 1908. The imperial Government responded by adopting the first Act regulating industrial relations, the Work Stoppages Act (Tatil-i Eşgal Kanunu, 1909), which banned trade unions in the public services sector. Between 1912 and 1922, the Balkan Wars, the First World War, and the war of independence fostered a paternalistic labour relations environment. The multi-ethnic composition of the Ottoman labour force, nationalistic movements and inter-communal tensions impeded the emergence of a strong and organized labour movement.

6.2.2   The Early Republican Era, 1923–46: A Paternalistic Labour Regime

In this period the country was ruled by a single party, the Republican People's Party (RPP; CHP in Turkish). From 1925, with the adoption of the Restoration of Peace Act (Takrir-i Sükun Kanunu), for more than two decades a virtual state of emergency was maintained, during which all political and societal opposition, including political parties, associations, unions and publications, was prohibited *de jure* or *de facto*.The authoritarian character of the regime was softened by paternalism which dealt with the physical, economic and social problems involved in the transition from the village to the city, and from rural to industrial life (Rosen, 1963).

In 1936 Turkey's first labour law was enacted. Shaped by the statist economic policies of the 1930s and the traditionally paternalistic attitude of the Turkish state towards labour–capital relations, the law was comprehensive and inclusive in terms of individual employment relations, at a time when there was no substantial industrial workforce or labour conflict in Turkey (Dereli, 2013).

The law reflected the state tradition which continued for decades. The law had two opposite and contradictory characteristics. On the one hand, it guaranteed basic individual employee rights, such as minimum wage, social security and limitations on working time. On the other, it banned strikes and lockouts and adopted a compulsory arbitration mechanism in the event of disputes. Trade unions were not mentioned. The measure embodied a typical paternalistic approach: the protection of employees individually, along with the prevention of collective empowerment. In 1938, inspired by authoritarian political developments in Europe, the Government passed the Association Act, explicitly prohibiting all organizations based on class, and banning the establishment of trade unions (for more detail, see Makal, 1999). The lack of organized business and labour, a state tradition, and the solidaristic ideology of the ruling party left little room for the emergence of corporatist industrial relations.

6.2.3   Unionism 1946–60: No Rights to Free Collective Bargaining or Strike Action

Following the Second World War, a degree of pluralism entered Turkey's political system. Reflecting this change, the prohibition on the establishment of trade unions and class-based political parties was lifted in mid-1946. Two socialist parties and several trade unions were established shortly thereafter, but were closed down by the Government. From the end of 1946 until the 1960s, left-wing politics and class-based unionism were put on hold; only unions under the influence of the ruling party or other mainstream political bodies were tolerated.

The Trade Union Act of 1947 provided for limited unionism, without the right to free collective bargaining or to strike. As illustrated by Professor Galenson, the activities of unions were so circumscribed by law as to exclude them from any effective role in industrial relations. They did not enjoy the right to strike, or to handle grievances at the factory level (Galenson, 1963). The Act also prohibited relations between political parties and unions and labelled unions as nationalistic organizations, in line with the mainstream ideology of the ruling party. Notwithstanding these restrictions, labour gained the right to establish unions without previous authorization, and cleared the way for trade union pluralism. The legacy of the 1947 Act on the formation and emergence of a specific type of unionism persisted for many decades. Following its passage, several unions were formed, mainly in state-run enterprises (most of the industrial workforce at that time being employed by the state), where they were under the controlling surveillance of the ruling party. These conditions generated a type of unionism that was pro-Government and paternalistic rather than strong and independent. This type of unionism continued for decades, as did the system of the free establishment of unions and trade union pluralism.

From 1950 until the coup of 1960, power was in the hands of the conservative Democrat Party (DP), under which policy regarding industrial relations and trade unions remained unchanged (Çelik, 2010). The private sector's role in industrialization had gained momentum by the 1950s. Turkey's first national trade union confederation, Türk-İş, was formed in 1952, ten years earlier than the first national employers' association (the relatively late emergence of which reflected the domination of state-run enterprises). Between 1946 and 1960, the right to organize evolved, although state intervention remained prominent and limits continued to be placed on on collective labour rights. Yet while unions still did not have the right to bargain (freely) and strike, unionization and workers' movements made some gradual advances, and organized labour gained valuable experience and self-confidence in its interactions with employers and the state (Koçak, 2008; Çelik, 2010). The government insisted that the level of industrialization was not sufficient to institutionalize industrial relations.

6.2.4 The Institutionalization of Industrial Relations, 1960–80

Turkey's modern industrial relations system, with the hallmark rights to organize, to bargain collectively and to strike, was established after the 1960 coup. The Constitution of 1961 which secured these rights was based on the principles of the social state and the rule of law, launching an era of what has been called 'limited societal corporatism' (Bianchi, 1984). For the first time organized labour was placed on equal footing *vis-à-vis* the state and employers, which brought workers into the political and economic domain as a powerful interest group, introducing a greater dynamism into Turkey's industrial relations system (Özkızıltan, 2013). As an example of the limited societal corporatism, in 1978, a social pact named the Social Agreement was agreed between the leftist government of Ecevit and the leading confederation Türk-İş, but it failed in a short time.

Over the next 20 years the industrial relations system as a whole was modernized and institutionalized, workers and employers organized freely, and collective bargaining became one of the chief determinants of wages, with positive effects in both the private and public sectors (DPT, 1968, 1973; Boratav, 2003). As collective bargaining gained ground, so did the social and political influence of trade unions. There was a dramatic increase in trade union density, and in the numbers of strikes and worker movements. Bipartite and tripartite dialogue between social partners and the state became somewhat more common (Koray and Çelik, 2007). The import-substitutive industrialization strategy paved the way for strong trade unions in both the public and private sectors. In the mid-1960s a class-based trade unionism which derived from private sector workers emerged, and the second-biggest national labour umbrella organization DİSK (the Progressive Trade Unions Confederation of Turkey) was established.

During this period, the adoption of Keynesian economic policies and import substitution may have contributed to an inclusive development from which all working people benefited. Real wages rose significantly: taking 1965 as the base year with an index of 100, by 1977 real wages measured 184 in the public sector and 138 in the private sector (TurkStat, 2005; Talas, 1992; Çelik, 2012a). At the same time, income distribution improved: the share of wages in functional income distribution was 21.5 per cent in 1963 increased to 36 per cent in 1977 and 1978 (Özmucur, 1995).

6.2.5   The 1980 Coup and After: The 1980s and 1990s

The institutionalization of industrial relations was interrupted by the new export-oriented economic policy which liberalized labour markets, and the coup of 1980 which eroded civil and social rights. The *coup d'état* of 1980 dealt a severe blow to the nascent industrial relations system. The 1961 Constitution was suspended, collective bargaining and strikes were pro-hibited, and union activities ceased. This was accompanied by the arrest and long imprisonment of many union leaders. The new military regime espoused economic policies based on export-oriented industrialization, large-scale privatization and liberalization of markets, including the labour market, and implemented structural adjustment programmes (Boratav, 2003; Yeldan, 2015[1]).

The rationale given for the wage stabilization programme enacted on 24 January 1980 was that Turkey's exports would not be competitive at existing wage levels, and that it was therefore necessary to find ways to discipline wages (Boratav, 2003). The overall goal of the new economic programme was a free market economy, the pursuit of which resulted in the strengthening of international and local capital against labour. The implementation of this was made possible by the military coup (Boratav, 2003); indeed, major employers of the time admitted that without the coup, it would not have been possible to put the structural adjustment programme of January 1980 into practice (*Cumhuriyet*, 1982). A new market-driven economic paradigm and a new industrial relations regime resulted in growing insecurity. Following the coup, collective agreements were concluded by the High Board of Arbitration (YHK), a compulsory arbitration board mostly composed of government and employer representatives. The right to collective bargaining and the right to strike were suspended for four years. The board removed crucial industrial relations institutions from the collective bargaining agreements (CBAs) such as the rules relating to representation and participation of workers at enterprise level, and rules on union and job security. Important elements of industrial relations established between 1960 and 1980 were abolished.

A new Constitution enacted in 1982 (and still in force today), along with Laws Nos 2821 and 2822, on industrial relations was passed in 1983. This created an authoritarian framework which limited labour rights and fundamental freedoms. Not only did it restrict freedom of association, the right to bargain collectively and the right to strike, but it also banned all political activities by unions, and severely restricted the right to assemble and the right to demonstrate, making these subject to permission from the public administration. The period after 1980 has been described as the most regressive era in Turkey's entire history in terms of social policy (Talas, 1992). The country's industrial relations system today is a legacy of this era.

Along with privatization, efforts to increase the use of non-standard types of employment, the flexibility of labour markets and the moderation of wages gained momentum. With the radical changes in economic policies, the protective social functions that the state had carried out between 1960 and 1980 gradually faded away. With the Motherland Party (ANAP) in office, from 1983 to 1991, employers' associations came to dominate the Government's policy on industrial relations.

6.2.6   The JDP Era: 2002 and After

The JDP came into power in 2002. Its parliamentary dominance was a result of the financial crisis of 2001, and an electoral system that enabled it to win two-thirds of parliamentary seats with one-third of the popular vote.

The social and economic goals of the new government, set out explicitly in political party and government programmes, include a more flexible labour market, a free market economy and a market society. This market-driven perspective extends to individual and collective labour relations, and the party is in favour of minimizing the state's social responsibilities, as well as privatizing and commercializing public enterprises and services. One of the important developments in this period is the systematic flexibilization of the legislation of individual labour relations. In the first year of the new government, a new labour Act no. 4857 was adopted (in 2003), inaugurating a more constrained era for individual labour relations. The new labour law encompassed many new flexible regulations which were not included in the former Act (no. 1475). The result has been the modification or abolition of many pro-labour practices and institutions that had been stabilized for more than 30 years.

The new government sustained the market-driven policies of its predecessors, and showed more resolve in executing them. Flexible employment practices, such as subcontracting and fixed-time employment contracts, which came into use under the ANAP in the 1980s, have become more deeply entrenched, including in the public sector, where the new government preferred subcontracting arrangements to recruiting permanent public employees. Between 2002 and 2011 the number of workers hired under subcontracting arrangements rose from 387 000 to 1.6 million (Öngel, 2014). There has also been a new wave of privatization. During the period of 1986–2003 the total revenue of privatization was about $8.2 billion. Between 2004 and 2016 the new government acquired a total of $60 billion from privatization.

For this reason, 2002 may be considered a major point of departure from previous labour regimes. Although the protective labour regime that began with the Constitution of 1961 was neutralized by the military coup of 1980, its real purge took place more than 20 years later. The new labour regime institutionalizes flexibility in individual labour relations, and at the same time demonstrates an authoritarian tendency in terms of collective industrial relations.

Table 6.1   Main labour market indicators in Turkey, 2016

Indicator	Turkey, 2016
Active population (aged 15+)	59 million
Labour force	30.8 million
Labour force participation rate	52%
Labour force participation rate of women	32.7%
Total employment	27 million
Employment rate	45.8%
Paid employees	18.4 million
Informal employment rate	33%
Share of non agricultural employment	81.3%
Unemployment rate (non-agricultural)	14.3%

Source: TurkStat (2017).

6.3   CURRENT TRENDS IN TURKEY'S LABOUR MARKET

The structure of labour markets has a direct influence on industrial relations, with the industrial and demographic structure of employment, and the types of employment, playing a critical role in union density. Turkey's active working-age population (aged 15 and over) is 59 million and the labour participation rate is 52 per cent (see Table 6.1). Total employment in Turkey is about 27 million; while the proportion of paid employees has risen rapidly in recent years, it still accounts for only 18.4 million. The great majority of employees (15.3 million out of 18.4 million, according to 2016 data) work under employment contracts; these workers constitute the foundation of unionization. The remainder are civil servants employed under administrative law (see section 6.5.1 below) (TurkStat, 2017; MoF, 2013). The Turkish labour market is characterized by high levels of unemployment, underemployment and informal employment.

Agricultural employment declined from 53 per cent of total employment in 1980 to 18.7 per cent in 2016; while employment in the service sector, which was around 26 per cent in the 1980s, rose to 54.2 per cent (TurkStat, 2017). At the same time, wage employment has been increasing rapidly: the proportion of unpaid family workers in the labour force fell from 29 per cent in the mid-1990s to 10.7 per cent in the mid-2010s; and the share of self-employed from 25 per cent to 17 per cent. Over the same period the share of wage-earning labour climbed from 40 per cent to 68 per cent (TurkStat, 2017). This trend was reinforced by the dissolution of agricultural structures and the growth in non-agricultural employment.

The informal employment rate was about 51 per cent in 2000, but it declined to around 33 per cent in 2016. Although the formalization of labour has made progress in recent years, still 8.7 million people, mostly own-account and unpaid family workers, remain outside the formal sector. Turkey has 3.1 million informal workers (under employment contracts) in the private sector. All informal workers are outside the formal industrial relations system, including domestic workers. Informal workers cannot affiliate to trade unions, due to the electronic union membership mechanism based on social security institution records. Recently, legal provisions have been adopted to formalize domestic workers in the social security system.

It might be expected that the decline in informal employment would strengthen trade unionism. However, there has been no observable increase in unionization. One reason for this is that the increase in formal employment is happening in the service sector, where unionizing is more difficult than in manufacturing. Another reason is the large number of small and medium-sized enterprises (SMEs) in the Turkish economy. Enterprises with 50 or fewer employees account for 61.5 per cent of all workers in Turkey, and those with 100 or fewer employees for 71 per cent (MoLSS, 2014). The penetration of unions in SMEs is extremely low. SME employers usually oppose union activities, and workers are reluctant to join unions for fear of losing their jobs (Dereli, 2013).

The shift from a public sector to a private sector economy has also weakened industrial relations. This trend is reflected in the erosion in public sector CBAs, which covered 900 000 workers in the mid-1980s and only 350 000 in the mid-2010s; the public sector share in the coverage of CBAs fell from about 62 per cent in the late 1980s to 36 per cent in 2016 (Çelik, 2012b; MoLSS, 2016). This change is a direct consequence of privatization, externalization and flexibilization (outsourcing and subcontracting) practices in the public sector. On the one hand, public enterprises have been privatized and public employment has fallen; on the other, subcontracting and outsourcing have replaced the direct employment of public workers and civil servants. Even so, trade union density and CBA coverage remain higher in the public than in the private sector.

6.4   THE LEGAL AND REGULATORY FRAMEWORK OF INDUSTRIAL RELATIONS

The legal framework for the Turkish industrial system is characterized by both continuity and discontinuity. Since the first Trade Union Act was adopted in 1947, there has been relative continuity in the system for the establishment of trade unions, including voluntary membership and trade union pluralism. But in terms of collective bargaining rights, there has been considerable discontinuity. The trajectory has at times been described as 'one step forward and two steps back'. Between 1963 and 1980 the law allowed the establishment of several types of unions, such as workplace unions, industrial unions, regional unions, federations and confederations for workers. The collective bargaining system covered the workplace, enterprise and industry levels. The right to strike was guaranteed for workers in respect of both rights and interest disputes.

The Turkish employment and industrial relations system is characterized by two distinct systems: one for employees and a separate one for public servants (those employed in the administration of the state), with few similarities in terms of individual and collective labour relations. Public servants acquired the right to organize in 1965 but this did not include the right to collective bargaining or the right to strike and to peaceful assembly. However, following the quasi-military intervention in 1971, public servants' unions were abolished.

In the early 2000s, some groups of public servants gained the right to organize, but not the right to collective bargaining or the right to strike. In 2010, some provisions of the Constitution were amended, granting public servants the right to collective bargaining under a system of compulsory arbitration. There are several unions and confederations for public servants in Turkey (see, for more detail, Uçkan, 2013), but these have been left out of the analysis here as they are regulated differently from other unions. While workers (in both the private and the public sectors) work under individual employment contracts, public servants are subject to administrative law. Public servants' unions in Turkey function as associations rather than trade unions.

Turkey's industrial relations legislation as a whole has not encouraged trade unionism; indeed, to some degree it has been hostile to the unions. The provisions of the 1982 Constitution relating to labour relations and other labour legislation of the years following the 1980 coup were largely shaped by the demands of the Turkish Confederation of Employer Associations, TİSK, whose leaders openly welcomed the new industrial relations legislation despite strong opposition from the unions (MESS, 2000).

The regulations of the coup era placed limitations on organizational rights. The public notarization system, which was adopted in 1983, ostensibly to prevent forged membership, turned into a cumbersome, costly and time-consuming process. Nonetheless, the provision remained in effect to 2013, when it was abolished and an electronic membership mechanism was adopted. Other serious obstacles to union organizing were the 'double threshold' (see below) and the competency system, by which unions have to meet defined thresholds in order to be deemed 'competent' to engage in collective bargaining. The latter enables employers or rival unions to block union activities by raising an objection to the competency certificates issued by the Ministry of Labour and Social Security (MoLSS), in which event all such activities must cease pending a final judicial decision. Furthermore, the lack of an effective job security system to protect against dismissals on the ground of union membership has made it all too easy for firms to systematically lay off unionized workers.

The labour legislation of the coup era remained untouched until 2010, when changes were made to the provisions of the Constitution relating to trade union rights. The provision allowing strikes to be prohibited or postponed (article 54/4) remains in force, the final decision resting with the Supreme Board of Arbitration (YHK), a body dominated by the Government and employers. Although the prohibition on 'political strikes and lockouts, solidarity strikes and lockouts, general strikes and lockouts, work place occupation, slowing work, diminishing productivity and other forms of resistance' has been lifted, the essence of article 54 remains unchanged. The first clause of the article limits the right to strike to 'interest strikes' in 'cases of disagreements during collective bargaining'. The amendment to article 53, meanwhile, prescribes mandatory arbitration for public servants (that is, all employees engaged in the administration of the state), denying those employees the right to strike.

In November 2012 the Unions and Collective Bargaining Law No. 6356 replaced the Laws Nos 2821 and 2822, dating from 1983. The new law, which provides the legal foundation of the current Turkish industrial relations system, was expected to overcome the problems stemming from the old legislation; however, it did not represent any significant change. Moreover, it is hard to argue that it is based on genuine consensus among the social partners. Employer associations, such as the Independent Industrialists' and Businessmen's Association (MÜSİAD), the Turkish Confederation of Businessmen and Industrialists (TUSKON) and the Turkish Union of Chambers and Commodity Exchanges (TOBB), were heavily involved in preparing the new Act (Çelik, 2014b). Crucially, Law No. 6356, although introducing some limited improvements, especially regarding the founding of unions, their internal activities and union membership, maintains the restrictions on the rights to bargain collectively and to strike.

6.4.1   The Right to Organize, Union Membership and Internal Governance of Unions

The new law has made it easier to found unions and has introduced some regulations that make the internal governance of unions easier. It has also removed the notarization requirement for entry into and withdrawal from union membership. Workers can now become members of a union digitally, via an e-membership system, and through the MoLSS. However, although the notarization requirement was a very serious obstacle to union membership, the new e-membership mechanism has also started to cause problems. For example, some employers are illegally obtaining the e-membership passwords of their employees and interfering with workers' union choices (Çelik, 2014a). Nevertheless, the e-membership route resulted in a rapid rise in union membership, from 1 031 000 in July 2013, before its introduction, to 1 514 000 in January 2016.

Law No. 6356 limits the formation of unions to industry level and prohibits the formation of workplace, enterprise or occupation-based unions. Nor does it allow union federations, city- or region-based unions, or unions representing retired people, farmers or the unemployed.

6.4.2 The Right to Collective Bargaining

The most important contradiction in Law No. 6356 is that while it allows only industry-level unionization, it prescribes a workplace- or enterprise-level collective bargaining regime. That is, the new law, just like the old one, takes the workplace and enterprise level as the sole points of reference, and does not allow economy-wide, industry, or profession-based collective agreements. Another persisting constraint concerns the competency requirement for collective bargaining. There are two main problems associated with the competency process. One is the industry and workplace or enterprise threshold; the other is the fact that only the MoLSS can issue the competency certificates entitling unions to undertake collective bargaining.

The Act did amend the double threshold system – 10 per cent all of workers in a particular industry and more than 50 per cent in an individual firm or workplace must join a union for it to be recognized – that had inhibited unionization for 30 years. At first, the industry threshold was reduced to 3 per cent for independent unions and 1 per cent for unions affiliated with confederations under the umbrella of the Economic and Social Council (ESC). In 2015 the Constitutional Court decreed that all unions shall be subject to the 1 per cent industry threshold. The law continues to maintain the workplace threshold of more than 50 per cent where a company is composed of a single workplace, while lowering the threshold to 40 per cent for enterprises composed of multiple workplaces, for example, banks. These high workplace and enterprise thresholds hamper union organization, the effective representation of workers and the exercise of their right to bargain collectively.

The MoLSS determines whether a union has met the industry and workplace or enterprise thresholds, and issues the competency certificates required to engage in collective bargaining. However, some authors are of the view that as a political institution, it is not always impartial and sometimes acts to protect unions close to the Government (Özveri, 2013). For instance, in certain years, when unions affiliated to Türk-İş enrolled the majority of workers at some state-run companies such as the General Directorate Tea Enterprises and the Ministry of Forestry, the MoLSS issued competency certificates to unions affiliated with Hak-İş, which has close ties with the ruling party (Çelik, 2015a).

The collective bargaining process can be brought to a halt if the employer or rival unions object to the competency document that the Ministry has issued. Competency lawsuits last for years, and the union cannot pursue any activities in the workplace until the final judgment. Employers, meanwhile, can use the legal process to hamstring a union and either force unionized workers to resign or lay them off; even if an employer is found guilty of dismissal on grounds of union membership, fines are too low to exercise a deterrent effect. According to a survey of the textile, metal, petrochemical and paper industries, between 1992 and 2009 the MoLSS issued 8144 competency certificates in these sectors, and employers or rival unions opened lawsuits in 944 cases (about 12 per cent). At the end of the judicial process, only 27 per cent of all cases won by unions resulted in CBAs, while the unions had lost about 60 000 members (Özveri, 2013).

Law No. 6356 regulates the CBA procedure in detail, specifying processes and phases that interfere with free bargaining by the parties. The number of workers covered by collective agreements remains lower than the number of unionized workers and there is no effective system for the extension of CBAs.

6.4.3 The Right to Strike

The most restrictive provisions of Law No. 6356 concern the right to strike. The law designates as illegal all strikes except those that arise from disputes during collective bargaining ('interest strikes'). Thus slowdowns, solidarity strikes, sympathy strikes and general strikes are prohibited and subject to heavy penalties, including large fines and the dismissal without compensation of participating workers. The law limits 'interest strikes' to specified durations, and stipulates that employers be notified ahead of time and that strike action take place within 60 days of the notification. The right to strike is granted only to workers in the strict sense. Public employees do not enjoy the right to strike.

The law also maintains the existing prohibitions on strikes in many sectors, including banking services, electricity, the petrochemical industry, natural gas production and urban transportation, as well as on strike action by civilian employees working for the Ministry of National Defence and the military. The ban on strikes in banking and urban transportation was pronounced unlawful by the Constitutional Court of Turkey following an application filed by the main opposition party, the RPP.[2] A further provision added to the Law of Capital Markets on 6 December 2012 banned strikes on the stock exchange and in other financial services. Moreover, the Government has the authority to postpone or suspend all strikes on the grounds that they are deemed to jeopardize national security and/or public health. Following the state of emergency declared after the failed coup in 15 July 2016, the government issued a statutory decree that changed the trade union law. A strike in the banking sector may be suspended on the grounds that it jeopardizes economic and financial stability. The authority has been used repeatedly for many years by Turkish governments.

6.5 ACTORS IN THE TURKISH INDUSTRIAL RELATIONS SYSTEM

6.5.1 Trade Unions

Before the coup of 1980, a pluralistic trade union model prevailed in Turkey, and workplace-based unions, regional unions and federations could be freely established. Following the coup, a uniform and centralized industrial unionism was enforced; workplace and profession-based unions, along with regional unions and federations, were not allowed (Dereli, 2013). As a result, centralization increased and the number of unions declined dramatically, from some 800 before 1980 to around 100 after that date. Because of the ban on workplace unions, most unions became defunct and/or merged with others. As of 2017, there are three trade union confederations and 169 trade unions (excluding those for civil servants, as explained above). However, only 56 of these trade unions meet the thresholds required to win competency to conclude collective agreements.

Most trade unions in Turkey fall within three confederations. The leading one is the Confederation of Turkish Trade Unions (Türk-İş), founded in 1952; the other two are the Progressive Trade Unions Confederation of Turkey (DİSK), founded in 1967, and the Righteous Worker Unions Confederation (Hak-İş), founded in 1976. Türk-İş, which has adopted the principles of 'bread-and-butter unionism' and 'non-partisanship politics' characteristic of the United States (US) trade unionism, and is generally aligned with centre-right political parties, is active mainly in state-owned enterprises. DİSK, founded by unionists of the socialist Labour Party of Turkey (TİP), adopted class-based unionism, is more closely aligned with socialist and centre-left politics and is most prominent in the private sector. DİSK was the second-largest confederation in Turkey before 1980. Hak-İş was founded by the National Salvation Party and is known to have formed close ties to the ruling party since the 2000s. There are also some small independent unions outside the three confederations. Türk-İş was formerly the largest confederation by far, ahead of DİSK in second place and Hak-İş in third place. However, owing to its links to the governing party, Hak-İş has gained ground: whereas in 2002 the respective shares of Türk-İş, DİSK and Hak-İş in total union membership were 71.5, 14 and 11 per cent, by 2017 the shares of Türk-İş and DİSK had fallen to 57 and 9 per cent, respectively, while that of Hak-İş had shot up to 32 per cent (MoLSS, 2002, 2017). There are also several unions and confederations for civil servants in Turkey, but these have been left out of the analysis here for the reasons mentioned above.

During the 1990s and 2000s, the three union confederations established two joint platforms called the Democracy Platform and the Labour Platform. Some professional and occupational organizations such as the bodies for engineers and architects also participated in these platforms. The main aim of these platforms was to defend labour and social rights and to organize joint activities such as demonstrations, campaigns and research. These platforms did not last after 2010, as a result of mounting political differences among participant organizations.

Trade unionism in Turkey today is a fragmented movement, subject to competition and rivalry. Although there are no formal ties between unions and political parties, there are informal links, and unions are subject to political pressure. Because there are no formal ties between trade unions and political parties in Turkey, the unions have little influence over political decision-making. In Turkey organized labour had not been part of the struggle for independence and the transition to democracy.

Neither the organic relationship between one or more political parties and unions that is observed in the United Kingdom and the Scandinavian countries, nor the strong ties and mutual influence present in some G20 emerging economies such as Brazil, China and South Africa, can be found in Turkey. During the 1960s and 1970s, Türk-İş forged strong ties with the US unionism (Çelik, 2010), which has continued to influence Türk-İş policies. Although Türk-İş became more politically active for a short while in the 1980s and 1990s, opposing the governments of the period, it fell back to its previous political stance in the post-2002 era, and since then has largely remained under the influence of the ruling party. In Turkey, then, organized labour lacks weight in political decision-making and democratic–corporatist industrial relations remain undeveloped. It is ironic that while organized labour does not play a role in politics, the ruling party gained momentum and influence over a significant part of organized labour. Since 2002, several pro-government union leaders have been co-opted and moved into the Parliament and Government. Trade unionists moving into national politics had to withdraw from their union posts.

Political alliances between some pro-government labour confederations such as Hak-İş and Memur-Sen, and the ruling party, have strengthened since 2002. These two confederations, which have complex and close ties with the ruling party, supported the government unconditionally and in return they gained more and more members among public servants and public workers. The membership of Hak-İş soared in a short time from 166 000 in 2013 to 490 000 in 2016. Memur-Sen, a public servant confederation, also dramatically increased its membership from 40 000 to 1 million. This 'miracle' is a result of a symbiotic unionism that has emerged in the post-2002 era.

Trade union density

Official Turkish labour statistics, as published by the MoLSS, have for many years contained errors regarding trade union density (Çelik and Lordoğlu, 2006). These are attributable largely to the lack of a reliable data-collecting system, fictive membership data arising from inter-union rivalry, double-counting, huge informal employment, and inclusion of void memberships. According to the statistics published by the MoLSS between January 1984 and July 2009, rates of unionization varied between 51 per cent and 69 per cent. A further difficulty arises from the evaluation of public service unions (covering government employees and officials) together with workers' unions. As noted above, the two types of unions are not comparable.

Given the impossibility of finding reliable data for union density in Turkey before 2013, the figures presented here are based on the number of workers covered by collective bargaining agreements. Table 6.2 shows union density for the years 1989–2012, excluding civil servants, calculated on this basis. The consistent and marked decline is striking: union density in Turkey in the 2000s was even lower than in the period following the coup of 1980. In fact, Turkey has the lowest and fastest-dropping union density of OECD countries, at about 6 per cent against an OECD average of 17 per cent.[3]

Finally, in January 2013, the MoLSS switched to calculating union membership on the basis of the country's social security records. The revised official statistics put union density for Turkey in 2016 at 12 per cent (MoLSS, 2016). However, there remains a weak point even in the new

Table 6.2   *Estimated union density, 1989–2012 (old system) (workers*
           covered by collective bargaining agreements, excluding civil
           servants)

Year	Coverage of CBAs (%)	Year	Coverage of CBAs (%)
1989	27	2001	12
1990	24	2002	12
1991	25	2003	10
1992	22	2004	11
1993	24	2005	9
1994	21	2006	9
1995	18	2007	8
1996	17	2008	7
1997	15	2009	7
1998	14	2010	7
1999	14	2011	7
2000	12	2012	6

Note: CBA coverage figures are based on two-year averages calculated from MoLSS labour statistics, as a proportion of the number of total workers, excluding civil servants.

Sources: TurkStat (1999, 2005); MoLSS labour statistics (for concerned years).

statistics: namely, that they do not take informal workers into account. When this element is factored into the calculation, trade union density based on the new system stood at 9.8 in 2016, rising slightly from 7.3 per cent in 2013 (Table 6.3).

Analysis of the data by sector shows marked differences in unionization rates across different areas of the economy, with particularly low rates in construction and services (see Table 6.4). Areas that are dominated by the public sector, such as general services, defence and agriculture, have higher levels of unionization. Looking beyond these public sector activities, the marked difference between the construction and services sectors, on the one hand, and manufacturing industry, on the other, is noteworthy. In manufacturing, the unionization rate (14 per cent) is higher than the overall rate (12 per cent in 2016), while in construction and services it is much lower (by 3–5 percentage points). With the service sector accounting for an increasing proportion of total employment, the implications are not favourable for unionization in Turkey in the future. In recent decades, a significant decline has occurred in employment in the public sector and manufacturing, traditionally unionized sectors.

Table 6.3   Trade union density and the coverage of CBAs (new system), 2013–16

Year (by January)	Total workers (excluding civil servants) (000)	Total formal workers (000)	Total union membership (000)	Coverage of CBAs (000)	Trade union density (%)	Official trade union density (%)	Coverage of CBAs (%)
	(1)	(2)	(3)	(4)	(3/1)	(3/2)	(4/1)
2013	13 640	10 881	1002	690	7.3	9.2	5.1
2014	14 391	11 601	1097	876	7.6	9.5	6.1
2015	15 043	12 181	1297	954	8.6	10.6	6.3
2016	15 512	12 664	1514	1004	9.8	12.0	6.5

Sources: Author's calculations from MoLSS labour statistics, 2013, 2014, 2015, 2016 (new basis); TurkStat (2015, 2017); Finance Ministry statistics.

Table 6.4   Trade union density by sector and industry, 2016

Industry	Trade union density (%)
Construction	3.1
Services	5.1
Tourism	3.8
Transportation[1]	9.8
Manufacturing	14
Defence and security[1]	35.5
Mining[1]	19.3
Energy[1]	27
General services[1]	33.3
Agriculture[1]	25.8
Banking	35.5

Note: 1. Mostly public sector.

Source: Based on official data of MoLSS (2017).

The labour force participation rate of women in Turkey is much lower than that of men, and the share of women employees in formal employment is about 24 per cent. The proportion of women in the country's total union membership is even lower, standing at only 17 per cent in 2015 (Table 6.5). One recently published survey revealed that in Turkey women are experiencing severe difficulties not only in becoming union members, but also in participating in the internal governance of unions (Urhan, 2015).

Table 6.5   Trade union density by gender, 2015

	Membership (000)	No. of workers (000)
Men	1130	9332
Women	234	3317
Total	1364	12649
Women's share (%)	17.2	26.2

Source: MoLSS (2015).

6.5.2   Employers' Organizations

Turkey has many employers' organizations. Three of the major bodies are confederations consisting of chambers based on mandatory membership: the Union of Chambers and Commodity Exchanges of Turkey (TOBB), the Union of Turkish Agricultural Chambers (TZOB) and the Turkish Confederation of Tradesmen and Craftsmen (TESK). These three mandatory employers' associations deal with sectoral issues of employers apart from labour–management relations. The umbrella employers' organization that addresses only industrial relations and labour issues is the Turkish Confederation of Employer Associations (TİSK), which is based on voluntary membership. Its membership comprises 20 employers' associations, and it represents employers in many bilateral and trilateral social dialogue bodies.

TİSK deals with trade unions in both private companies and state-run enterprises. The affiliation of public enterprises with TISK has attracted sharp criticism from the trade unions: Türk-İş, for example, has alleged that the inclusion of public employers as members of TİSK gives them the right to act in the same way as private sector employers, with a particular concern that public resources could be diverted to support TİSK's lockout funds (Koray and Çelik, 2007).

TİSK states that 9600 workplaces are affiliated with its constituent employers' associations (TİSK, 2015). However, as there are no official and comparable data about the membership of employers' associations, the figure cannot be verified. The number of workplaces registered under the labour laws in Turkey is around 1.6 million, of which about 1.4 million have fewer than ten employees (MoLSS, 2014). Owing to a lack of data, it is almost impossible to comment on employer organization and collective negotiation in these workplaces.

According to 2012 and 2013 data, the number of workplaces with collective bargaining agreements is around 24000. Most of these are workplaces with more than 50 employees (TurkStat, 2011). As might be expected, larger workplaces are more likely to belong to employer organizations and to engage in collective bargaining. Some 40 per cent of the workplaces using collective bargaining are members of an employers' association; others bargain individually with trade unions. Although most bargaining takes place at the workplace or company level, in some sectors, such as the metal, textile, glass and chemical industries, multi-employer bargaining is conducted between an employer association and one or more trade union(s); the agreements thus reached are called 'group CBAs'. Employers' associations may also bargain with unions on behalf of a single company. Employers' associations have a strong influence in the collective bargaining process across the country: the CBAs they conclude with trade unions act as trend-setters, influencing individual CBAs. In other words, collective bargaining in Turkey happens largely between trade unions and employers' organizations.

6.5.3 The Role of the State

The state in Turkey maintains a role in industrial relations as an employer, despite its dwindling prominence both in the economy and in employment. In the 1980s, 36 per cent of employees worked in the public sector; by 2010, with privatization intensifying in the new century, the proportion had fallen about 10 per cent (Çelik, 2012a).

The continuing role of the state as employer is obvious in the collective bargaining process for public workers (excluding civil servants). This process is centrally coordinated by the Türk-İş trade union confederation, which reaches a non-binding framework agreement for CBAs with the Government on the basis of which individual trade unions conclude CBAs at the level of each state-run enterprise. As noted above, the legislative provisions that apply to government officials are very different from those that apply to other employees, and as a result they are omitted from this review of the Turkish industrial relations system.

Alongside its role as an employer, the state also has strong regulatory, arbitration and conciliation roles in Turkish industrial relations. In a continuation of the paternalistic state tradition, the state regulates all spheres of industrial relations in detail. There are several rules and procedures peculiar to industrial relations. These rules not only arrange the relations and solve disputes, but also restrict autonomous industrial relations.

The state plays a role as a conciliator and arbiter to solve collective labour disputes that arise from interest conflicts in the Turkish collective bargaining system. The collective bargaining process is coordinated and audited by the MoLSS, which also issues the competency certificates for collective bargaining and coordinates the official mediation process in the event of disagreement arising in collective bargaining. Unless an official conciliation or mediation mechanism is governed by the MoLSS, it is unlawful to go on strike or lockout. If no agreement is reached through mediation, the workers may go on strike. In case of strike bans and suspensions, which are common, official compulsory arbitration mechanisms are enforced. Turkey has a compulsory arbitration mechanism which comes into play in the many contexts in which strike bans and/or interventions apply under the labour legislation. The Supreme Arbitration Board consists of eight members: two representatives each for employers and workers, who sit alongside three members assigned by the Government and under the presidency of a judge.

The state also monitors and supervises individual and collective labour relations. The MoLSS has a labour directorate focused on industrial relations and an inspection directorate that supervises individual labour relations, especially health and safety at the workplace. Within the judicial system, labour courts handle workplace disputes and adjudicate individual and collective cases. The Government has the authority to issue a decree for the extension of a CBA to all enterprises, but does not make use of this policy tool. Rights disputes arising from the non-application of CBAs are settled in the labour courts.

6.6 INDUSTRIAL RELATIONS AND SOCIAL DIALOGUE INSTITUTIONS

In order for social dialogue between different groups in society to function well, organizations of social partners must be independent, and willing to resolve their problems through negotiation, consultation and information sharing. Turkey has some formal mechanisms that could facilitate social dialogue at the national level. However, lack of a culture of cooperation and codetermination between employers and workers, unwillingness to engage on the employer side, and government indifference, have inhibited social dialogue.

6.6.1 Social Dialogue from National to Enterprise Level

The main Turkish entity created to facilitate social dialogue at the national level is the ESC, established in 1995 and given constitutional status following the 2010 constitutional amendments. The ESC is supposed to convene four times a year; but in fact it has met just eight times since 2000, most recently in 2009. The ESC is composed of 15 government representatives, 12 employer representatives and 12 worker representatives, and is chaired by the Prime Minister or Deputy Prime Minister. The dominance by government inevitably skews the council's response to the effects of economic change. Another important tripartite body, the Commission on Minimum Wages, sets the national minimum wage; this body consists of five representatives each from the Government, employers and employees (for more on the minimum wage, see section 6.7 below).

Bipartite dialogue between employers and labour can be seen as the first step towards a well-developed tripartite social dialogue platform, where not only labour relations issues, but also socio-economic policies at the macro level, including those that have an effect on labour, could be discussed. As yet, however, Turkey is not in a position to move in this direction, as workers' representation at the workplace and enterprise level has not been adequately established in law and institutionalized; the only limited channel for workers' representation is the trade union shop steward system where CBAs exist.

Below the national level, bipartite social dialogue at the workplace and enterprise levels is severely underdeveloped. Insofar as it exists, social dialogue in the Turkish private sector is strictly limited, with no formal mechanisms other than CBAs. Collective bargaining at the enterprise level is almost the only opportunity for labour to have an effect on decision-making.

There is a provision in the Turkish Labour Act No. 4857 (2003) regarding collective dismissals for economic, technological or structural reasons. In such a case, the employer is supposed to provide the union and the regional labour directorate (local unit of MoLSS) with written information to justify the decision, and take measures to minimize job losses and negative effects on the workers concerned. However, this process relies on there being a trade union in existence at the workplace, which is by no means always the case.

The fact is that the vast majority of Turkey's workers (including almost all those in SMEs) suffer from a lack of representation, information and consultation. This weakness in social dialogue and participation is largely attributable to the country's historical legacy. As noted above, Turkey lacks the federalist or corporatist tradition common to European countries or Latin America, and the Turkish state has historically played a paternalistic role rather than engaging in participatory relationships with other elements of society.

6.6.2 Collective Bargaining

In contrast to its centralized union structure, Turkey has a decentralized collective bargaining system. This weakens the influence of unions over collective bargaining. The scope of collective bargaining is the most critical aspect of collective labour relations. Without an effective collective bargaining extension mechanism, the number of workers covered by CBAs is lower than the number of unionized workers. MoLSS statistics indicate that while the total number of unionized workers by the end of 2015 was about 1.5 million, the number of workers under collective agreements was about 1 million. Thus, more than 33 per cent of unionized workers fall outside the scope of collective agreements. By the end of 2015, the coverage of CBAs stood at just 6–7 per cent, held down by the lack of extension mechanisms, the cumbersome competency system, and the lack of industry-level and national-level negotiations.

Unsurprisingly, the coverage of CBAs in the private sector is lower than in the public sector. According to calculations based on MoLSS data, the number of workers covered by CBAs in the private sector in 2015 was around 600 000; that equated to 4.5 per cent of the total number of private sector workers, down from 7.8 per cent in 1995. While the number of private sector workers rose from 5.6 million in 1995 to 15 million in 2015, the number covered by CBAs during that time has risen hardly at all (Table 6.6).

Table 6.6   *Coverage of collective bargaining agreements in the private sector, 1995–2015*

Years	Workers in the private sector (000)	Private sector workers covered by CBAs (000)	CBA coverage in the private sector (%)
1995	5584	438	7.8
2002	7483	416	5.6
2003	7675	393	5.1
2004	8510	401	4.7
2005	9305	424	4.6
2006	9918	400	4.0
2007	10 572	361	3.4
2008	10 019	316	3.2
2009	9811	336	3.4
2010	10 748	380	3.5
2011	11 777	435	3.7
2012	12 404	462	3.7
2013	13 033	513	3.9
2014	13 685	645	4.7
2015	14 306	643	4.5

Source: MoLSS labour statistics and TurkStat.

Table 6.7 Strike severity rate, 1985–2015

Years	No. of workers at formal sector (000)	No. of working days passed in strikes (000)	Strike severity rate[1]
1985	2614	194	74
1990	3445	3466	1006
1995	4410	4838	1097
2000	5254	368	70
2005	6919	176	25
2010	9914	37	4
2011	11030	13	1.2
2012	11939	36	3
2013	12484	308	25
2014	13240	365	28
2015	13399	129	10

Note: 1. No. of working days that passed in strikes per 1000 workers.

Source: Author's calculations based on MoLSS labour statistics.

6.6.3 Strikes and Other Industrial Conflicts

In line with diminishing union density, the number of strikes has fallen precipitously. A very intense period of industrial conflict, with mass participation, followed the strikes and 'spring protests' that occurred in the public sector in 1989, and in the private sector in 1990 and 1991. Through the early 1990s, the frequency of strikes increased rapidly, peaking in 1995; thereafter the number of strike actions went into sharp decline, though the falling trend stabilized after 2002. Between 1985 and 1995 the number of workers participating in strikes averaged some 60000 per year; that number dropped to 9000 between 1995 and 2000, and to around 5000 after 2000. Through the 2000s, the numbers have been virtually stagnant (Çelik, 2012c). Table 6.7 shows how the use of strike action has declined: strike density, calculated as the number of working days passed in strike action per 1000 workers, was 1097 in 1995, 70 in 2000, and just 3–4 in the beginning of the 2010s. But recent years a slight upward trend or revival in labour disputes and strikes in formal industrial relations.

Intensifying privatization, the pressure created by economic crises, and the repeated use by the Government of its power under article 54 of the Constitution and Law No. 6356 to ban or suspend strikes have contributed to the falling number of strikes. Since 2000, a number of strikes have been suspended on the grounds that they endanger national security or public health (Çelik, 2008). At the end of 2016, the trade union Act was amended

Table 6.8   Strikes suspended by the Government on the grounds of national security and/or public health, 2000–2017

Year	Industry	Grounds	No. of workplace/ company covered	No. of workers covered (approx.)
2000	Rubber	National Security	3	5000
2000	Municipality	Public health + National security	10	13 000
2001	Glass	National Security	15	6000
2002	Rubber	National Security	3	5000
2003	Rubber	National Security	1	353
2003	Glass	National Security	13	5000
2004	Glass	Public health + National security	13	5000
2004	Rubber	National Security	3	5000
2005	Mining	National Security	1	400
2014	Glass	National Security	10	5800
2014	Mining	Public health + National security	2	1500
2015	Metal	National Security	38	15 000
2017	Metal	National Security	4	2200
2017	Banking	Economic and financial stability	1	14 000
2017	Glass	National Security	10	5500
2017	Chemical	Public Health	1	500
Total			128	89 253

Source: Compiled by author from Turkish *Official Gazette*.

and 'economic and financial crisis' adopted as a reason to suspend any strike in the banking and finance sectors. Following this amendment, a big strike in the Turkish banking sector was suspended in March 2017 on the ground of economic and financial crisis. In the 2000s, 16 big strikes were suspended or banned, covering 89 000 workers (Table 6.8).

The suspension of any strike under current Turkish labour legislation means an indefinite ban, because the law imposes compulsory arbitration at the end of the 60-day period of suspension, unless the parties have either come to an agreement or voluntarily sought arbitration. While suspension is justified on the grounds of risk to national security and/or public health, it is applied not only to action affecting essential services whose interruption would endanger the life, safety and health of the whole or part of the population, but also to strikes in any service or industry, including rubber, metal and glass. Claiming that any strike in such industries threatens national security is implausible. It is extremely difficult to exercise the right to strike in Turkey, where, as shown in Table 6.8, the suspension of a strike is not an exceptional situation. Moreover, the judicial supervision of the right to strike has declined and jurisprudences on strike suspensions has altered course in recent years. In the past, the Council of State, which supervises suspension decrees of the government, always ruled that suspension of any strike on economic grounds was *de facto* unlawful, and a violation of the right to strike. On the contrary, since 2014 the Council of State has upheld all strike suspensions (Çelik, 2016).

Despite the decline in lawful strikes, spontaneous and *de facto* strikes, resistance and non-procedural protests continue to occur outside of formal industrial relations. Many of them occur as wildcat strikes, or out of trade unions' control. In May and June 2015, an intense wave of wildcat strikes and protests occurred in the Turkish automotive industry, with the participation of some 10 000 workers. These strikes and protests have affected leading companies in the automotive industry, and represent a unique moment in the history of Turkish industrial relations (Çelik, 2012c, 2015b). Some recent research reveals that there has been an upward trend in spontaneous and wildcat industrial action. In 2015, a total of 178 strikes occurred as a result of labour disputes; 144 out of them fell outside of the formal industrial relations system (Association on Labour Researches, 2016).

6.7   THE MAIN OUTCOMES OF THE INDUSTRIAL RELATIONS SYSTEM

Sound industrial relations can have a positive effect on wages and income distribution. Figure 6.1 shows that from the 1960s to the 1980s, during which Turkey had a strong industrial relations and social protection system, real wages and labour productivity developed in parallel, with workers benefiting from economic growth; but following the *coup d'état* a gap rapidly opened up between real wages and productivity, as growth continued but workers were deprived of the benefits. In the period after 1980, industrial relations institutions and social protections alike grew weaker. The exceptional case in the post-coup era is the spring movements of 1989–91. Major labour disputes and strikes (both formal and informal) during 1989–91 played a positive role in wage increases, as is seen in Figure 6.1.

The average wages of workers covered by CBAs are considerably higher

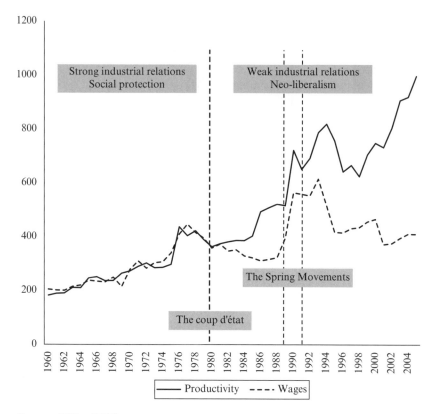

Source: Yeldan (2015).

Figure 6.1   *Labour productivity and real wages in Turkish manufacturing,*
              1960–2005 (1950: 100)

than those of workers not covered. Taking the monthly gross income of
workers not covered by CBAs to be 100, the gross monthly wage of workers covered by CBAs was 202 in 2004, 208 in 2008 and 189 in 2012 (Figure
6.2). However, because the percentage of workers covered by CBAs (as
mentioned above) is so small, the effect of the industrial relations system
on wages remains very limited, especially in the private sector and in
SMEs: the proportion of workers subject to collective agreements in
enterprises with fewer than 250 employees is just 1.3 per cent (TurkStat,
2011).

Organized labour in Turkey has a limited role in the process of setting the minimum wage, which is usually determined by a consensus of
employers and the Government. The decision reached by a majority vote

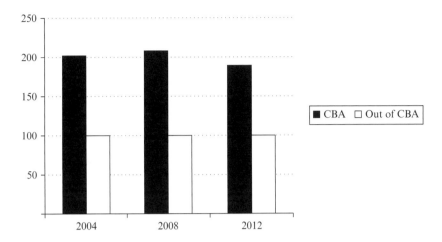

Source: TurkStat (2012).

Figure 6.2   Gross monthly wages of workers under collective bargaining agreements (workers not covered by CBAs: 100)

of the Minimum Wage Commission is final; and there is no scope for appeal. The minimum wage has only been mutually agreed upon by all concerned three times out of sixteen occasions between 2000 and 2016. Workers objected to the minimum wage thirteen times. For these years, the minimum wage was set by the Government's and the employers' votes. The employers have objected to the minimum wage only once. This disproportion in response brings into clear focus the bias in the minimum wage determination process. The Turkish minimum wage setting system, a tripartite mechanism, came into effect at the beginning of 1950s on a regional basis, and shifted to a national system in the early 1970s. There has been no substantial development in the minimum wage setting system since that time.

While per capita income increased by around 4 per cent every year between 1996 and 2012, the real net minimum wage increased by just 2.9 per cent every year over that period. The minimum wage in Turkey has not contributed to reducing inequality and to inclusive development (Yağcı, 2014).

Similarly, in private manufacturing, real wages have stayed well below worker productivity. The difference between the increase in productivity and the increase in real wages between 1988 and 2008 is striking. As can be seen in Figure 6.3, the productivity index that hovered around 100 in 1988 had reached 310 in 2008, while the real wage index had reached only 112.

Source: Yeldan (2012).

*Figure 6.3   Productivity and real wages in Turkish private manufacturing,
                1988–2008*

In other words, wages and productivity have been delinked. Labour did
not benefit from growth. This trend has continued in the years since 2008
(Yeldan, 2012).

However, it is worth noting that the years 1988–92 were exceptional. In
that period, real wages and productivity per capita overlapped. In fact, at
times real wages even moved ahead of productivity. The main reason for
this improvement in real wages was the 'spring protests' of 1989. These
resulted in a considerable increase in real wages in the public sector. After
that, wages in the private sector also increased. The coverage of CBAs at
that time was about 25 per cent, as seen in Table 6.2.

The share of waged employees in national income has been falling since
the mid-1990s. In 1991, this share approached 65 per cent; but it fell back
to 30–35 per cent in the 2000s (Figure 6.4). The peak in 1991 occurred
because of worker protests that began that year and went on for the next
three years. In this context, CBAs provided real wage increases. 1995 was
the climax in terms of the number of workers involved in strikes: some
200 000. The balance of functional income distribution has deteriorated
since then, to the detriment of labour. Between 2008 and 2016, the
Gini coefficient declined only from 0.41 to 0.40 (TurkStat, 2009, 2015).

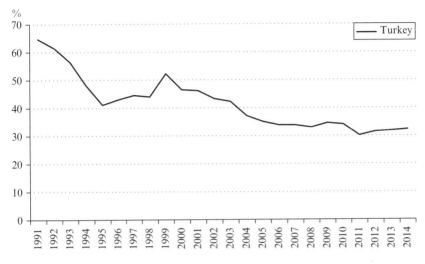

Source: EC (2015).

Figure 6.4   *Adjusted wage share: total economy as percentage of GDP at current market prices (compensation per employee as percentage of GDP at market prices per person employed)*

6.8 CONCLUSION

The paternalistic legacy of the early republican period delayed the institutionalization of industrial relations and had a long-standing influence over the trajectory of Turkish industrial relations. The trajectory of industrial relations in Turkey has been shaped by internal and external dynamics. A hybrid industrial relation system, was institutionalized, and modernized in the era 1960–80. These two decades were an exceptional in the evolution of Turkish industrial relations and saw a convergence on a modern industrial relations paradigm. But discrepancies between the modern industrial paradigm, the Turkish state tradition and the reticence of employer organizations resulted in a discontinuity of this institutionalization.

The transformation of the economy of Turkey by a wave of liberal economic policies in the 1980s also eroded the limited institutionalization of industrial relations. The modernizing of Turkey's industrial relations system after 1960, was seriously interrupted and weakened by the adoption of the new export-oriented economic policies of the 1980s which aimed to integrate the economy in global markets, and by the 1980 military coup. Between 1960 and 1980, Turkey's industrial relations system produced positive effects on labour wages and income distribution, and helped to ensure that labour was included in economic development. From the 1980s to the present, this has been reversed: union density and the coverage of collective bargaining agreements declined significantly, and unions lost their role as key players in social policy.

The weakness in Turkey's system of industrial relations was exacerbated in the 2000s under the new government and the influence of unions over the income distribution and inclusive development has ebbed yet further. The decrease in the ratio of wages to national income and productivity, the political inactivity of the unions, the paucity of bilateral and tripartite social dialogue, and the lack of democratic–corporatist mechanisms, have all prevented unions from enjoying positive outcomes in terms of income distribution and inclusive development. Inequality is characterized by most workers earning no more than a minimum wage, and not receiving the gains of productivity improvements. Despite the historical development of Turkish industrial relations and an increase in wage employment, Turkey still awaits the emergence of a strong industrial relations system and convergence on a modern labour relations paradigm. It seems that this may take a long time.

NOTES

1. I am indebted to Professor Erinç Yeldan for sharing his unpublished paper.
2. Decree No. 2013/1 of the Constitutional Court, dated 22 October 2014.
3. For the reasons outlined above, the OECD does not rely on Turkey's official unionization statistics, but derives its unionization figures for Turkey by the method suggested by Çelik and Lordoğlu (2006); see Visser et al. (2014).

REFERENCES

Ahmad, F. 1995. 'The development of class-consciousness in republican Turkey, 1923–45', in Quataert, D. and Zürcher, E.-J. (eds), *Workers and the Working Class in the Ottoman Empire and the Turkish Republic*. London: I.B. Taurus.
Association on Labour Researches. 2016. '2015 İşçi Eylemleri Raporu' (Report on Labour Movements in 2015). http://emekcalisma.org/Raporlar/RAPOR.pdf (accessed 12 March 2017).
Bianchi, R. 1984. *Interest Groups and Political Development in Turkey*. Princeton, NJ: Princeton University Press.
Boratav, K. 2003. *Türkiye iktisat tarihi 1908–2002* (The history of Turkey's economy) (revised and expanded 7th edn). Ankara: İmge Kitabevi.
Çelik, A. 2008. 'Milli güvenlik gerekçeli grev ertelemeleri' (Strike postponements on the ground of national security), *Çalışma ve Toplum*, **3**(18), pp. 87–132.
Çelik, A. 2010. *Vesayetten siyasete Türkiye'de sendikacılık 1946–1967* (Trade union-

ism in Turkey from paternalism to political participation 1946–1967). Istanbul: İletişim Yayınları.

Çelik, A. 2012a. 'Çalışma ilişkilerinde esneklik ve kuralsızlaşma (1980–2010)' (Flexibilization and deregulation in labour relations (1980–2010)), in Makal, A. (ed.), *Çalışma ilişkileri tarihi* (Labour relations history). Eskişehir: Anadolu Üniversitesi.

Çelik, A. 2012b. 'Türkiye'de çalışma ilişkilerinde kurumsallaşma (1960–1980)' (Institutionalization of labour relations in Turkey (1960–1980)), in Makal, A. (ed.), *Çalışma ilişkileri tarihi* (Labour relations history). Eskişehir: Anadolu Üniversitesi.

Çelik, A. 2012c. 'Türkiye'de 2000'li yıllarda grev ve grevdışı eylemler: Çalışma hayatında "pax Romana" mı?', (Strikes and other labour protest in Turkey in 2000s: Pax Romana in labour relations?) in *IV. Social Right National Symposium Proceedings*. Istanbul: Petrol-İş Sendikası.

Çelik, A. 2014a. 'E-sendika üyeliğinde şifre hırsızlığı' (Forgery in e-membership system), *Birgün*, 6 March.

Çelik, A. 2014b. 'Uluslararası çalışma normları ve çalışma ilişkilerine etkileri açısından 6356 Sayılı sendikalar ve toplu iş sözleşmesi yasası' (An evaluation on trade unions and collective labour agreements Act (no. 6356) in terms of international labour standards and its effects on labour relations), Trade Union Organizing and Social Justice working paper, Istanbul: Friedrich Ebert Stiftung Derneği.

Çelik, A. 2015a. 'Turkey's new labour regime under the Justice and Development Party in the first decade of twentieth century: Authoritarian flexibilization', *Middle Eastern Studies*, **51**(4), pp. 618–35.

Çelik, A. 2015b. 'The wave of strikes and resistances of the metal workers of 2015 in Turkey', **4**(10), pp. 21–37, http://researchturkey.org/?p=9830.

Çelik, A. 2016. 'Grev Ertelemelerinin 30 Yılı' (The thirty years of strike suspensions in Turkey), in Savaş, A., Süzük, A., Koç, C. and Koç, Y. (eds), *Emek Yıllığı 2015* (The 2015 Year Book of Labour). Istanbul: Yazılama Yayınevi.

Çelik, A. and Lordoğlu, K. 2006. 'Türkiye'de resmi sendikalaşma istatistiklerinin sorunları' (Problems of official trade union statistics in Turkey), *Çalışma ve Toplum*, **2**(9), pp. 11–30.

Cumhuriyet. 1982. '12 Eylül olmasaydı 24 Ocak kararları başarıya ulaşmazdı' (Without September 12 coup, January 24 decrees would not have been achieved), *Cumhuriyet*, 26 January.

Dereli, T. 2013. *Labour Law and Industrial Relations in Turkey*. Alphen aan den Rijn: Kluwer Law International.

Devlet Planlama Teşkilatı (DPT). 1968. *İkinci beş yıllık kalkınma planı 1968–1972* (Second five-year development plan 1968–1972). Ankara.

Devlet Planlama Teşkilatı (DPT). 1973. *Üçüncü beş yıllık kalkınma planı 1973–1977* (Third five-year development plan 1973–1977). Ankara.

European Commission (EC). 2015. *European Commission Economic and Financial Affairs, AMECO data base*. ec.europa.eu./economy_finance/ameco/user/serie/ ResultSerie.cfm (accessed 4 December 2015).

Galenson, W. 1963. *Labor in Developing Countries*. Berkeley and Los Angeles, CA: University of California Press.

Koçak, H. 2008. '50'leri İşçi Sınıfı Oluşumun Kritik Bir Uğrağı Olarak Okumak' (1950s as a critical moment of the formation of working class), *Çalışma ve Toplum*, **3**(18), pp. 69–86.

Koray, M. and Çelik, A. 2007. *Avrupa Birliği ve Türkiye'de sosyal diyalog* (Social dialogue in the EU and Turkey). Ankara: Belediye-İş Sendikası.

Makal, A. 1999. *Türkiye'de tek partili dönemde çalışma ilişkileri: 1920–1946* (Labour relations in the single party era in Turkey: 1920–1946). Ankara: İmge Kitabevi.

MESS (Turkish Employers' Association of Metal Industries). 2000. *Gelenekten geleceğe* (From the tradition to the future) (Vol. 1). Istanbul.

Ministry of Finance (MOF). 2013. 'Kamu Sektörü İstihdam Sayıları' (Employment in public sector), Department of Budget and Fiscal Control, http://www.bumko. gov.tr/TR,908/kadro-istatistikleri.html.

Ministry of Labour and Social Security (MoLSS). 2002. *Labour Statistics 2002*. Ankara.

Ministry of Labour and Social Security (MoLSS). 2014. *Labour Statistics 2013*. Ankara.

Ministry of Labour and Social Security (MoLSS). 2016. *Labour Statistics*. Ankara.

Ministry of Labour and Social Security (MoLSS). 2017. *Labour Statistics*. Ankara.

Öngel, F.S. 2014. 'Türkiye'de taşeronlaşmanın boyutları' (The dimensions of subcontracting in Turkey), *DİSK-AR*, Winter, pp. 38–51.

Özkızıltan, D. 2013. 'A political economy of insecurity? State and socio-economic actors in the making of industrial relations in modern Turkey', PhD dissertation, University of Bath.

Özmucur, S. 1995. *Türkiye'de gelir dağılımı, vergi yükü ve makro ekonomik göstergeler* (Income distribution, tax burden and macro economic indicators in Turkey). Istanbul: Boğaziçi Üniversitesi.

Özveri, M. 2013. *Türkiye'de toplu iş sözleşmesi yetki sistemi ve sendikasızlaştırma (1963–2009)* (CBAs competency system and union busting in Turkey). Ankara: AÜ SBF.

Rosen, M.S. 1963. 'Turkey', in Walter Galenson (ed.), *Labor in Developing Countries*. Berkeley and Los Angeles, CA: University of California Press.

Talas, C. 1992. *Türkiye'nin açıklamalı sosyal politika tarihi* (Annotated history of social policy in Turkey). Ankara: Bilgi Yayınları.

Turkish Confederation of Employer Associations (TİSK). 2015. 'Hakkımızda' (About us), www.tisk.org.tr/hakkimizda.

TurkStat. 1999. *Labour Statistics 1997*. Ankara.

TurkStat. 2005. *Statistical indicators, 1923–2004*. Ankara.

TurkStat. 2009. *Living Conditions and İncome Distribution Survey, 2008*. Ankara.

TurkStat. 2011. *Structure of Earnings Survey*. Ankara.

TurkStat. 2012. *Labour Cost Survey Results*. Ankara.

TurkStat. 2015. *Household Labour Force Survey*. Ankara.

TurkStat. 2017. *Household Labour Force Survey*. Ankara.

Uçkan, B. 2013. *Türkiye'de kamu görevlileri sendikacılığı* (Public servants unionism in Turkey). Istanbul: Legal Yayıncılık.

Urhan, B. 2015. *Sendikasız kadınlar kadınsız sendikalar* (Women without unions, unions without women). Istanbul: Kadınlarla dayanışma Vakfı.

Visser, J., Martin, S. and Tergeist, P. 2014. 'Trade union members and union density in OECD countries: Sources and definitions'. https://www.oecd.org/els/emp/ UnionDensity_Sourcesandmethods.pdf.

Yağcı, F. 2014. '1980'lerden günümüze dünyada ve Türkiye'de gelir dağılımı' (Income distribution in the world and Turkey from 1980s up to date)', in

Friedrich Ebert Stiftung (ed.), *Sosyal adalet ve sendikal örgütlenme*. Istanbul: Friedrich Ebert Stiftung.

Yeldan, E. 2012. *Growth and Employment in Turkey*. Ankara: ILO Office for Turkey.

Yeldan, E. 2015. 'Real wages and labour productivity', unpublished paper.

Index

Accelerated and Shared Growth
   Initiative for South Africa
   (ASGISA) 89
African National Congress (ANC) 16,
   72, 74, 89, 104
Agarwala, R.N. 56–7
agricultural employment 191
All China Federation of Industry and
   Commerce (ACFIC) 162, 163
All China Federation of Trade Unions
   (ACFTU) 15, 151, 154, 158, 160,
   161, 162, 164
All India Trade Union Congress
   (AITUC) 34–5, 61
ANAMATRA 146
apartheid 69, 71
arbitration cases 165
Argentina 8, 9
associated unions 159
Association of Mining and
   Construction Union (AMCU) 77,
   105
authoritarian flexibilization 185
automobile industry 43–4, 51
autonomous workers 146

Badigannavar, V. 51, 52
bank of hours 137–8
bargaining councils 75, 79–80, 81,
   91–2, 92–8
bargaining power 51–2
beedi homeworkers 53–4
Bhattacherjee, D. 7–8
Bhorat, H. 84, 94–5
Black Business Council (BBC) 78–9
Bolsa Família programme 140,
   142
Bonner, C. 56, 60
Brazil 1, 8, 9, 10, 11–22, 38, 115–50
   changes in labour relations in the
      2000s 129–36

collective bargaining 142–3, 144,
   145
Constitution of 1988 14, 15, 122–3,
   135
dispute resolution 119, 120, 127–9
evolution of industrial relations
   119–23
extension of rights to domestic
   workers 130, 135–6
industrial relations and the political
   and economic context 136–46
labour reform of 2017 144–6
Law on Cooperatives 1994 137
minimum wage 131–2, 137, 138,
   139–40
PLR 18, 130, 134–5
structure of the industrial relations
   system 116–19
trade unions, *see* trade unions
union tax 118, 122, 130, 132–4
Building and Wood Workers
   International (BWI) 56
Business South Africa (BSA) 73, 78–9
Business Unity South Africa (BUSA)
   78
Butcher, K.F. 94

capital–labour division 3
casual workers 44–5, 48
casualization of employment 159–60
CCMA 76, 80, 99
Central Pay Commission 33
Central Única dos Trabalhadores
   (CUT) 121–2, 133, 136
Chen, F. 165
Chile 8
China 1, 10, 11–22, 151–81
   12th Five-Year Plan 161
   1994 labour law 155
   aligning economic policy and labour
      policy 160–62